To Test the Joy

Cocoanut Island, Hawaii

To Test the Joy
Selected Prose and Poetry

Genevieve Taggard

Introduction by Terese Svoboda
Edited and with essays by Anne Hammond

RECOVERED BOOKS
BOILER HOUSE PRESS

Contents

II: The Exquisite Skin of Self

III: Marvelous Now is Man

IV: A Nothing Vast

"Work gloriously, words. We plug here the great circuit.
Riches and rest, and before you die, some bliss."

from "Dedication for a Book", *Calling Western Union*

Introduction

by Terese Svoboda

Genevieve Taggard, along with radical poet Lola Ridge, was
named by feminist critic Louise Bernikow as twice neglected
in her seminal anthology *The World Split Open: Four Centuries of
Women Poets in England and America, 1552-1950*. Twice neglected
because they were women and radicals, part of "the buried history
within the buried history" of American poetry. This collection,
the first of Taggard's to appear since 1980 and the first to cover
her whole career, including both poetry and prose, has been
collated from thirteen out-of-print volumes as well as a number
of previously uncollected pieces. Best known for her progressive poetry in *Calling Western Union*, Taggard also wrote about
passion in women, their beauty and wildness, often with formal
constraints, in poetry as polished as Louise Bogan's, as bleak as
Weldon Kees's. Her interest in rhyme and meter seems to have
evolved out of a desire for collective expression, that of song,
instead of its predictable rhythms or musical attributes. Three
composers set her work to music, including her friend Aaron

Copland, then a Lefty, who wrote her poem "Lark" as a choral work. This egalitarian impulse, the desire to share rather than to claim freedom, runs through nearly all of Taggard's poetry and is rooted in her profoundly Edenic Hawaiian upbringing, which is where the collection begins.

Taggard spent her childhood eating minnows raw, climbing date trees, and playing with centipedes on the beach. She was no simple admirer of South Pacific sunsets. In describing a hula dancer in "The Tourist," she evokes in the performance even "The poison heavy sleepiness of death" that "Made all her figure's slender golden grace/Seem like censer in an altered place." She recalls the "horrible smell of bubbling sugar" in "A Haole Scrapbook," which perfectly evokes the imperialist takeover of the islands when, at the age of four, she saw the American flag raised and the natives she loved weeping. She was one of the few Americans, let alone poets, to express despair over the annexation of the islands. "For Hawaii Brought Low" begins:

> Let me be voice for that proud, lovely race.
> Let me be words for them, who are so mute;
> Let me be lips to tell the hushed disgrace
> Of these, my people.

Taggard is also egalitarian in style. As fellow poet Josephine Miles writes: [Her poetry] combines the free and the constrained in a way that seems to me full of surprises and graces. Rhyme wanders in and out, lines vary in length and emphasis. ideas break off or firmly assert themselves." The jagged-lined "Aleatory Wind," a poem about experimental American poetry, concludes:

> "Unreal," said the European, "No ghosts.
> No culture."

> I took a stone of weeping in my right hand.
> And a stone of laughter in my left.

Her love poems, written as if only the use of tight form could contain such great emotion, are no delicate paeans to the lovestruck:

> Love you surely, but in a prone
> Dogged way, more like a stone;
> As if a stone's touch gave a cue
> To a clearer love of you.

> From "Letter in Solitude"

In Taggard's aubade "Doomsday Morning," the lovers are defiant, "working havoc," and "deaf to God who calls and walks/Like an engine overhead." To anyone objecting to their union, her fiat is essentially *Go to hell*: "Let your final darkness fall!/And God may call and call and call."

Taggard also had decided views on the "natural" efficacy of the opposite sex. "What's in the men nowadays — the women have the fire & the ardency & the power & the depth?" she writes to fellow poet Josephine Herbst.[1] She believed in what she considered the more natural "bisexual" source of creativity. In the preface to her *Collected Poems 1918-1938*, she argued that they "hold a wider consciousness than that colored by the feminine half of the race. I hope they were not written by a poetess, but a poet."

She also made clear her position on the most perplexing issue for progressives: children. In 1925 she published "Legend," a story about abortion, in Margaret Sanger's *Birth Control Review*. "One baby a year. Better die," confesses an immigrant woman in Vermont where Taggard raised a daughter on her own. Edmund

---

1   Quoted in Drake, William, *The First Wave: Women Poets in America, 1915-1945*, Macmillan Publishing Company. NY: New York, 1987, p.180.

5

Wilson praised her poem "With Child" as "the only respectable poem on child-rearing that I remember to have ever seen."[2] Her writings about motherhood, abortion, birth control, the struggle of female artists, and marriage — "Like every one else I have wanted it. And yet having it, it is not all I want" — will resonate with contemporary women.

She believed in documenting action, "word-in-deed." "It is a "Necessity to eat,/Necessity to act," she states in "Life of the Mind," exhorting poets to write the truth of their experience. "The words in the books are not true/If they never act in you." In the story "Engaged," the narrator, waiting for an abortion, observes that "Everyone looks at the girl's back as she goes in, before the door closes. There is a lot to see in that instant, in that girl's back. While she is there in the room, she isn't much, but when she gets up to in at the door, you want to call her back and tell her that you love her."

In "Ode in a Time of Crisis," Taggard's subject is also contemporary — the plight of the immigrant:

> Now in the fright of change when bombed towns vanish
> In fountains of debris
> We say to the stranger coming across the sea
> Not here, not here, go elsewhere!

In addition to her powerful writing on the issues of gender and social justice, she studied the metaphysical, wrote an essay on John Donne, and compiled a collection of contemporary metaphysical poets. Her biography of Emily Dickinson, whom she felt was the only true poet of the genre, practically single-handedly saved the poet from obscurity. She favored the leftist Edna St. Vincent Millay for her use of the sonnet, as well as the work of Robert Frost, writing in her review of his *Collected Poems* that for him

---

2   Wilson, Edmund, *The Shores of Light*, Farrar, Strauss & Young. NY: New York, 1952, p.349.

"science is merely an extended metaphor — that is, that science is attempting to describe the unknown in terms of the known." She also co-founded the magazine *Measure*, again with the flourish of the progressive egalitarian, sharing the role of editor with seven other writers. Intuiting that new technology — radio and film — would help democratize art, she chaired a panel on new media at the New School's American Writers Congress of 1939. But she could be caustic in her evaluation of so-called progress: "The age [the 1920s] hadn't come to grips with anything much more serious than the problems of rancid meat."[3]

Editor Anne Hammond has arranged Taggard's poems, essays and stories in chronological order, interspersed with graceful biographical essays. Why did Taggard's work all but disappear after her death in 1948? Politics. Consider the title of just one of her poems: "For the League of Dead Nations." Also, she honeymooned in Russia. Literally. Her second husband, Kenneth Durant, (her first, a writer, ended up in an insane asylum), directed the Soviet news agency TASS in the US. She wrote with much more urgency after that second marriage, believing her poetry could act as a positive force for change. That didn't go over well in the 1950s, and many on the Left believed that redbaiting by her Sarah Lawrence colleague and poet Horace Gregory hastened her death due to complications of hypertension at the onset of the Cold War.[4] But Taggard's legacy — exotic yet quotidian, fierce and sensual, and sometimes metaphysical — can now be rediscovered.

3   Taggard, Genevieve, *May Days: An Anthology of Verse from Masses-Liberator*, New York: Boni & Liveright, 1925, p.2.

4   Wald, Alan M, *Exiles from a Future Time: The Forging of the Mid-Twentieth Century Left*, Chapel Hill: University of North Carolina Press, 2002, p.10.

I
The World All Gilded

The Tourist

He saw the hula flower in her hair
Drop to her bosom where it rose and fell:
Forgotten was her lover; slow her stare
Felt for his eyes; her warm body's smell —
The yellow-stamen perfume on her breath,
The poison heavy sleepiness of death
Made all her figure's slender golden grace
Seem like censer in an altered place.

Swinging she danced the hula, and the moon
Hung on the mountain honeying the night:
Her dress of flowers whirled about her — strewn
Along the grass the fire-petals died.
Then like a bat against that disc of light
Leaped up her lover, and the lonely wide
Hollow and shadow echoed as he cried.

Hawaiian Hilltop, [p.18]
Previously published *Liberator 2* (August 1919), p.25

The Futile

The stone falls, the bird flies, the arrow goes home,
But we have no motion, we scatter like foam.

O, give me a song to sing for your sorrow,
A song that will lift, like a wave from the reef,
You and myself, that will fling like an arrow
My poor scattered words to the target of grief:
I want to forget, to remember no morrow,
To go with the petrel, to go with the leaf....

We would fly with all things to the goal of their flying,
We would turn with all things to the magnetic star,
But we never can live, because of our dying,
And we never can be, for the things that we are.

We alone of all creatures — the stones more than we —
Have no end, no motion, no destiny.

For Eager Lovers, p.3

For the League of Dead Nations

What husks of last year's winter close you in,
To-morrow's world — what dead, what wrinkled skin
Of ancient parchments, laws, beliefs! What dried
Worn tattered layers keep the life inside,
Where slender as a sword, and tender green,
It trembles, pushes, patient and unseen:
Vibrating atom, fronded silken thread,
Some day to shake, to sunder back the dead
Two halves of hemispheres, to pierce the crust
Of the ages' rubbish, crowns and cults and dust!

See, iron arms, that cluster all the wide
Plateau of liberty — see, fortified
Dull spikey towns — you cannot hold your own
Against one seed a fecund earth has grown!
Alarmed you stand, alert to meet your foe,
Ready to battle blow for thundering blow;
Nor do you see this sprout of common wheat,
The blade between your firm implanted feet.

Liberator 3:3 (March 1920), p.10
[Published as "Revolution" in *For Eager Lovers*]

Talking Water

If you will poise your forefoot in my pool,
I will not loose a ripple, Beautiful.
Crackle the fern-stems, arch aloft and stare,
See! There's no fright for you, anywhere.
A leaf shall not lift, nor a shade shake
You and your shy love away from my lake.
I know the noon is ablaze for you,
This gaunt forest, a maze for you:
Kneel near this drop of water on stone,
No one comes plunging. You are alone.
To-day I am opal, tinged with blue,
My color deepens with the glassy heat,
And I listen for hoofs. Am I timid, too?
Noon is my enemy! Thrust in your feet!
Trample this silver, trample this sand,
I will not startle you, Little One; stand
Slim as the larch, there, I'll not take
Even your shade to the naked ache
Of my lessening waters. If you lean,
Another faun, like you, but green
Will flick his ears and curve his throat,
His shadow hoof will lift between
These pebble-splotches. Will you float,
Mingle and drowse and touch me, Beautiful?
If you come down some blown noon to my pool,
I will be quiet, I will be cool.

For Eager Lovers, p.40

14

First Miracle

There was a time when Mother Nature made
My soul's sun, and my soul's shade.

A cloud in the sky could take away
The song in my heart for all day,

And a little lark in a willow-tree
Would mean happiness to me.

My moods would mirror all her whims;
Trees were my strength: their limbs, my limbs.

But, oh, my mother tortured me,
Blowing with wind, and sighing with sea.

I flamed, I withered, I blossomed, I sang,
With her I suffered pang for pang,

Until I said: "I will grow my own tree
Where no natural wind will bother me."

And I grew me a willow of my own heart's strength,
With my will for its width, and my wish for its length:

And I made me a bird of my own heart's fire,
To sing my own sun, and my own desire.

And a vast white circle came in the air,
And the winds around said, "Don't blow there."

I said, "Blow on — blow, blow, blow, blow,
Fill all the sky, above, below,
With tempest, and sleet, and silence, and snow!

"Wherever I go, no matter where,
My bird and my willow-tree are there.

"However you frown, no matter how,
I will sing as I am singing now."

For Eager Lovers, p.5

Dead Man

Sap stirs near me, roots stretch and seize,
Sundering stones.
And rivers waken, start in monotones
Their later tunes.
Oaks bend their knotted knees
In labor, and the full earth groans
Like women big with their increase;
While underground my body lies,
With open eyes,
In this stiff pose of peace.

For Eager Lovers, p.67

Sea-Change

You are no more, but sunken in a sea
Sheer into dream, ten thousand leagues, you fell;
And now you lie green-golden, while a bell
Swings with the tide, my heart; and all is well
Till I look down, and wavering, the spell —
Your loveliness — returns. There in the sea,
Where you lie amber-pale and coral-cool,
You are most loved, most lost, most beautiful.

For Eager Lovers, p.32

Forever Lost

Forever lost — like birds forever flying,
Searching bleak space,
Circling, and with the south wind crying
Across earth's face:

Arrowed I fly, and like them lost forever,
Having once seen
Scarlet in a jungle, by a deep river —
Scarlet and green.

For Eager Lovers, p.28

For Eager Lovers

I understand what you were running for,
Slim naked boy, and why from far inland
You came between dark hills. I know the roar
The sea makes in some ears. I understand.

I understand why you were running now
And how you heard the sea resound, and how
You leaped and left your valley for the long
Brown road. I understand the song

You chanted with your running, with your feet
Marking the measure of your high heart's beat.
Now you are broken. Seeing your wide brow
I see your dreams. I understand you now.

Since I have run like you, I understand
The throat's long wish, the breath that comes so quick,
The heart's light leap, the heels that drag so sick,
And warped heat wrinkles, lengthening the sand....

Now you are broken. Seeing your wide brow
I see your dreams, understanding now
The cry, the certainty, wide arms, — and then
The way rude ocean rises and descends....

I saw you stretched and wounded where tide ends.
I do not want to walk that way again.

For Eager Lovers, p.29

With Child

Now I am slow and placid, fond of sun,
Like a sleek beast, or a worn one:
No slim and languid girl, not glad
With the windy trip I once had,
But velvet-footed, musing of my own,
Torpid, mellow, stupid as a stone.

You cleft me with your beauty's pulse, and now
The pulse has taken body. Care not how
The old grace goes, how heavy I am grown,
Big with this loneliness, how you alone
Ponder our love. Touch my feet and feel
How earth tingles, teeming at my heel!

Earth's urge, not mine — my little death, not hers;
And the pure beauty yearns and stirs.

It does not heed our ecstasies, it turns
With secrets of its own, its own concerns,
Toward a windy world of its own, toward stark
And solitary places. In the dark,
Defiant even how, it tugs and moans
To be untangled from these mother's bones.

Liberator 4:12 (December 1921), p.28

Everyday Alchemy

Men go to women mutely for their peace;
And they, who lack it most, create it when
The make — because they must, loving their men —
A solace for sad bosom-bended heads. There
Is all the meager peace men get — no otherwhere;
No mountain space, no tree with placid leaves,
Or heavy gloom beneath a young girl's hair,
No sound of valley bell on autumn air,
Or room made home with doves along the eves,
Ever holds peace like this, poured by poor women
Out of their heart's poverty, for worn men.

For Eager Lovers, p.46

Elegy in Dialogue

See... we find pathways
All over-grown,
Prod an old spider,
Turn a damp stone,
Until in a loop a spider spun
We start at a silver skeleton.

This is death — this exquisite
Quiver of hollow coral... try,
The delicate thing is all awry —
Put it in order, gently, knit
These dangling stems together tight;
Put on the flesh; put in the light;
Peer at the wee imagined face;
Pretend you cannot — pretend you can
Start a little thud in the skeleton man.

So we shall struggle — you or I:

One of us will shortly die
And leave the other alone in the end,
Stunned, too weary to pretend.

Dear, this is not death! This delicate tangle,
Caprice of bones at an uneasy angle —
This is the trellis frame beneath
The bruised and crumbling spray of death:

Death is a reckless lunge — a sprawl
Of naked limbs on a narrow wall.

So shall we struggle, you or I.
One of us will shortly die
And leave the other a callow mask —
An idiot smile to remember by,
And a granite body to conjure and turn.

Against such massive unconcern
One will labor; the other lie —
Christ — so quiet...
      Tell me why...

Measure 37 (March 1924), p.5

For Hawaii Brought Low

Let me be voice for that proud, lovely race,
Let me be words for them, who are so mute;
Let me be lips to tell the hushed disgrace
Of these, my people. Let my sharp words shoot
Cutting to death the righteous, scheming brood
Of these, my people who have plundered them.
Rude let me be, who are their blood, as rude
They were who broke this flowering stem.
For them, sweet singers, let me not be dumb
In this, their silent day, when they lie down
Simple and sad, aware that they have come
To the death that brooded in my people's frown.
If I can tell of them, so they be heard
My own small griefs may go without a word.

American Review 3:2 (March-April 1925), p.142

Fall of Dew

Sweet mortal boy who walks with me
Nearer and nearer the sleepy sea

Wherein we shall be separate
Drowning singly — it is late;

Now while my mind is clear and airy
I want to hurry, hurry, carry

All I may ever keep with me
Before it vanishes, to the sea;

Toward the salty sea I take
Dew from a little inland lake;

A lake that lay on a leaf, where
You wrung water from the air;

The sea has nothing to say to this;
I will dilute her salt with bliss;

However silent, it has been.
I am sleepy and serene.

Words for the Chisel, p.75
Previously published, *New York Herald Tribune*
(20 September 1925)

The Vast Hour

All essences of sweetness from the white
Warm day go up in vapor, when the dark
Comes down. Ascends the tune of meadow-lark,
Ascends the non-time smell of grass, when night
Takes sunlight from the world, and gives it ease.
Mysterious wings have brushed the air; and light
Float all the ghosts of sense and sound and sight;
The silent hive is echoing the bees.
So stir my thoughts at this slow, solemn time.
Now only is there certainly for me
When all the day's distilled and understood.
Now light meets darkness: now my tendrils climb
In this vast hour, up the living tree,
Where gloom foregathers, and the stern winds brood.

For Eager Lovers, p.65

Engaged

She had gone to work for a week of mornings now, feeling as if she had an enemy inside her body. All the nights for a week she had stiffened and cringed in her bed and begged God not to give her a baby. She was not going to work this morning, but it was the same ferryboat. She went to the rail and tried to take her mind between her hands and make it look fixedly at the city, pushing up its gray towers against the sky.

"God doesn't answer. God's away on a vacation."

She was pleased with this sentence. God and her lover were both away on vacations at the same time.

"I'm not losing my nerve in the least," she said. "I still watch the seagulls. I still look at the early sun on the water. I'll make sense of it somehow today. I'm getting used to the idea now."

It was such a lovely, disarming morning, that her body unstiffened a little. The caught feeling between her breasts went away, and left her giddy, saying and re-saying these motherly sentences to herself. Perhaps she could decide what to do before the ferryboat got to the other side, before it bumped against the piles of the slip; it would be nice to have one's mind all made up, and her mouth drawn resolutely when the boat jerked with that bump.

For instance, before she walked off the boat, she might have decided to marry him. In spite of her heart. ...

There was the hat of the girl who worked in the same office!

To meet the blithe ways of the office-girl was the most intolerable thing she could think of. Get away, get away from the office-girl — the neat, mannerly, opinioned office-girl, who would look at her shoes all muddy from tramping the hills last night; look at her hair only half done. The office-girl always talked of where you could get bath towels cheap for your hope-chest.

But the office-girl came over, leaning on the breeze, breezy herself.

"Hello, Lady Fair. Had breakfast yet? Let's!"

Well, it might help to eat; anyway, to do something, go down the stairs, talk about anything. It will be easy in a minute. Eating on the ferryboat always made you feel as if you were starting off on a journey, as if you were running away. ...

There was a pregnant Portuguese woman over by some piles of rope on the lower deck. She had a striped shawl on her head. Oh, what a monster of a woman. She was smiling at the sea-gulls! The woman looked up at a bird that veered into the sky; she staggered on her flat feet.

Down more steps, before a mirror where you see first your muddy shoes and your ankles, then your legs, the bottom of your skirt. And nothing looks wrong yet. Even a smile can be managed, a big laugh for the office-girl, and a quick glance to see how the smile looks, how brave the whole face looks.

The office-girl has thin white fingers and an engagement ring. The ring flashes while her hands butter the corn muffins. The ring comes from a red-haired doctor who probably knows all about this dizzy feeling, who would tell her to get married quick and take care of herself. She danced with him once. He was a good dancer....

Which is it, the ring, or the office-girl talking of hope-chests and bath towels and embroidered sheets? Anyway the ring stabs at her, seems to comprehend why her cramped blue hands across the table push away those steel knives....

Bump, and a second bump. There is the slip. What is it that might have been decided before hitting those piles? Well, anyway, here is the city and a chance to walk, to think, and yet not think too hard. Leisurely, with a cool head — not in a panic any more.

The office-girl determines to ride to work.

"I'm going to walk," says the other girl.

"Oh, come on, squander a whole nickel."

"No."

"Well — see you in ten minutes."

The morning sunlight is all gone out of her now. Even that walk in the hills last night, and the quiet beauty that covered a heap of stones up there where she sat alone, is far off. Here comes the city, framed by the arch of the ferry building door, whistling, clanging, smoking with the day's work.

She chooses to walk in the dirtiest streets, where people look desolate but still keep on living. Walk through the mean little parks, listen to street birds and the talk of old, red-faced men, the drip of water in fountains, look at the Chinese women sitting with their oiled hair in the sun, don't even avoid the rigid dead cats in the gutters.

After a while she gets a feeling of numbness; she is indifferent to the hateful thing inside her. She knows she can't solve the problem of what is right about it. It is too mixed up with all the dark beginnings. "Anyway," she says spaciously, "I'm on the high-tide. Let me ride the wave, not understand it."

A lovely mood is coming over her. She takes an envelope out of her purse, and tries to write.

"Along with the smoke of your factories and sky-scrapers,
I will send up the smoke of my soul, casual city.
I will pile the rubbish of old swamps, tangled vines,
Torn-up stumps, into a mouldy autumn heap;

(Well, it is wordy poetry, numb poetry, dead poetry. Nobody in the world would think she meant very much by tangled vines!)

Where with fire they become a white vine,
Trailing and caressing ugliness,
Folding and unfolding into the air breathed by your multitudes,
casual city."

II

Hours later, when she has ceased to be pleased with her poem, she decides not to marry him.

Her body dreads violence so today. It is a sharp agony, as if a knife cut her, today, for anyone to look at her. She doesn't want to be touched. That was why it had seemed needful to marry him. Her body wants a bed and a night-gown and sleep. She wants to be insensible and stupid, like the big swelling Portuguese woman.

But when she decides not to marry him she is happy. It is almost as if she were right again, a girl, back in college talking about freedom and life, a light-footed girl. She gets up and begins to walk, trying to walk as she walked then, pretending to dance. The people in the park look at her. Suddenly she feels heavy, wounded, altered, old.

She goes down to a chewing-gum machine and looks at herself in the mirror. She can only see part of her face at a time. It isn't a nice face any more. Her chin looks weak.

She decides to wash her face somewhere, to have a shine.

That will make a difference with her chin. She buys a newspaper. There is a great deal of very important news in it, she says to herself, perched up in a shoe-shine chair. The boy slaps the flannel band over her shoe-tips. Just think, he was born once, came out of some woman, like the Portuguese woman, curled up like a pink cockle-shell, and grew up and shined her shoes. She wanted to draw her feet in to herself, to tell him to stop. She couldn't have him bending down, cutting the mud off her shoes.

"That's all right." She got down, fumbling with money. "I'm in a hurry." It was hard to get down without tripping and catching on the steel foot-holders. She felt clumsy, she who had always been so scornful of heavy people.

"Here I am, old and clumsy." She walked off repeating old when she stepped with her right shiny foot, and clumsy when she stepped with her muddy left.

"Is that what love does to a girl?"

"But what we have together isn't love."

It gave her great relief to say, "It isn't love." She had never dared to say that before. Now she stood waiting for the horizontal traffic to pass and said louder and louder, almost in a frenzy:

"It isn't love. It's hideous. It's hideous."

She found that she was talking out loud. In another moment she would have said into the ear of a cane-swinging gentleman, "I won't make a baby out of that."

In the wash place there is a telephone book with a yellow section. Doctors advertise themselves. Two of them sound as if they might listen to her.

Her face still looks blurred in the wash-place. When she smiles her lips stretch like rubber bands. There are hostile glances, astonished scrutinies from women with little girls and babies, in the wash room, but she undoes her dress and tears off the laundry marks on her underwear. She throws away the envelope with the poem on it because her name is on the other side.

So she goes, a little dizzily, across to the nearest doctor, stopping at a drug-store to get out the yellow advertisement, torn from the phone book. For a while she reads the labels on the jars of drugs behind the counters. But not one of the clerks looks as though he would reach down the right bottle, if she should ask.

In the building where the doctor ought to be, his name is gone from the little black-velvet board. When she asks the elevator girl, the girl stares and says that the doctor is in prison.

"It will be hard," she comments.

Down the block at the curb is a familiar car, familiar blue monogram on the door, and cut-glass vase full of fresh flowers. She remembers a blue-eyed freshman that she rushed for her sorority in that car. She repeats to herself some of the chatter she had given the poor baby. Oh, how splendid and sophisticated and strutting she had once been. The profile of her face slides by across the limousine window. Now she would like nothing better than to crawl in there and lie down on the soft cushions, let the car slip away, and go plunging off somewhere.

Then she sees the coat-tails and the backs of her friends on the *Star*, Sam and Joe. They are laughing. The paper is put to bed for three hours. Sam and Joe are off to a matinee after lunch. They are matching for something now, as they go down the street, saluting cops and flower-women.

Before she knows it, there is the other doctor's place, across the street, far up on the building. Yes, there is his name in big black letters on six windows.

And a cab is just coming up to the door with a beautiful girl in it. They go in together past a policeman. It is a dirty place, and the elevator man is a hunchback. He looks at her, at the beautiful girl (who seems by now not so beautiful), opens the iron door with a sniff, and points at another door down the hall.

There are more girls inside, who all look up. They all sit or stand as she feels that she sits, with a great self-conscious girdle around her waist. They are all alike, with uneasy hands, moving as if their corsets or their bodies hurt.

One girl has blue eyes, like that freshman's. Another has red hands and a wide wedding-ring. She is crying. Most of them are silent, stiff as stone, hardly looking at each other, just keeping their eyes to themselves, cursing their luck.

One by one they go into a side door. There is a kind of mute raising of faces every time a girl goes in. Everyone looks at the girl's back as she goes in, before the door closes. There is a lot to see in that instant, in that girl's back. While she is there in the room, she isn't much, but when she gets up to go in at the door, you want to call her back and tell her that you love her.

At last the nurse says, "You're next, girlie, ain't you?"

Inside the nurse's room, she begins to say things that are hard to say.

"Now, dearie, you don't have to go and make a speech. All you young kids think you've got to tell us something. Just put down your money!"

"How much is it?"

"Say, don't you know anything about this business? It's twenty-five. Who sent you, anyway?"

Thank goodness, it's no more than twenty-five.

When she says she found the name in the telephone book, something goes wrong. The nurse puts the money back on the desk, almost shoves it at her.

"Now, that's not what we care for in a customer usually."

Close scrutiny. The nurse goes behind the screen. A woman has been groaning a little back there. The girl seems to be forgotten. They help someone into the hall, and the doctor tells the nurse to get a cab.

After a while a little man comes out wiping his hands on a towel. He looks at everything she wears, at her muddy shoe, her shiny one. There is a lot of talking.

"Can you rest ten days after the operation, and no questions asked?"

"I – I don't know. Do I have to? Yes; yes, I can."

"Not at home?"

"No," swiftly. "At a friend's. I'm a stranger here. I'm from up north. I can stay quiet."

"You see," says the little man, looking at the fat of his thumb, "there's danger, and we can't take no risks." And they talk some more.

"After lunch," he says at last, and puts on a coat and derby. "Three o'clock. Miss Boyd, tell the rest of the girls outside to go home and come tomorrow."

At three o'clock she is back again with a second-hand copy of Whitman. She takes the book with her, when the nurse says, "Now come along in, girlie."

At half-past four she stumbles down the iron stairs — seven flights, stepping slowly, escaping. On the street she holds Whitman against her, wonders if she will ever hold a baby, and tries not to walk like a drunken woman.

III

The sun is sweet in the tangled grass on the hill, just before she gets home. It slants down into the little roots of some weedy flowers. People are playing tennis beyond the hill, calling in the late afternoon air. Girls are coming home from the movies, saying good-by to each other at street partings.

It is almost time to collapse now, to lie down, perhaps cry. When she gets to her room she will lock the door and put up her writing sign; let them think she is writing through supper.

Her door stands open down the hall. Just as she gets there she sees her mother in her own room by the window, sewing.

This is her mother's favorite place, because she likes to watch the sunset as she sews.

"Jean, is that you?"

She was starting to tiptoe away.

"Come in, here, in your room. Aren't you back early?"

Early!

"I'm grimy, mother. Just a minute while I wash a bit."

"Look here," says her mother, who has been creaking away by the window. She holds up some white stuff. "I feel like a girl again. I've been making doll dresses for the church fair! Tell me about your day, dear."

Dante's face is there on the wall at the bottom of the bed as she stretches out. Lean old hound, Dante. "We'll be damnably mouldy a hundred years hence." Nonsense. Gentle mother, doll dresses, church fairs....

The snappers down the front of her dress rip open and loosen the band of pain. Mother's rocker creaks on and on.

"Are you too tired to talk to mother?"

"Never too tired to talk, mother." This she manages with a little laugh. "But I'm just about too tired to work in that awful office any longer. I've decided to give it up, and freelance a while. And college is coming — my biggest year. I want to loaf a little, mother. Not that college is so much, but I seem to want a little quiet space."

"Well, I'm glad. I've felt all along that you were under a nervous strain in that city work."

"I went looking at park fountains today. They'll take an article on historic fountains at the *Star*, I'm pretty sure."

"And you could help me at home, too, for a change. I'd like to have you to myself a little. There are several letters for you, and three phone calls down on the telephone-stand. And I think that Horace phoned long-distance, saying he'd be back to-night, and is going to drive right over to see you."

"Oh, dear!"

"I'm not sure of it. Your father took the call."

The creak of the chair again, and then mother's voice hesitatingly, "Don't you want to see Horace?"

"I don't want to see anybody."

"Well, you rest now, anyway, while I go down and glance at the dinner. I'm glad you're done with the office, dear. Suppose you finish putting in the lace on this little neck for me."

Mother dropped the doll dress right upon her, and went out humming to herself. The needle slid off the thread onto the rug. She sat and stared at it, stared until her father came to tell her about Horace.

In spite of his coming, she was going to bed.

Father thought it rather hard on Horace.

"Oh, tell him that I'll expect to see him tomorrow, or tomorrow night."

Father went away dubiously down the hall. He liked Horace.

And now if she could only tell herself what *she* would say to Horace tomorrow night. Some elaborate way of saying, "Go away! Don't touch me!" Perhaps by tomorrow she would have hundreds of words, hundreds of ways.

The sleeping-porch got blessedly dark, and wounded as she felt she lay limp and at ease, at last, after so many rigid nights. Perhaps she would lie there and bleed to death, as the doctor had said she might, if she wasn't careful.

Either die or go to sleep, before Horace drove up.

IV

But she did neither. He came with quite a toot of his horn, tore open the door and plunged to the porch where father sat waiting.

"Gone to bed. Well, I like *that*. Go tell her to get up and come

38

and see what I brought down with me. The most wonderful little twelve-pound bass you ever saw! For her; on ice. Come out and see it."

Father went out and complimented Horace.

"Now, where's the girl?" she heard him say, laughing a little, trying not to be hurt. She felt for her kimona and wrapped it around herself and went to the railing.

"Here I am, Horace. Hello!"

"Well, Jean, you *are* a pill. Here I drive down a hundred and twenty-five miles to see you tonight. Just because there's the kind of moon you like. Haven't even had supper."

Father went in with a soft click to the door. Horace stood looking up.

"You can't cheat me out of a kiss tonight, do you hear?" With a little grunt he dashed at the window-sill below, swung up to the porch and caught her angrily in his arms.

It was an unsatisfactory kiss.

"Why don't you *kiss* me?" he growled.

He took off his cap and levelled his face at her.

"Look here, Jean. I drive down all that way dreaming of the woman you used to be — a woman with a little affection in her. Can't you ever be that again?"

Yes, he was bitterly disappointed.

"Here we are in all this romantic pose and everything. You in a window of roses. But I must say, Jean, you don't play the Juliet part very well."

"No. I don't. I know I don't. Juliet was fourteen."

Here he was. She tried to tell him that she had discovered something. "It isn't love. It's hideous. It's hideous," she kept trying to tell him.

But he was talking louder. "Well, I hate to say it, Jean, but you're fully forty tonight. I'd almost rather have found you out gadding with one of those newspaper boys than here, looking at me this way. Aren't you ever going to be the same again, Jean?"

He waited.

"I'm always prepared to find you gone out with another man."

She couldn't stand and push him off much longer.

"I'm tired. I wish you'd go home, Horace. It's terrible to stand here in the moonlight and roses. I'm — I'm afraid I can't be much of a sweetheart tonight. Go home, Horace. Tomorrow you'll forgive me."

But Horace was looking at her breast that showed when she leaned down to say she was sorry. He wrenched her nightgown open, fastened his mouth to her in fury.

"Do you want to drive me crazy?" he said under his breath, and lifted his face — so full of drawn passion, so like a hungry little boy — the face that always made her into nothingness....

She had fooled herself. She thought that in not having the baby she was not having Horace any more. Up there with the prostitutes and the antiseptics and the level pain, she had begun to dream of her own heart's love, of love and loving.

Now she knew she had fooled herself. Her bones would turn to chalk, and she would find herself caught, hatefully smothered all over again, one of these sharp moonlit nights.

The college clock struck ten times. It was broad moonlight. The night was vast. The soft dark hills were full of lovers.

Horace was groping between her breasts blindly.

She wasn't Juliet. She couldn't admire herself any more. She wasn't even the blue-eyed prostitute girl in the doctor's office. She was a wife to this man.

"I'm sorry. Am I a brute?" Horace was kissing her throat. "Poor little girl."

This day might even happen all over again.

Liberator 5:9 (September 1922), pp.5-10

Emily Dickinson

[Review of *The Life and Letters of Emily Dickinson* by Martha Dickinson Bianchi and *The Complete Poems of Emily Dickinson*, with an introduction by her niece Martha Dickinson Bianchi.]

Because it is the familiar fate of most rare spirits and great innovators to be foolishly misvalued, one should not be surprised, having found in her poetry a most astonishing Emily Dickinson, to turn through the first half of her "Life and Letters" — that is, the Life, by her niece — and find only a mundane reproduction along family lines. Where are the bold and capricious and impassioned colors that lie so marvelously beside the nun-like gray and spiritual azure of her nature? Not here. This is the supreme irony of the book: Emily's family still has her under lock and key; so far as such devices are powerful at all, they are still, forty years after her death, the chief concern of this single surviving Dickinson. Reticence, good taste, Amherst sensibilities — all the forces that stifled and warped the living girl are here again, silencing the events of her life and destroying her letters, as perfect in many instances as her poems. I have merely to refer the reader to the 1894 edition of the letters and certain passages in the later chapters of this volume to illustrate Mme Bianchi's shortcomings. As to the maltreatment of the poetry in the past, let anyone compare the facsimile reproduction of "Renunciation" in *Poems: Second Series* with the printed version, in that series edited at the request of her sister Lavinia by Higginson and Todd. In every instance this freshest of spring water has had to come through the filter of common and cloudy minds.

Such outrageous tampering with the facts in the life of a nearly inexplicable woman, and with her priceless writing, cannot, however, be the only significance — serious as it is — of the publication of this book. For those who do not know the real Emily there remain her letters and certain significant incidents in the narrative to send them flying toward discovery.

Although the total story, as told in black and while, is not particularly illuminating, a wealth of detail remains for any one who cares to write his own spiritual biography of Emily. Like Margaret Fuller, the woman of action in that narrow and remote society, Emily, the artist and ascetic, clearly had a father. Again like Margaret, at an early age she calls herself a Whig and suggests that she would like to vote and read politics. We discover that she lived by Keats for sensuous richness, by Browning for outspoken zest (calling *Men and Women* a "broad book"); cherishing the extravagance and waggery of Dickens, and brooking over the fortunes of Elizabeth Barrett, George Eliot, and Emily Brontë, her far-away kin.

Of the central drama of her life, from which came such fragments as

> So we must keep apart,
> You there, I here,
> With just the door ajar
> That oceans are,

> And prayer,
> And that pale sustenance,
> Despair!

we have very little, but for imagination enough. The truth of the story here has recently been disputed by a family friend who insists that the real tale is neither so conventionally noble nor so simple. From the present book we gather that the man Emily Dickinson loved was a minister in Philadelphia who begged her to run away with him and, when she refused, took his wife and child to the Pacific coast, dying there many years later. God and death, throughout Emily's whole passionate utterance, take on a new meaning when remembered with these facts. She rebelled against drab morality and theology — she rebelled against death and loss and anguish — but death and God became in the end the symbols of her fulfillment.

Putting poems, letters, and life side by side, another much-suppressed clue emerges. God and father are evidently closely linked, and the recluse and unmarried spinster daughter of a rich man had a significant economic problem when seen by the light of

> Twice have I stood a beggar
> Before the door of God!
> * * *
> Burglar, banker, father,
> I am poor once more!

But you will not get to the bottom of Emily Dickinson even in the letters. Here our difficulty is not the niece, but the great original herself. The letters, like the poems, suggest a depth quite beyond any plummet except that of another such spirit. Certainly Emily had her beginnings and many of her conclusions in human and natural dilemmas; and some of these are herein shown. Within herself she performed miracles — that hardest and slowest miracle, chiefly, of self-mastery and self-expression.

Two emotions seem to do battle back and forth: there is the constant triumphant note of her victorious self, and, struggling with that, a less obtrusive anguish and rebellion, always spoken in language too cryptic to trouble those about her. Most poignant of all is this line to a child too young to understand — written curiously enough to the Martha Dickinson who edits the present volume: "Dear Mattie: Be sure to live in vain, dear. I wish I had. Emily."

As to explaining the artist, there is no explanation. How such a woman could write "The Railway Train":

> I like to see it lap the miles,
> And lick the valleys up,
> And stop to feed itself at tanks;
> And then, prodigious, step
>
> Around a pile of mountains,
> And, supercilious, peer
> In shanties by the sides of roads;
> And then a quarry pare
>
> To fit its sides, and crawl between,
> Complaining all the while
> In horrid, hooting stanza;
> Then chase itself down hill
>
> And neigh like Boanerges;
> Then, punctual as a star,
> Stop – docile and omnipotent –
> At its own stable door.

a few years after the first of these whistled into Amherst, and in doing so, write perhaps the only poem, for all our conscientious attempts, that makes art of the machine age — this puzzle, beside many subtler ones, we shall not solve.

Nor shall we discover here the secret of her strange technical power, unless in the stray remark that Emily was something of a musician. Her verse, which is to our whang-bang school poor technique, accomplishes the most miraculous sound-flutings; her assonance-rhyme, like her thought, is a tone that opens in the central atom of feeling, outward. Her images, magnificent, tempered, utterly her own, make her the only genuine Imagist.

In the collected work we are face to face with a startling personality and one of unusually diverse qualities. Emily's poems are played on plucked strings, on an instrument of great variety and range. Her scope is wide, and the tones are many — she finds infinite subtleties between the gaps of our crude scale — but there is only one method, the direct stroke of a bold hand. She had no bow as has Edna Millay, who by one long sweep gives us a lyric line of marvelous power. This inability to link words endlessly with gathering speed has kept Emily from having an understanding audience. Her gift is static — "to scalp the naked soul" by an instant's sound and image.

However they may outdo her in cumulative melody, Emily surpasses our contemporaries, Edna Millay and Elinor Wylie, in the simple matter of range. From the silver bliss:

> I taste a liquor never brewed,
> From tankards, scooped in pearl;
> Not all the vats upon the Rhine
> Yield such an alcohol!
>
> Inebriate of air am I,
> And debauchee of dew,
> Reeling, through endless summer days,
> From inns of molten blue.
>
> When landlords turn the drunken bee
> Out of the foxglove's door,
> When butterflies renounce their drams,
> I shall but drink the more!

> Till seraphs swing their snowy hats,
> And saints to windows run,
> To see the little tippler
> Leaning against the sun!

she runs the clear half-notes downward to:

> The heart asks pleasure first,
> And then, excuse from pain;
> And then, those little anodynes
> That deaden suffering;
>
> And then, to go to sleep;
> And then if it should be
> The will of its Inquisitor,
> The liberty to die.

Two poems on death, numbered in this collection XX and XXII, stand alone, I think, in the whole world's literature. No other poet has said what is herein said. The nearest approach would be the utterance of a Shakespearean woman with Hamlet's soul. But perhaps the bleak and religious Emily has been over-stressed at the expense of the capricious and nimble one. "Papa Above! Regard a Mouse" and

> Lightly stepped a yellow star
> To its lofty place.
> Loosed the Moon her silver hat
> From her lustral face.
> All the evening softly lit
>
> As an astral hall —
> "Father," I observed to Heaven,
> "You are punctual."

merely suggest the merry irreverence that runs like a stream, through light and shade, in her work.

We find the images — lightning "skipping like mice" and a snake "unbraiding like a whip-lash in the sun" — a wealth of

46

homely memory and fancy. But we cherish above even these delights the utterance of the impalpable. "Pain has an element of blank" begins one poem. And again this:

> Elysium is as far as to
> The very nearest room,
> If in that room a friend await
> Felicity or doom.
>
> What fortitude the soul contains,
> That is can so endure
> The accent of a coming foot,
> The opening of a door!

Poor Emily who could not write like Lowell and Longfellow! She could not. She wrote in secret, for herself alone, and now we find her, in the company of the maddest and most stubbornly realistic men, Blake, Shakespeare, and Browning.

The Nation 119:3092 (October 8, 1924), pp.376-378

A Haole Scrapbook

For the third time, the other night, I met a man who had spent a few weeks in Hawaii and knew more useful things about its geography, commerce, politics, industry, anthropology, and geology than I ever did. The man was surprised when he found that I had lived there eighteen years. I had not been able to contribute one respectable fact to the discussion.

What have I to show for those tropic years?

Well, to count up: Like Rupert Brooke's Great Lover or like any jackdaw — certain unique colors and significant sounds; the very special angle of a particular tree; the sense of eight or nine barefooted years walking over coral roads shimmering in the noon sun, climbing tamarind trees and exploring the part of our valley known as Kalihi-kai, with its red volcano dust and rain rutted roads....

And the memory of two native girls, Kane and Lani, together with the terror of my school days, Portuguese Merry Perry; John Frank, the native boy who taught me to play baseball and shout

Wellakahou; the memory of the young and beautiful Isaac at the whose funeral we sang, "When the swallows homeward fly...."

Then the droll captains who hung on their whitewashed gates in the early evenings while their native wives pounded poi within; the never ending terror of tidal waves at night, with the quaint fear attached, that such a wave would imperil the Plymouth Rock chickens asleep in the yard below the garden. A feeling for a tropic sea, sky, atmosphere....

My fellow guest who had exchanged a few words with me (very like a countersign) concerning the beauty of the Pali, and the joys of hotel life at Waikiki, then took up the pineapple industry. It was too much like a geography lesson; pineapples meant too many absurd personal things to me. This talk was as canned and tasteless as any canned article. The traveler deferred to me and — with a look that implied, "I don't believe you ever saw the place, but if you did, you will have something to say about *sugar*" — switched things to that subject.

Again, I felt like a child who has been called upon to recite his lesson when he has been looking at picture books. My pictures started with a schoolteacher's house on a wild sea-thundering coast – sea to one hand and miles of bristling sugar cane to the other, and at the back, long ridiculously thin and high stems of the cocoanut tree that threshed about in the storms, but never broke. Above the sugar cane forest, like fattened and straightened cocoanut trunks, shot up the great smokestacks of the mill, and the horrible small of bubbling sugar came to us day and night.

No, I had nothing intelligent to say about the sugar industry.

I wondered why my childhood couldn't be like any other child's. Why must I be supposed to have so much marketable conversation about me? It was not my habit to cross question my companions on the boot and shoe industry in the New England states.

Once, in the midst of a similar difficulty, I discovered an old man who told me how the ground looked beside his favorite swimming hole in Missouri. He said it had cracks in it where the sun baked it after it was beaten down by many wet feet. I could see that little section very well as the old man talked, and I knew that I had nothing to say about the islands that was not as usual and simple as that. For those who love general information, my childhood was wasted. One girl stares every evening at an elm, and another at an algarroba — and in the end there is a difference. But that difference is intangible.

Yes, the outlines of trees, and the fruit you risk your neck for, and the insects you kill and fear, and the kinds of child hardship and toil you perform and endure, these make a childhood — and the subtle difference of memory. One glance at me, and if you are subtle enough you can tell that I used to eat live minnows....

That was in the days when Mr. McKinley was president, before and during the Spanish War, when boys and girls in America were collecting stamps and cigar bands. If you were a boy and a native and a good swimmer, you went to the wharves in the late afternoons and dived for nickels that the people on the big steamers threw to you, but if you were a girl, and a *haole*, and a very poor swimmer, you stayed with your sister playmates and ate live minnows.

And this is the way it is done. You take up your dress as you always do when you are lugging home mangoes or bringing in wood, and wade into the sea where the water is clear and quiet. There, as you stand looking down, you will see, of a sudden, something like a floating net in the water that changes its outline as it moves – a little cloud of silver. That you dip up, and your dress is think enough to act as a sieve, so that soon you have a million or so sweet little dancing flakes in your lap. Then wade to shore and eat them promptly; if you are very much *haole*, bite off the heads and spit them out; but your little Hawaiian friends will think you are putting on airs if you do, let me warn you.

There were other things to be eaten: wild plums, guavas, and mangoes, if the birds didn't find the ripe ones each day before you did. Then, in season, there was Mrs. Gulick's date tree. Climbing that was always a timid proceeding, because it stood right in the middle of the picket fence and part of it was undoubtedly hers – but so also was part of it undoubtedly ours. And that part we took, and more, if there was any. We went up the side toward the road, curling our toes into the niches made by cutting the old dead branches, until we got to the prickly, feather duster head of the old tree. Ah, and alas, how many thorns existed for one date, and how your friends below ate them all up as you threw them down. Perhaps the same plot exists with variations, in New England, for apples or chestnuts.

Nearly all our games involved eating something. We made mud pies which we did not attempt to eat. One tally for universal childhood. We played a Japanese game called peewee. In the movies once I caught a glimpse of the same game, I think, played in a Mexican alley. We had recurrent passions for hop scotch, and for jacks and marbles. Our most intense times, however, were concerned with finding things to eat outside our mother's icebox.

Now and then someone suggested getting ponninies. The day had to be very dull indeed before ponninies became our object. Certainly no one would go for them until every fern tub that might be hiding a curled up centipede had been overturned. And there was rarely a day when one of the twenty fern tubs hadn't a centipede for our delight. He would be a little stiff when we got him off and stay stiff from the damp rot of the tub until we had sliced off his pincers. The brown beetled, enameled thing would keep us amused for the afternoon, and when the bravest of us picked him up and let him run all over his hands, then indeed the afternoon was a success.

Sometimes the supply of centipedes failed. And every fruit tree in our father's tropical garden proved, when carefully combed, to have not even half ripe fruit. No, nothing on the strawberry-guava bush, nothing on the Eugenia tree, no alligator pears ready yet, no papayas, no mangoes, not even a sour little Chinese orange or a water lemon, nor fruit of the passion vine over the trellis by the veranda.

Then, in despair, you go on the ponninie hunt.

You hunt the ponninie with a long kitchen knife and a pie pan. And you wear your shoes. The ponninie, let me make it plain, is the simple cactus that grows in deserted and rocky places, where rattlesnakes would be found in this country. In place of snakes we had a tree that only hurt you when you came to eat its fruit. Besides the long white spines on the cactus leaves, were the millions of invisible specks that covered the fruit itself. The white spines, once in your hand, could be pulled out with some wincing, but the others stung like a nettle, and never came out except with time, or a vigorous rubbing of dirt over the tingling hand.

After ponninies, came mango season; and after mangoes the algarroba beans came on. Bean season woke a new intensity in all of us, not the hunger for food but the hunger for accumulating and possessing beans – which in sufficient quantities meant spending money. Algarroba beans are longer than string beans, hard and bright yellow. They grown on a kind of mesquite tree and fall to the ground or onto a tin roof with a succession of thumping noises. All the cattle in the islands used to eat these beans, and all the children used to pick them. They sold at ten cents a gunny sack, the year I determined to make my fortune. Three good days' labor went to filling a sack. We plundered the whole valley for beans.

Much of it was simple backache, but some of it was science. First, you skim across a bare bit of ground and pick up the beans on the wing, then you drop them as you can pick no more, into little piles, the two handfuls every few feet dotting the whole cleared space so that it looks like a big comforter with regular knots laid out in squares. Then you must walk as the witches used to, between piles (stepped on beans are no good), as if they were heated ploughshares.

I made up a chant about them one day when I was cramming the last of the third sack into place on the wheelbarrow:

> Algarroba beans, algarroba beans,
> It's easy when they fall,
> But to pick them up at all,
> That's the trouble, algarroba beans.
>
> My back aches, algarroba beans;
> I get ten cents a sack
> And my tired back; —
> Algarroba beans.

In the cool of the evening we went to see Mr. Judell, the rich man who bought our beans. He had a stable in Honolulu where all the tourists got horses for riding to the Pali and to Waikiki, and he kept his horses shiny and fat on our beans.

We trundled them down in our squeaking wheelbarrow: my three bags, and my sister's one, and two belonging to Gladys Simpson. Hers, if I remember rightly, had litter in the bottoms of the sacks. I felt very righteous because mine hadn't. There were at least ten thousand clean fat shiny beans in each of my bags. As I took my turn at the wheelbarrow it struck me that I had no way of proving which were mine, and Mr. Judell might open hers and think ill of me. We had had a quarrel over the ethics of litter and she had sassed me back and claimed the right to fill her bags as she chose.

Well, on we creaked, and the big moon came out to look like the blank face of my conscience. Mr. Judell was waiting on his veranda. He came down and let us through the gate and lifted off the bean sacks with his slender white hands. Then he turned to Gladys.

"Come here', he said and counted six shining dimes into her palm. They were brand new dimes, and a pang went through me that he should be cheated with litter. I looked at him and wondered what I should say. He lit his cigar and his face glowed a minute. I remember his face very well. We went off dragging the wheelbarrow after us; Gladys carried the dimes still.

Several years later it became known that Mr. Judell was a leper; he sold his stable and went to China to try a cure. By that time I had spent my three dimes and I was old enough to reflect that he was more thoughtless of us than Gladys had been of him, that night. The silver moon, the silver dimes, and the way lepers look, deadly silver all over, have always been connected in my mind — with algarroba beans.

The wild plum trees grew on one edge of the taro patch, and Mrs. Gulick's date tree grew across the road on the edge of another. The two patches were connected by an underground channel of water about two feet wide that ran under the road. Too many people depend on the crop of a taro patch to allow it to become the playground for the neighborhood children; but the irrigation ditch that runs around its four sides is not so sacred to the existence of its owners. We had tried wading through the taro patch once in a sort of game of hide and seek, pulling up taro plants as we ran, and we were treated very much as my mother was, when she and her friends played in an Illinois oat field all one Sunday afternoon. In both cases someone got a terrible beating and everybody got a scare.

Chinamen owned these patches (Pokays[1] we called them), and they didn't mind if we paddled about in the ditches. So between seasons we swarmed over the dikes that ran like rude tick-tack-toe designs between the hills. Everybody dared everybody else to crawl through the mud and water of the underground ditch that ran beneath the road at first; but nobody tried it.

Frogs managed it. We got one big fellow who lived on the Moana Lua side, to go Waikiki (that is, east) into the sheltered

---

1   This is Taggard's spelling of the Hawaiian word "pake" (pronounced "pah-kay"), now considered an ethnic slur in Hawai'i.

cove of the ditch near the more prosperous taro patch. He kept on hopping after our sticks ceased to reach and prod him on, and at last came out trailing a little necklace of water weed with all the pomposity of a stout Cortez gazing on a new and equally wide Pacific.

Gold fish, and black fish, and fish with trailing little goatees on their nether lips also lived in the bigger ditch, and floated or darted over a brown-green ribbon of sleek, water rippled weeds. Wading was ever so pleasant until we found that the fishes with the goatees or some unseen eel or fresh water beetle had a stinger for the feet that were thrust rudely into the silt of the ditch bottom. It was John Frank who got his toe pinched, and he swore his worst word, *Wellakahou*, as he sat nursing himself on a hot dry rock. We were peering down until our eyes had grown accustomed to nothing but gradations of blackness — and the depths he had muddied gave no sign of a desperado nipper. The bewhiskered fish got the blame, and we made his life miserable every time he wavered into sight. So much for the tradition of villainous whiskers.

That was the day of the great sunset…. As we came out of the coarse hilo grass, smelling strongly of rotten taro and taro patch slime, we all looked up. No one had told us that Kilauea was erupting — we did not know that a great river of sluggish lava was creeping up on the island towns. We had been accustomed to sunsets that turned the sky into arches of rainbowed light, but this was not like those flutings of color. This was a totally new sunset from start to finish, and its effect was very simple, one of utter terror and beauty.

The whole sky was a dome of deep crimson. From the blue mountains to the sea, it cupped over us, speckless, clear color from end to end. The great sun seemed to be running in rivers of red on the level horizon. Such small ignorant beings we became, under such a sky. We lost our feeling and our look of childhood, and seemed for a moment, under that light, shrunken like little, alien old women and men, standing upright in a world that had nothing to do with the cool wavering of fishes, or the jerks of a damp frog.

I think we ran home — at least Lani and John Frank and I did. We wanted our parents and lighted kerosene lamps and supper, very much indeed after that desolate grandeur. Gladys Simpson, who had come from the slums of San Francisco, was untroubled by what we saw and branched off for a final thrash at the wild plum tree.

After the volcano's eruption and the skies of smoke by day and fire by night, we manufactured volcanoes and lava flows — so strong in her young are the inclinations to imitate nature. We began in the sand box, where model volcanoes and well regulated lava flows were always on display for a time. Earthquakes we could not manage, and tidal waves were too terrifying. There had really been one on the island of Molokai during those discolored weeks.

One evening, soon after, we went to the beach to go moonlight bathing. The moon had not yet risen. There lay the sea, and we who thought we had no terror of her hurried in. But the moon was slow, the water cold and lifeless. The sky and sea were like ink, and now and then, far and high above the horizon, what seemed to be the foam crest of a cliff-like wave gleamed and fell. There were little silences and distant rushings and withdrawals. Suddenly the water around my rigid legs became a fluid horror, and I fled out and back up the sand with the imagined wave fast in pursuit.

That black night (for the moon never came) was a consummate agony. The grown up folks, who got all their hints as to the possibility of catastrophes from the newspapers, couldn't feel the terror in the air that I breathed. They would not go, and I started off alone for the dear sealed up little valley that lay beyond reach of the monstrous waves. All the way home the trees teased me by making the sound of ocean perfectly before me and behind me. My Japanese nurse put me to bed and sent her husband to tell my mother that I was safe at home. She sang a monotonous song that undid the spell of the wind in the trees, as she tucked in the mosquito net.

If the government hadn't sent a band of convicts to work on the rock pile across the road, our volcano game would have ended with the wet sand models and red tissue paper lava flows. It was summer vacation, and the convicts lived in the back yard of the school grounds and worked on the leveling of the land that was to be the new school, just up the valley road. Since this was the place, of all the empty lots, where the fattest algarroba beans grew, we disobeyed our parents and slipped through the picket fence to watch the convicts keep house. When we needed excuses, we said that we went for beans.

The new school was being built from the bluish grey rock that jutted from the ground, covered with cactus and wild banana bushes. These buried boulders the convicts had to blast apart and carry back to the old school grounds, where they cut and polished them for the square building blocks. Out in the heat they worked, with rags tied round their heads to prevent sunstroke, sweat pouring down their faces, tugging as if by the force of their arms alone to get the rocks out of the clutch of the ground. Over them stood the cactus plants, with their flat arms outstretched. That made a picture against the happy blue sky — men with bent backs and straining neck muscles, and the cactus looking like so many crosses.

After watching the blue and white striped men for a morning, we tore off to our own secret rock in the far corner of the chicken yard where the stubborn dirty white birds would roost instead of using their whitewashed perches. We had hammers and a huge nail. After much arguing, we fastened on a certain rocky point and began to bore a hole with the nail, as the convicts had done. One of us sat on a rock as they had done, and lifted and dropped the iron nail as they had the rod, while another pounded between-times. In our miniature way, we had a hole for the fuse and the

58

dynamite after some hours of toil. A grey powder gathered at the bottom of the little hole, and this we cherished. We supposed it to be one of the necessary ingredients to every explosion. At last the nail would go no farther. With carefully steered blowing, all the powder on the rim of the hole was dusted in. Someone, feeling perhaps a vital lack, suggested that we use insect powder as well, the powder our fathers burned in the evenings to keep away mosquitoes, while they read the Honolulu papers. This was added to the eruptive powers of stone dust. We made a fuse, about as effective as the old confident arrangement of string and bent pin for catching trout. Our fuse was string soaked in kerosene. There was a white boy in our bunch, now, and he claimed to know how to make fuses. His father was in the army and could, he claimed, by the same method, blow up all the Pacific Ocean. So we had implicit faith in our engine of destruction.

Then we stayed away. How many days we stayed away! For the white boy said that it would take days; that the fire on the fuse would reach the powder and eat downward into the earth and under it, for yards and yard, like the roots of a tree, until suddenly it shook and tore the black earth wide open. We went off, ostensibly interested in other things, but waiting almost instant by instant for the great growl of our artificial Kilauea. What made things worse — the convicts were blasting five or six times a day, and so five or six times a day our hearts leaped with joy … and stopped, and then sank. Those premature pangs of success came too often to leave us any relish for the actual occurrence. At last I went back to the old lichen covered rock and found a lazy rooster crouched asleep over the awful tunnel of our imaginations.

The convicts made us forget our dismay, however. They were jolly at mealtime, very domestic in their little camp, fussy about the looks of things, and they seemed to be happier than we children were. It was strange to see them smoking pipes where, in the school season, the little Japanese girls played jacks. They said, or rather their cook said for them, that in the world they had found it difficult always to get a meal, a job, a bed. Now they had all these, and no worry. Their *luna*, or boss, was easygoing. He too, had a meal, a job, a bed — why should he hurry them? They worked no harder than they had before they "enlisted", as they put it.

All these impressions I got from the cook, a Negro, who was being punished, my father told me, for marrying three women. Perhaps the others were not so carefree as he was. He whistled and talked to me as he stirred up a grey paste for pancakes. It was a lot like playing house, I thought, except that he had to wash dishes.

Then one day he showed me his treasures, while the potatoes boiled. From a flannel bag he shook out a dozen gleaming black balls – nuts they were, filed and polished and carved, until they looked like lumps of precious stones. I had seen crudely polished ones before. The most precious possession of the schoolmate was a half filed kukui nut like this. But these were carved in strange and marvelous designs, with whole scenes in the space of a fingernail: men and women in carriages, with parasols and silk hats; children flying kites, and sharks seizing fishermen; and then landscapes, Diamond Head and the Pali and Punchbowl.

Very solemnly the cook took up a nut that seemed to have little scratches all over it.

"I give this to you." He was very excited, and he rubbed the face of the nut with his fat, agitated thumb. "Something better for a little *haole* girl than Kanaka pictures."

I put out my hand and took it, and peered at the scratches, a little disappointed. I secretly wanted the shark and the fisherman.

"It is the Lord's Prayer carved and set with gold", he said. "You can only read it with a magnifying glass."

These vague random memories go through my head when travelers tell me of a Hawaii I have never known: the land of the tourist who spares a week for seeing this little dot on the map, who lives in a hotel like the hotels in New York, rides around the island in a carefully closed in Rolls-Royce and a cloud of dust. Can it be the same place as the one inhabited by John Frank and Merry Perry? Sometimes I think I made it up.

And then I found someone who remembers, quite independently of me. A blue eyed Irishman at a friend's house suddenly turned to me and said, without a word about the Pali, or the sugar industry:

"Do you remember Mrs. Maquiana?"

I nodded.

"And Mrs. Gulick?" he queried.

"Yes", I cried. "And her date tree!"

"And Captain Macy, and the Kalihi-kai swimming pool?"

That was Freddy O'Brien. Such a pity he had never known John Frank! John Frank, the greatest swimmer of all the native lads, stood on the big rock that overhung the Kalihi-kai swimming pool, the last day I saw him. His fathers had fished there, with spears and torches. The fish, white and languid, went back and forth, that day, in a shaft of sunlight that knifed the yellow-green water. John Frank stood on the stone worn into a little hollow by the feet of his forefathers. He didn't own the stone. It was on a white man's estate now.

"*Wellakahou*", shouted John Frank, and cut the water with his joined palms.

I sat on the stone when he left it and strung myself a lei – it was a goodbye lei made of ilima flowers. The first span of my years — the first ten years spent in the islands — was ending the next day.

John Frank's smooth black head popped up from the water. "How long you going stay in the States?" he asked me, as if it had just become clear that I was really going.

"Three months", I said.

"Mangoes getting ripe soon", he offered.

A sudden pang at the thought of missing mango season went through me. John Frank had dived again. The water was sooty black and quiet. Then in a whirlpool came a brown arm. This time he popped up with a well formed idea:

"Too bad you gotta be *haole*", he said and went under again. Off and on, I have thought so too, all my life.

Bookman (June 1924), pp.391-398

The Lo! School in Poetry

We are always being told why it is easy for a person living in California to be a poet. Let me tell you why it is hard. But first let me avoid the quicksand subject: Just how is a poet made? And all its cousins, and its uncles and its aunts — is he made at all? If his environment does have anything to do with his genius, which is better for him, joy or sorrow, struggle or recognition? In the older speech: doesn't he purify his soul by a longing for something he cannot have? In the manner of the day: isn't his wish for beauty more important than his satisfaction? Isn't wish-fulfillment the urge of all art? And so on...

Answer these questions as you have always chosen to answer them, and go on with me to the spectacle of the poet of major intensity growing up in the bronze background of California's sunburnt hills, with her kneeling, fern-like acacia, her fog-laden trees, her fig-leaf bay of green, wind-veined water.

With this landscape before his eyes, the old formula declares the poet unable to function because he has become that unusual creature, a beauty-nurtured man; because he is fulfilled without the need of aching words; because he touches Nature fearlessly with no interim for singing.

I agree that he finds it hard, but my reason is simpler. It comes in the census reports. California is a vast place; the few people who cling to its footholds have been there only a short time. Beyond the desert and the Rockies it lies — a huge, open, varied, unique land, with a freshly made civilization scattered across its surface, but penetrating neither down into its soil, nor abroad, into its recesses.

For all the accompanying activity, a huddled civilization. Man is always afraid of the enormous empty aspects of the earth. They negate him, ignore his outcries, silently and persistently demanding that he reject his mortal consciousness for their immortal, unquestioning agnosticism; constantly insisting that he yield and blot out his frail self in their taciturn cycles. Such towering, overhanging Nature is a rude, ruthless, man-mocking obstacle to any labor of the human spirit. Only in a very old country is there an impudent Tomas An Buile to speak up in the face of God himself.

Even the most Wordsworthian poet must use words, man's coinage, and perhaps say "I"; certainly he must value feeling and expression, which nature scorn, and these are for the moment personal, however universal they may thereafter appear. In his heart of hearts he knows he is no high-priest — as Nature's amanuensis, he is a fraud. No poet ever did express that lady. How mocking an earthquake or a lava flow, or even a rain storm is to the mortal who has supposed himself in her confidence. We shall never take off the Kantian spectacles, nor utter one word savage or serene enough to be counted as Nature's own.

When I saw the crouching bungalows that sit not ten feet apart in the little country towns of California, I was very scornful indeed. Around these shrinking little houses, miles and miles of sunlit air and undulating country wait without inhabitant. But I, who think I love Nature, go into the house very hurriedly, of a perfect night. Five minutes of inhuman beauty is all that I can stand.

So it is with most of us. Until we have enough people around to make the venture less lonely, we do not beard the genius of the place. Quaintly enough, this is nothing more than an inferiority complex in the face of Nature. Either the poet remains silent, or else he writes of her splendor and man's degeneration. In California, particularly, the poet is always saying that he is not good, noble, wise, mighty, and overwhelming as Nature herself. Yet an Emily Dickinson, with the soul of a self-sufficient and impudent child, calls Nature to account if she chooses.... But she spent her life in a New England garden.

Nature's material aspect has imposed on man's spiritual reality, and he cannot even properly compliment her until he conquers her.

When the census goes up, when man and women are not so like people living in cities of refuge, barricaded against the beauty and sheer bulk of a vacant earth, the West may have poets who dare to take their environment on less obsequious terms. That will be the beginning of really expressing it, in the only manner we shall ever express it at all, by showing its effect on man.

In our new and hesitant land, those who have not been intimidated and silenced, have been warped. What poetry we have has too often come from the will, not the emotions, and deliberateness is always a blight. The Californian has not been the sole sinner in this respect, but the color of his emotions, unconsciously determined by improving land values, has led him to offend by extravagant phrases while his fellow-poet elsewhere has learned to be wary of overstatement. There have been in their time as many poems written with the galvanized determination to express the Chicago Pig Pens and Niagara Falls, the New England Interior and the Middle-Western Corncrib, as there have been poems to Mt. Tamalpais and the Golden Gate. The very poets who are now expressing American have sinned this sin to some extent: Frost, Lindsay, Robinson, Lowell, and Sandburg — all, in fact, except Edna Millay, who has let us see backgrounds where they belong, in a glimpse, through a window — inadvertently always, never crammed awkwardly to the fore. Her countryside was in her blood, not in her note-book, and she expressed it because she could not help expressing it, if she were to write at all.

California, much like the rest of the United States, has tried too hard; and where Sandburg gave us concrete detail that led nowhere, our poets reiterated one sterile word: *beauty, beauty, beauty* ... and that also led nowhere.

The Western poet is seldom a modern, in the sense that the free-versist is. He is either better or worse. For the most part he belongs to the Longfellow-Whittier school — the Lo! Here, and Lo! There, school in American poetry — a school that never absorbed its environment, but always held it at arm's length in the gesture of a curio-lecturer. "Snowbound" could only be written in an age that was yet untouched by sensuous pleasure in the coming of snow. "Hiawatha" and "Evangeline," the pretentious epics of the new world, have hardly a speck of Continental dust on their prosy feet.

How then, if deliberateness is fatal to art, has Frost, for example, given us New England?

I suppose because something more urgent than Frost's will-to-express is behind his poetry. So many people live in those ragged farm-lands, and so many more lie buried there. When man puts his own dust beneath his feet, he makes some kind of electric connection with the creative spirit. If thousands have felt poems in their passive souls when they looked at birch trees, one at last will come who finds the tree no longer alien to his language.

Quite fittingly, there has never been a poem written to a eucalyptus tree. There could not be, until this special tree had gone into the experience of many people so long and so deeply that when a poet comes to write of it he has no sense of its novelty, but only the feeling of its everlasting uniqueness. Just now the eucalyptus tree is *news*; anything said of it, try as we may, has chiefly a reportorial and journalistic quality.

The old New England school of poetry is gone; the free-verse school is gone; everywhere the new, instinctive poet is springing up, a simple and unpretentious impulse makes him sing; he is writing not great poetry, perhaps, but good poetry, certainly. And a few of the older poets have changed with this change, and are now abandoning themselves to their material. All of Frost's hill-wives and farm-hands can be traded for one little lyric about the snow and some pine-woods and a horse in a sleigh... a lyric that gives the whole of New England (and not a single fact) in a dozen lines.

There will be, in time, such poems to hold the immensities of California in a brief compass. If we hang our meditations in her trees, and our impulses from her precipices, and stir her dust with the whirlwinds of our desire, some swarthy Keats or electric Shelley will come, in a hundred years or so, and find the land alive.

Continent's End: An Anthology of Contemporary California Poets, ed. George Sterling, Genevieve Taggard, and James Rorty, San Francisco: Book Club of California, 1925, pp.xxv-xxxi

May Days

I liked putting these poems together because the choosing of them took me over and over the old bound volumes, and in doing that I discovered a continuity — and a severance.

That is, I stepped back abruptly through the looking-glass into a literary and political world that seemed both familiar and strange — a preposterous world, but never for a moment an alien one. What I saw had the same fascination that the face of your father at the age of sixteen has, when you come upon it peering from an album, for the first time after years of pre-occupation with your own generation. Of course, only part of father's face is here. To put the whole portrait together I would have to get files of *Others*, *Seven Arts*, and the *Little Review*; find pictures of the first suffrage parades, and the speeches of social reformers reported in the *New York Times*; follow the editorial risings and sinkings of the *Nation* and the *New Republic*; and see by some act of the imagination, the expression on the faces of the crowds who went to the Armory Show in 1912 to watch the Nude descend the stairs.

A war and a revolution, and five or six famines have something to do with the severance I felt. Behind the human extremity of those slow war years we discover the preceding period in parade down Fifth Avenue; — white horses, purple banners, and a phalanx of well-shod middle-class women, demanding, — and getting, the ballot! Elsewhere, a little off the center, we find Frank Tannenbaum and Arturo Giovannitti stirring liberal opinion with the news that for a few in the commonwealth at least, this is not quite the best possible world —

> "Factory windows are always broken,
> Something or other is going wrong.
> Something is rotten — I think, in Denmark..."

That was the state of mind. Something was wrong. Probably in Denmark. Where else? Not terribly wrong. Just wrong enough to insure a holiday.

And the holiday had numerous events and several attractive features. There was zealous social work, backed by optimistic social theory; humanitarian crusades abounded, gracious amateur movements made a mushroom growth. This activity was never ruthless or bitter, but earnest, idealistic, — always Christian.

Our awakening was like us. There was not much reflection or arduous labor. Austerity and desperate struggle were absent. It was a happy, well-bred and lively society, although it desired to be much more. The air was clear and exciting and the hour was the hour of seven on a spring morning. May days, indeed.... Dignity was not the fashion. Boredom, ennui, were not the fashion. There was so much to be said, done, thought, seen, tried out. The youth of the land was getting out of doors and all winter taboos were being broken:

> Bliss was it in that dawn to be alive
> But to be young was very heaven.

Later, after the first spurt of activity had spent itself, the whole mood of the time flowered in Woodrow Wilson. He and his words ended one period and began another — began it with the vow of the despoiled youth to be anything in the wide world, but never again Woodrovian. In him, as in his generation, ended the beautiful belief in the beautiful efficacy of — beautiful words. Even the gangling free verse movement had not shaken that faith. Our rightful President before he went to France, was vaguely idealistic, earnest as earnest goes, Christian (as that goes). He could be. The age hadn't come to grips with anything much more serious than the problems of rancid meat. Even the I.W.W. and the extreme left wing of the revolutionary movement shared the verbosity and romanticism of the time. Everybody was playing. And the *Masses* editors were playing hardest of all.

It was easy to read the *Masses* in those days. I say easy after following all the indignant letters protesting against Carl Sandburg's "Billy Sunday," or Billy Williams' "Ballad," (G.B.S. was one of the protestants that time) or Floyd Dell's articles on birth control. It was easy in spite of all the shock it gave the college-professor, college-student audience, because its shock was pleasurable for those who could stand it and centered chiefly on breaking down prudery and traditional dogma. It hit few class or economic sore spots — not because it did not aim at them, but because class fear in the reader had not been genuinely aroused. It he could skip the fine print of Max Eastman's monthly "Knowledge and Revolution," he could swallow the rest — usually. At any rate this early reader seldom began to fidget, fearing bloody upheaval, — seeing himself, wife and baby flung out of security into a great flux. This magazine was so obviously the voice of a harmless minority. Although its editor pounded away at the distinction between reform and the seizure of economic power by the working class, he failed to keep them separate in the mind of the middle class intellectual because events themselves had not yet made them separate.

Because this magazine of rebellion was edited in spite of its title, for the bourgeois liberal, to give him the freedom he had grown needy of, and because although it did talk in a very specific and realistic tone of voice about the proletariat, it did not talk *to* the proletariat, scoffers said, rightly enough:

> *They draw nude women for the MASSES*
> *Thick, fat, ungainly lasses, –*
> *How does that help the working classes?*

When it came to it — really helping the working classes a little later — scoffers, along with the bulk of the other readers, found the magazine exceedingly hard to read. But by that time they were not confined to the *Masses* any longer. That early note of gleeful scorn for the Bourgeois and his lady, his ideas about sex, literature, art, politics, furniture, et cetera, has been the cue for nearly all the best sellers ever since. The 500,000 Americans who sat up nights with *Main Street* in 1920, and *So Big* in 1924, and Ring Lardner in 1925, would read the early *Masses* with chuckles of delight, if they could get them. Lewis, Lardner, and Ferber are not as hard nor as clear as their spasmodic original. The *Saturday Evening Post* method has helped dilute the murex for the billboards, while the too intense blue has been left for the serious artists. Sherwood Anderson, John Dos Passos, Edmund Wilson, John Howard Lawson and Eugene O'Neil would have written, *Masses* or no *Masses*, but they would have had to spend more time under water grubbing along on the floor of the ocean if the dredging had not begun earlier. The little magazine revived by John Sloan's group for the publication of its drawings, and gradually altered into a newsletter for the hungry idealist had as curious a range of contributors as of readers. Gelett Burgess, Inez Haynes Gillmore, William English Walling, Lincoln Steffens, Amy Lowell, Jimmie Hopper, Will Levington Comfort, Mary Heaton Vorse, Harry Kemp, Sherwood Anderson, Ernest Poole, Charles Edward

Russell, Witter Bynner, Irwin Granich, William Rose Benét, J.E. Spingarn, Margaret Widdemer; — if this rabble made up its contributors, you ask, just what was the magazine as a whole trying to say? Nevertheless the family was congenial. Because its foe was so impervious and so vast it found more likenesses than differences within its ranks. The widest implications of even a revolutionary doctrine may throw a grateful shade in a great desert. Reginald Wright Kauffman and Pablo Picasso lay down together between the same editorial sheets.

All this you may observe — the grotesque bright green landscape — through the peephole of the old numbers. Having glimpsed this I changed my position to the landscape itself for a moment to see the *Masses* in its milieu.

It was born of a general upheaval still too close to us to be accurately described. In 1912 there were other live spots, since overrated however, I believe, by schismatic disciples. The *Masses* seems to have vanished from the gaze of the literary historian – underground it went, to cut channels in the bed rock, and left the *Little Review*, *The Glebe*, *Seven Arts*, *Others*, *Soil*, *Camera Work* and Miss Monroe's *Poetry* in full view above ground. But with the exception of *Soil* these magazines lacked even an acquaintance with the qualities that made the *Masses* dynamic; they lacked native humor, and realistic philosophy, had too much defensive aestheticism, and too little natural or racial intoxication. They were all fearfully immaculate and upper class. They were High Brow. They distrusted the country and the country distrusted them — rightly, I think, as the fungus growths that any nation or time can produce for a season out of the determination of a few editors. We have had several such growths in the past; such a group produced Stephen Crane and Harold Frederic during the 'nineties.

And *Soil*, the exception, is the example which proves the futility of a sociological pioneer who carries crooked maps and poor tools in his knapsack. Its editor under a layer of radical sounding talk, believed finally in the familiar salvations of more education, Henry George and Community singing.

The *Masses*, in spite of its readers, and the economic status of its editors, in spite of its editorial background, in spite of almost everything, — was revolutionary. It takes very few individuals to make a new age or explode an old one. That is, if the individuals themselves have hold on a vital substance. For me, and I think for numbers of others, there were few people writing in America in 1913 with the desire for a realistic grasp of our life as a whole. Creative artists dare not bite off more than they can shew; accordingly the novelists of the day who were in love with America, were deliberately seeing the country as a confusion of parts, and choosing for themselves one part of the many. So far as I know there were only three people who saw then what we all see now — the identity of the land. At any rate only three registered themselves indelibly: Max Eastman, Jack Reed and Floyd Dell.

I may be doing some personal injustice in classifying them as they appear to me now. There will be ample time later to discuss them as rich and fascinating single figures. In this preface I think of them as interplaying forces, not as they are now, but as they were then. They were more than three people when you put them in close contact: they drew to themselves a swarm of excellent artists and social satirists, — Max Eastman, realistic philosopher and poet; Floyd Dell, teacher and intimate psychologist; Jack Reed, man of action and human symbol for the time. This was a living combination and the ideas that grew from it had kinetic energy. They were more than these embodied abstractions, but being figures in a historical drama they must, having chosen to play the roles, take all the foreshortening and warping that go with the simple outlines of large events.

Seen thus, working together, they are for America the most significant group that ever managed to dominate, for a time, an entire generation. They, and the *Masses* as their instrument, were of tremendous importance for every young middle or working-class person just then coming alive within their radius. Their recorded sense of contemporary life has been a store house to which the diverse and quarrelling publicist world has gone for its energy – the liberal editors of the *New York World*, *Vanity Fair*'s humorists, Amalgamated organizers and pamphleteers, the *New Republic*'s decorous contributor, the *Nation*'s earnest one, and the present proletarian intellectuals who conduct the *Daily Worker*, all have to some extent consciously or unconsciously reflected *Masses-Liberator* tutelage. Only one other man, I think, belongs with Max, Floyd, and Jack, in their curious role of father-teacher-hero to that generation of young Americans, and he, George Bernard Shaw, is an English-Irishman, side-stepping sex with windy apologies and wedded in politics to the Fabians.

What was it they did? Well, to begin with, all three of them, although they would deny it, gave up being single-minded artists. They had started, all as poets (which they might consider unimportant), when something else caught them. They became obsessed by the unity of our life, the dance of it, and when they found themselves, after following the dance with abandon for a time, they were no longer poets — merely. In them was a fatal social-mindedness that made being artists a temptation which they put aside somewhat reluctantly, for pressing matters in hand.

Floyd Dell expresses the struggle best in his own words. His writing abounds with the phrase 'escape from reality' — the 'escape' being preoccupation with a fantasy, — or as we put it, the writing of a great poem, a great novel, a great play. That was the temptation he and his companions resisted. They turned their backs on 'escape' in the *Masses* days.

And to what purpose? There was this America — its politics, love life, industry, humor, architecture, education, poetry, dancing, clothing, drama, sport, language ... When the *Masses* group, cartoonists, artists, and editors touched these subjects it was their combination of sophistication and naïveté that made what they said so difficult to resist. These were in just the right proportions; proportions that allowed part of the soul to remain childlike while another part acquired worldly wisdom and discovered its delicious heritage of homely sound sense. The native shrewdness, the drawling humor that is called American because Mark Twain and Mr. Dooley and Abraham Lincoln had it, was coming up through the outlet afforded by this magazine, under layers of surface solemnity. The *Masses* set up its little tent between the two most social-minded tendencies then active in the American community — between the group that was liberal but Christian and the group that was rational but dull. It entertained them both with blithe impudence, being to some extent the child of both. The parents looked on as modern parents do, in awe of the little creature. Presently the child found its mission, — that of debunking the society into which it had been born. A point of view, known as Marxian, hitherto expressed in this land chiefly in undomesticated foreign gutturals, because, when simplified and translated into the idiom of Lincoln and Jefferson and Tom Paine, the new Yankee wisdom — shrewd, racy, materialistic.

And the awakening came too soon. The world moved threateningly beneath everybody's feet. Big strikes, outrages; the Mooney case; the McNamara case, — a nest of textile strikes shoved it on. Much grist for the mill, and good honest grinding. The European war stretched across the Atlantic. Holiday time almost over. It wasn't all going to be a battle of ideas, no indeed. A long way to Tipperary, Chicago slaughter-houses, Isadora Duncan dancing, and the bright, eager faces of suffrage parades glittering down the great avenues, Fifth, Michigan, Commonwealth. The *Masses* had a movement on its hands — people following, going where it led. It had created that following and now it had to take it some place. And a fight coming — America came into the war.

The world, abandoning even liberal Christianity and rationalism, went off its head. The *Masses* folks saw the spectacle. They knew that something might be done — but what, exactly? They kept their balance if nothing else, — in a world that began to whirl faster than a merry-go-round. Until Wilson's second election their heads were clear and until their trial most of alert young America was going to school in the *Masses* office.

When the trial came the three men tugged in separate directions and the triangle cracked.

Mr. Glintenkamp had drawn two pictures, and an assistant editor had printed them while Max and Floyd were away, busy in the larger turmoil. "The Liberty Bell in Collapse" made a frontispiece; another entitled, "Conscription," a few pages over. The magazine for August was refused the mails. In October followed another picture by the same artist: a naked young man with a too beautiful young face, a skeleton measuring him. Hot stuff. But they had all been doing hot stuff for years — Art Young, Boardman Robinson, Clive Weed, Robert Minor, Maurice Becker, Cornelia Barns, John Sloan, George Bellows. Only suddenly it wasn't simply Hot Stuff. It was treason.

Or so it became apparent — slowly, in spite of a cordial letter from President Wilson, visits with George Creel, and the decision of one judge in their favor. The post office would have none of them at first, remained silent for a time, and then when the *Masses* went to court for the lost mailing privileges, turned swiftly and brought about the indictment.

The next spring, in April 1918, Max Eastman, Floyd Dell, Art Young, Merrill Rogers, and Josephine Bell were tried on the charge of "conspiracy to obstruct recruiting and enlistment." With Morris Hillquit and Dudley Field Malone to defend them.

In the interval between November 1917 and March 1918 there had been no magazine. The *Masses* was fading into the protective coloration of the *Liberator*.

The first jury disagreed. A new trial was ordered. A second jury disagreed. The editors had won — and lost. Jack Reed got off the magazine, reorganized under a compromise with the war spirit; died in Russia, lies buried in the Kremlin with Lenin. Not gifted as a facile or complex thinker, he escaped the blind-alley of opportunism, and took the road to death and enduring glory. "Fog", his strange epitaph, printed in this anthology assures him a no less permanent title as a poet.

Floyd, who had never advocated much more than parliamentary socialism, and who believed, as many Bolsheviks do today, in conscription, was willing to go to jail but reluctant to go for an abstract principle he considered worthless. He stayed with the *Liberator*, to emerge at last as a popular novelist for the generation he had so long instructed.

Max determined to be a realist and keep the revolutionary home-fires burning. This is his reply to Jack's letter of resignation from the editorial board:

> I haven't a word of protest — only a deep feeling of regret.
>
> In your absence we all weighed the matter and decided it was our duty to the social revolution to keep this instrument we have created alive toward a time of great usefulness. You will help us with your writing and reporting, and that is all we ask.
>
> Personally, I envy you the power to cast loose when not only a good deal of the dramatic beauty but also the glamour of the abstract moral principle is gone out of this venture, and it remains for us merely the most effective and therefore right thing to do.
>
> Yours as ever
>
> Max Eastman

This is what perhaps nowadays we should call a rationalization.

His followers who agreed with him that a sincere radical does not run about the world courting martyrdom, still felt that a revolutionary leader does not purchase immunity from jail by repudiating his revolutionary opinions.

Prosecuting Attorney: "Will you tell us if the sentiments therein expressed (concerning "The Star-Spangled Banner"), which I have just read to you are your sentiments today?"

Defendant: "No, they are not, Mr. Barnes. My sentiments have changed a good deal. I think that when the boys begin to go over to Europe, and fight to the strains of that anthem, you feel very differently about it. You noticed that when it was played out there in the street the other day I did stand up ... I felt very sad; I felt very solemn, very sorrowful, because I thought of those boys over there dying by the thousands ... with courage, and even laughter on their lips, because they are dying for liberty ..."

Whether or not this retreat was a tactical error, Max did do what he set out to do. He did go on with the *Liberator*, forcibly modified as it was, and preserved what he could of the badly shattered body of the new philosophy. Significantly, because of his old quality of intellectual courage, Max was a Bolshevik when several of the present most prominent leaders were still anarchists, mensheviks, or industrialists.

In its last days when the *Liberator* could not decide whether it wanted to be either a propagandist or an artistic magazine, or both, it declined rapidly — all that had been brilliant turned wastefully violent; what had been masterful was either harassed or sentimental. The magazine, like a seismograph once again vividly recorded the tremors of the day, before any other group could quite tell what was happening ... In November 1924 the *Liberator* because incorporated with *Soviet Russia Pictorial* and the *Labor Herald* as the official organ of the Workers Party — rechristened the *Workers Monthly*. The futile magazine of the last years had a new birth as a revolutionary publication of the first rank.

But the *Masses-Liberator* spirit was gone — not so much dead as dispersed and divided. The magazine, until the war, was like a self-fertilizing tree. Social passion and creative beauty grew from the same branches. Now there has been pruning and grafting, — we have in consequence two trees — the air is sultry — there is no cross pollinizing. The artists who were attracted to the *Masses* for its art have gone one way; the revolutionists another. The two factions regard each other with hostility and suspicion. They consider themselves mutually exclusive and try their best to remain so. In the main the artists have become reactionaries or at best liberal camouflage for reaction. The revolutionists are impatient of all expression that fails to rubber-stamp the specific doctrines of the latest party creed. From one point of view the artists are loafers. From another, the revolutionists are — not artists![1]

In such a disheartening world the *Masses'* robust interchange between the two kinds of temperament seems amazing and impossible. Bellows, Sterne, Sloane, Minor, Lankes, Young, Barber, Becker, Davis, Barnes, Robinson, numbers of others in the prolific years, did not lie awake nights fighting off the essential significance of the contemporary scene as material unfit for art. Barnes, the most native of the older group, runs from the first volume until the bitter end. Gropper was the paper's last great social satirist. In him and in those who came before him the best of the *Masses'* spirit bore its fruit. The poetry, from first to last, was never so whole, native, radical — and still so powerful, as

---

1 *cf.* "Pletnev proves ... that the products of proletarian poetry ... are significant cultural and historical documents. But this does not at all mean that they are artistic documents.... Undoubtedly, the weak, the colorless, and even the illiterate poems may reflect the ... growth ... of a class, and may have an immeasurable significance as a symptom of culture. But weak ... poems do not make up proletarian poetry, because they do not make up poetry at all.... It would be monstrous to conclude that the technique of bourgeois art is not necessary to the workers. Yet there are many who fall into the error. 'Give us,' they say, 'something even pock-marked, but our own.' This is false and untrue. A pock-marked art is no art and is therefore not necessary to the working-masses. Those who believe in a 'pock-marked' art are imbued to a considerable extent with contempt for the masses." Leon Trotsky, *Literature and Revolution*, pp.202, 204.

this drawing. The poets tended either to a Tennysonian convention or to journalism. There are a few exceptions worth all the failures. If the *Masses* had continued another twenty years, this anthology might have preserved for English literature not four great poems, but forty.

But it ceased, and the buds on the two trees wither for lack of each other. It is the artist's fault because he is afraid of revolution. It is the propagandist's fault for giving the artist a job he cannot perform. And it is nobody's fault, as well, but simply the effect of a world change.

From now on, as long as this division hold, our art will have little fertility. Certainly it will be hard to put roots deep into a soil pre-empted by propagandists who insist that the artist bear only one kind of fruit. The artist's concern is not to persuade or educate, but to overpoweringly express. A good revolutionist should allow the artist this freedom, since he knows very well that only liberals seek to persuade, or to lure other half-hearted liberals into action.

The working class needs artists. It has no one to convince of its quality but itself. The exploited mass that owns neither the earth or its own toil or the fruits or implements of toil will sooner or later have all these. Whether it will have its artists before or after these, we do not know. What they will be like we can only guess. But the beginnings of that art in poetry, will, I think, be found in the *Masses-Liberator* anthology, 1912-1924.

May Days: An Anthology of Verse from Masses-Liberator, New York: Boni & Liveright, 1925, pp.1-15

A Poet Out of Paradise

Genevieve Taggard was two years old when she arrived in Hawai'i with her schoolteacher parents in 1896. There, she grew up in the company of children of many races, attending the public school in Kalihi where her mother and father taught. From her religious and politically liberal parents, she learned early about social inequalities and the injustices suffered by the indigenous population under the colonial occupation of American business interests. In her first memoir of her Hawaiian upbringing, "Haole Scrapbook" (p.49), she alluded to her disillusionment with the oppressive American colonial presence on Hawaiian society in her part-Hawaiian friend John Frank's disenfranchisement from his rightful heritage. At the end of that memoir, learning of her impending departure from the islands, Frank tells her, "Too bad you gotta be haole" (meaning, generally, an outsider). This might have been interpreted as his regret that she came from a different world, to which she now had to return. But for Taggard, it also meant it was too bad that she would never be able to free herself from the stain of cultural complicity in the American overthrow of the Hawaiian culture. This may shed an important light on the question of why she never returned to Hawai'i.[1]

After leaving Hawai'i in 1914 to attend the University of California at Berkeley, Taggard began to realise the scale of the damage that American colonisation had inflicted on the place and its people. Attracted to socialist circles at the university, her growing commitment to racial and economic equality made her aware of the extent of the exploitation of the Hawaiian populace by the American takeover of that sovereign nation in 1893.

Taggard brought with her an aura of Pacific exoticism about which she remained deeply ambivalent in her early work. At the same time that she was becoming politically aware of her separateness from her homeland, she recognised in her poem "To a Hawaiian Girl" (published in *Liberator* in March 1920) that having known and loved "an Island and a Sea" would also keep her emotionally "ever foreign" in the continental US. This tension between two geographies and two cultures would remain with Taggard and her poetry throughout her career. The critical reception of her early collection, *Hawaiian Hilltop* (1923), however, shows her work to have produced a more universal expression, transcending the "local" in poems that were "Hawaiian in order to be human."[2]

The Tourist" (p.11) is a poem that explores that tension, in the context of gender conflict. Written in 1917 during her student years at Berkeley, it presents a scene of Hawaiian dance performed for the visitor, with unresolved implications of seduction and thwarted desire, in a foreigner's fantasy of hula. The narrative casts the "lover" against

---

1   For a detailed portrayal of Taggard's years in Honolulu, see A. Hammond, "Genevieve Taggard: The Hawaiian Background to a Radical Poet," *Hawaiian Journal of History* 49 (2015), pp.149-177.

2   Frank Ernest Hill, "Hawaiian Magic," *Measure* no.38 (Apr 1924), p.18.

the outsider "tourist," but the whole energy of the poem centres on the sensuousness of the dance, not so much as sexual invitation but as a state in which the physical senses, tactile, visual and olfactory, portray the dancer as an agent of vital and even spiritual power — by the movements and the presence of her body she can command even "the sleepiness of death" and bring a mundane setting to an "altered" state, approaching an "altar"-ed sanctity. By the actions of her dance, the moon, the mountain, and the flowers' fragrance are intensified. By shifting her gaze from her lover to the tourist, and in the energy of the dance, she ignites desire and controls the actions of her male counterparts. This was an altered paradise, but one in which power was invested in the feminine life force.

"The Tourist" was first published in the radical magazine *Liberator* in 1920. Taggard had been was introduced to one of its editors, Max Eastman, when he delivered a talk at Berkeley in the summer of 1919. Taggard was then editor of the university's literary journal, *The Occident*; Eastman had just published his book of poetry, *Colors of Life* (1918) and considered himself a "fervent evangelist of revolutionary socialism." Intellectually stimulating and strikingly handsome, he had been regarded as one of the country's New Intellectuals.[3] That combination of art, political enthusiasm, and sex appeal was irresistible to Taggard, and they were soon romantically involved. She already knew his poetry and he was flattered to see her favourite passages marked in her copy of *Colors of Life*.[4] On Eastman's part, he remembered having loved Taggard's poetry, and their correspondence reveals a love/hate relationship that persisted through their marriages to others into the 1930s. At that first encounter, Eastman apparently offered her a position on the

---

3   Robert Rives LaMonte, "The New Intellectuals," *The New Review: A Critical Survey of International Socialism* 2:1 (January 1914), p.45.

4   Christoph Irmsher, *Max Eastman: A Life*, New Haven and London: Yale University Press, 2017, p.146.

staff of *Liberator* and, although this never materialised, its promise was enough to lure her to New York. There she found herself at the centre of a vibrant political and literary scene, and was soon immersed in the most current ideas on poetry, politics and women's rights. Addressing the power of the feminine and taking a critical position on colonialism and cultural imperialism Taggard's poem "The Tourist" had placed her squarely in the middle of those issues.

"The Tourist" was also noticed in the pages of the *Liberator* by the Harvard-educated poet and critic Robert Wolf, who later described the poem as "one of the strangest and most magic pieces of sensuous beauty in the English language." Having joined the Communist Party in 1919, Wolf was working as a freelance journalist in Washington D.C..[5] His report on the testimony of Ludwig Martens (the *de facto* Soviet ambassador, deported the following year) before the Senate Sub-Committee on Foreign Relations, appeared in the same issue of *Liberator* as Taggard's poem "To a Hawaiian Girl."[6] By then, he had already determined to seek her out. He traveled to the magazine's offices in New York and persuaded Max Eastman to introduce them. They soon became a couple and married in March 1921. Wolf was Taggard's first husband; the character he described in his Martens article as "advisor and press agent to the Soviet bureau," Kenneth Durant, would become her second.

Taggard and Wolf moved to Farmington, Connecticut, near Hartford and in easy reach of Manhattan by train. Wolf was trying to write a novel. Leaving her job at *The Freeman*, Taggard spent her time writing reviews and developed many of the poems that

---

5   Robert L. Wolf, [rev. of *Hawaiian Hilltop*] "Reviews: Once Over," *Liberator* (February 1924), p.31. Lydia Fiske Emery, unpublished biographical chronology for Robert L. Wolf.

6   Primarily a political magazine, promoting the new Bolshevism, *Liberator* also featured poets such as Louis Untermeyer, Jean Starr Untermeyer, Babette Deutsch, and Carl Sandburg.

would go into her first major book, *For Eager Lovers* (1922). Her correspondence with her friend Josephine Herbst shows her hard at work with both her poetry and short stories, including "Engaged" (p.29), which she planned to submit to *Liberator* but was sure would never be published "short of a new social order"—the ideal of socialism which she said "determines me artistically."[7]

One is tempted to read the sense of entrapment and eclipse of identity in "Engaged" as a possible early response to the constraints of her own marriage. It features the problems of young women intent on an independent life of love and work, but thwarted by a class-bound society still resisting birth control and criminalizing abortion.

In November 1921, heavily pregnant, Taggard set off with Wolf by train headed for California. They halted their journey in Chicago for the birth of their baby Marcia. Continuing on to San Francisco, they rented an apartment on Russian Hill, where the plan was for Wolf to continue to work on his novel and Taggard to teach poetry in Berkeley and to edit with George Sterling and James Rorty an anthology of contemporary poetry of California, *Continent's End*. Her introductory essay for that book, "The 'Lo!' School in Poetry" (p.63), shows her sharpening her critical skills and developing her prose style.

Their near neighbours on Russian Hill were Charles Erskine Scott Wood and his partner Sara Bard Field. Field was a women's rights advocate of the previous generation; she had organized the state of Oregon for women's suffrage, and was one of the campaigners who presented the national petition for the women's vote to President Wilson in 1918. She was also a poet. Field and Taggard grew very close in this period; Genevieve read Sara the poetry of Emily Dickinson and Edna St. Vincent Millay. And they

---

7   Taggard to Josephine Herbst, 12 September 1921, Genevieve Taggard Papers, New York Public Library.

had quite a few friends in common, among them George Sterling, William Rose Benét, and Doris Stevens, Field's closest personal friend who had been a friend to Taggard in Greenwich Village.

Field, a socialist since the turn of the century, and Wood, who described himself as a "philosophical anarchist," shared Taggard's socialist beliefs. Field felt that Taggard's upbringing in Hawai'i instilled in her a "feeling toward social justice." While Wolf wrote in solitude in a cabin up the coast in Bolinas, Taggard found emotional support and inspiration in their company. Years later, Field remembered fondly the three of them having had long talks on the subject of poetry and, particularly, of their shared belief in "how poetry and so-called propaganda could be united without blemish to poetic ideals."[8] With Shelley as their model, these conversations proved rich ground for Taggard's desire to create a poetry in which a deeply felt social commitment and a desire for lyric transcendence could be fully integrated.

Before Taggard and Wood had left for California, she had helped found a poetry magazine titled *The Measure*. The title was taken from Robert Frost's poem in his book *Mountain Interval*, "The Aim was Song":

> And then by measure blew it forth.
> By measure. It was word and note,...

Originally conceived by Maxwell Anderson, Frank Ernest Hill and Louise Townsend Nicholl, *The Measure* was established by a collective of eight writers, who took turns in the role of "acting editor" for three monthly issues at a time, beginning with the first issue in 1921. Louis Untermeyer later rated *The Measure*

---

8   Sara Bard Field, "Sara Bard Field: Poet and Suffragist," *Suffragists Oral History Project*, Interview conducted by Amelia R. Fry with introduction by Dorothy Erskine. Berkeley: Regents of the University of California, 1979. Online Archive of California.

Front cover illustration from *The Measure*.

in importance alongside Harriet Monroe's *Poetry* magazine,[9] although the founders hoped it would function as an alternative to that more established tradition.

As the magazine's critical voice developed over its five years of publication, both innovative and traditional elements were included in the contents, but its overall emphasis was on the modern lyric tradition as represented by Robert Frost and Edna St Vincent Millay.[10] The cover illustration gives a sense of the poet (with feet still in contact with nature though not quite firmly on the ground) measuring himself against an awe-inspiring cosmos.

9   Deborah S. Greenhut, "The Measure: A Journal of Poetry," *American Literary Magazines, The Twentieth Century* (ed. Edward E. Chielens), Westport, CT and London: Greenwood Press, 1992, pp.195-198.

10   Andrew Thacker, "Poetry in Perspective: *The Measure*", in Peter Brooker and Andrew Thacker, eds., *The Oxford Crucial and Cultural History of Little Magazines: Vol.II*, Oxford: OUP, 2015, pp.322-333.

Wolf retuned to Connecticut in early 1923 and Taggard joined him that summer. With two published books of poetry, *For Eager Lovers* (1922) and *Hawaiian Hilltop* (1923), Taggard settled into the creative life of the working poet. Her poem "Elegy in Dialogue" (p.23) was published in *Measure* the following spring. The title of this poem is almost an oxymoron: a dialogue is by definition delivered by two voices, but in this elegy although the poet addresses the other there is no conversation. Questions posed fall unanswered. The death that is fearfully anticipated is not necessarily that of a person, but of the relationship. There are hints of this in the strains beginning to show in the marriage: Robert's desire for other sexual partners, his increasing mental instability, financial worries, all of which may well have underpinned such a song of lamentation.

The poem begins with a couple walking though the past, in which "pathways all overgrown" suggests that ways to reach each other have been blocked by neglect. They discover a dead insect in a spider's web, a central metaphor for the struggle against the inevitability of death. The lines "so shall we struggle — you or I. / One of us will shortly die" occur twice in the poem. The two images of death — the quiet still-lifes of the insect in the web or the dried blossoms are opposed to the "reckless lunge" out of control — giving us contrasting views of two different minds in conflict with each other. These are the two faces left alone (separately and alternately) when death arrives: one wears a "callow" mask of immaturity, the other an "idiot" smile expressing only incomprehension. By the end of the poem, the failure (death) of the marriage seems to be immovable as the unyielding stone, in "a granite body to conjure and turn." But with this note of ambiguity, even the apparently lifeless granite may be receptive to the magic that "conjuring" love can generate and "turn" — transformed — into an object of hope.

Taggard's work appeared in *Liberator* from 1919 through 1922, and even while she was teaching in Berkeley she was gathering ideas and making preparations for an anthology of the poetry from *Masses* (1912-1918) and *Liberator* (1918-1924), suggested to her by Max Eastman (an editor of both magazines) before she left for California in 1921.[11] In this period when she was giving critical shape to her ideas about the directions of modern poetry, she was also still firmly anchored in her admiration of socialism. In 1924 she wrote to J.J. Lankes, whose wood-engravings graced the pages of *Liberator* from its inception, asking to reproduce some of his work in the book. For its cover or title page, she initially suggested the words "Hammer and Scythe" — possibly a reference to the flag of the newly-formed Soviet Union.[12] At the end of her editorial essay, she announced she would donate any royalties to the International Workers' Aid, a charity to combat poverty and hunger in Russia in a time of drought and crop failures.

The aim of the book *May Days* (1925) was to gather the best poetry from the two radical publications more or less continuously edited by Max Eastman and Floyd Dell, *Masses* and *Liberator*, but in her critique of these cultural productions she was also assessing her own political development. In her introduction to the book she found the reformist socialist voice of the *Masses* magazine now lacking urgency and action, while applauding the energy and experimentation that drove the modernist literary project. Taggard criticised *Masses* for not addressing pointedly enough class divisions and economic inequalities, while conceding that it was dynamic in its time, and revolutionary; though the audience for its sense of rebellion would have been primarily the bourgeois liberal. She had to admit, though, that it was the *Masses* that had translated pre-1920 Marxism into a fundamentally American idiom.

---

11   Taggard's "A Note on the Poetry" credits Robert Wolf with the suggestion of the project, but correspondence shows that Eastman offered it to her in 1921.

12   Lankes to Taggard, 31 March 1924, The Papers of Genevieve Taggard, New York Public Library.

From the vantage point of 1924, Taggard found that the artistic temperament and the political focus of contributors to these two magazines had now diverged and become for the most part mutually hostile. For all that was best in the spirit of the *Masses* Taggard used the metaphor of a tree where "social passion and creative beauty" grew from the same branches, the union of a creative and an ideological consciousness she had dreamed of with Sara Bard Field and Charles Erskine Scott Wood in San Francisco. *Liberator*, on the other hand, failed to produce a similarly fruitful bounty – its branches yielded only harsh doctrinal teachings and political treatises, without the complementing sweetness of art.

II
The Exquisite
Skin of Self

Memoir

Such bliss he had, such agony,
And what he had he gave to me.

I shut the door of our small house,
And lived with agony's carouse:

I opened the door and let in
Others to live down the din;

And all the time his bliss was there
Eluding me like silver air,

And when I caught his silver glee
It was too magical for me.

I broke his bliss, I hushed his woe,
We stood in our empty house to go

Packed and coated on our quest;
He went east, I went west,

Until at length we met before
The narrow panel of our door;

We stood and faced each other as
Long as life-times take to pass;

Into the house I led him then,
I shut the door on living men;

And now we watch grope to and fro
The ghost of bliss, the ghost of woe.

Words for the Chisel, p.38
Previously published in *The Nation* (10 December 1924)

To One Loved Wholly Within Wisdom

Someone will reap you like a field,
Pile your gathered plunder,

Garner what you bring to yield,
Turn your beauty under;

In cruel usage, in such
Sickle-cutting, heaping,

Certain women toil too much,
Weary of their reaping;

Someone else may winnow you;
Someone else may plunder;

I have cut too many new
Swathes, and broken under

Soil that should have fallow lain
To be greedy either

For the shattered stalk, the stain
Where the clusters wither.

Words for the Chisel, p.33
Previously published in *New York Herald Tribune*
(8 November 1925)

Galatea Again

Let me be marble, marble once again:
Go from me slowly, like an ebbing pain,
Great mortal feuds of moving flesh and blood:
This mouth so bruised, serene again, — and set
In its old passive changelessness, the rude
Wild crying face, the frantic eyes — forget
The little human shuddering interlude.

And if you follow and confront me there,
O Sons of Men, though you cry out and groan
And plead with me to take you for my own
And clutch my dress as a child, I shall not care,

But only turn on you a marble stare
And stun you with the quiet gaze of stone.

Words for the Chisel, p.39

Picture

These triumphant hills have stood
Waiting for human magnitude;
They have seen
Only the humble and the mean:
The hurried farmer, haying, heaping
Acres of grass before the storm;
Smoke from houses, winter reaping,
And the heavy uniform
Furrow ... These hills have seen
Only the meager and the mean;
Awkward women weeding rows;
Children brandishing at crows;
Men building barns and cutting wood
In an eternal solitude.

Words for the Chisel, p.41

Only the Frost

Good night, good night. And this warning:
I'll be kind and cold-hearted with you —
I will take you with me any morning
Up the path where this evening we flew
To the lap where we lay in the hills.

There, where the lavish sun spills
To the level of the hollow,
Where the sun-motes flicker and fall
And the flakes of the sparse leaves follow,
When you see the sure sun crawl
Where you saw the huge moon hover
And the swallows go southward, over —
You will wonder you loved me at all!

You will know you wanted, and made
A girl-lover of moon-shade.

Morning, and the sane light chills
The love, the loved, and the lover;
Why search for the little thing lost
On scarlet leaves, under frost?
There is only the frost in the hills.

Words for the Chisel, p.59

Words for the Chisel

The moss will creep upon your name
And fill the cleft of mine
And scraggley grasses grow and frame
The granite's oblong line.

This unsubstantial air we cleave
To rear us massive form
Will aid the moss, the viney weaver,
The little clumsy worm

Within whose body all the crust
Of earth is powdered so
Often, with such patient lust
Against such granite woe.

Words for the Chisel, p.11
Previously published in *Pasadena Star-News*
(26 December 1925)

The Enamel Girl

Fearful of beauty, I always went
Timidly indifferent:

Dainty, hesitant, taking in
Just what was tiniest and thin;

Careful not to care
For burning beauty in blue air;

Wanting what my hand could touch —
That not too much;

Looking not to left nor right
On a honey-silent night;

Fond of arts and trinkets, if
Imperishable and stiff

They never played me false, nor fell
Into fine dust. They lasted well.

They lasted till you came, and then
When you went, sufficed again.

But for you, they had been quite
All I needed for my sight.

You faded. I never knew
How to unfold as flowers do,

Or how to nourish anything
To make it grow. I wound a wing

With one caress, with one kiss
Break most fragile ecstasies....

Now terror touches me when I
Seem to be touching a butterfly.

Travelling Standing Still, p.18
Previously published in *New York Evening Post
Literary Review* (4 June 1928)

Dilemma of the Elm

In summer elms are made for me,
I walk ignoring them and they
Ignore my walking in a way
I like in any elegant tree.

Fountain of the elm is shape
For something I have felt and said....
In winter to hear the lonely scrape
Of rooty branches overhead

Should make me only half believe
An elm had ever a frond of green —
Faced by the absence of a leaf
Forget the fair elms I have seen.

(A wiry fountain, black upon
The little landscape, pale-blue with snow —
Elm of my summer, obscurely gone
To leave me another elm to know.)

Instead, I paint it with my thought,
Not knowing, hardly, that I do;
The elm comes back I had forgot
I see it green, absurdly new,
Grotesquely growing in the snow.
In winter, an elm's a double tree;
In winter all elms trouble me.

But in summer elms are made for me.
I can ignore the way they grow.

Travelling Standing Still, p.49

Understand the Eye

Opposite the infinite
Is the single eye set.

In its core the infinite lies, —
A mighty jewel, claspt to finite size.

There, there in indivisible
Purity the old lights dwell

Poured by the aged light of some
Star on the eye-ball's convex room.

Opposite the infinite
Is the single eye set,

There to behold curved space that goes
Opening the lavish starry rows,

There by a slowly gathered gaze
Weaving star-rays on star-rays;

Or single, pierced, nugget of clear sight,
Shut on its eye-hinges for night.

O, opposite the infinite
Is the single eye set:

The depth, the tunnel of sky
Held to the lance of the eye

Blunts the beam, lines out-spread
From the eye's head.

Curve to curve, with no end
The thick beams bend,

And the cave of far space
Tips to the cave of the face.

This is the great dignity, —
The repose, of the eye.

Travelling Standing Still, p.51

Letter in Solitude

Here are autumn certainties:
I will love you and the trees
Go on yellowing and the sun
Stand and pour its radiance down.

Count the seasonal certainties:
I will love you and the trees
Color like a carnival,
Color and refuse to fall,
To show a new aspect of trees
More nearly like themselves than these.

I will love you as I have said:
After all the leaves are shed,
And the sky is fastened down,
And the valley depth is brown,
And the ruts begin to freeze,
There are other certainties.

Surely love you, but with none
Of that radiant tint of sun;
As if a cloud had curled across
The sun, and clung like lichened moss;
Love you surely, but in a prone
Dogged way, more like stone;
As if a stone's touch gave a cue
To a clearer love of you.

However absently the eyes
Thinking their inner thoughts may stare

They match within, the sharpened size
Of hillshapes in the cutting air.

And so, by seeing uncovered ground
And outlines gaunter all the time
I see love also winter-bound
And think more simply into rhyme.

And since love gets its tempered sense
From the large fact of altering earth,
I love the winter, stubborn, dense,
And love the storm my love is worth.

Travelling Standing Still, p.53
Previously published in *The Dial* (October 1927)

Tired Girl

Put her away some place between two hills,
Away from the sea and the sun.
She has so much to think of — must she run
On your bright bosom always, Mother Earth?
Put her away, and let some other birth
Bring her back to the sound of the sea, and the sun.
After she ponders under silent hills,
Beneath your warming bosom, Mother Earth,
She will have words for her beloved one.

Travelling Standing Still, p.20

Monologue for Mothers
(Aside)

I am a coward now, and never shall
I walk the earth in confidence again.
And I have let death know I am afraid
At this late date.
          His steps come at my back
As viewlessly as feet track some one with
The fortune of a nation, — just behind ...
Halt when I halt, and pick me up again.

(A hinge, just a rusty hinge,
Nothing to ague at,
Still, how I scuttle and cringe!
What was that?)

The coarse stuff of myself folded no longer
Around the small pure person, the new child; I tremble,
I am afraid, I have found
How slender the shoulders, the rare bones, and how fine

The little deep-blue veins that show along
The temple bone. The world is evil. Greedy air
Sucking too near could sip her inward breath, — I go
So timidly now, who had so many prides.

Who scorned the craven wings across the nest,
The squawking warning of the parent bird,
Neck stretched far out, peering and peering still,
East, West, North, South for infant enemies.

Come, crane your neck, an instinct says;
Perhaps the great sky holds hawk! a hawk!
If eagles come, combat them with your eyes.
Hold off a reptile with one mother-gaze.

(Beauty writhing in the snake,
Alert in the bad eye
Of the great hawk, good Beauty make
Cause with this child. I cry:

Beauty, be her swords to cut
Enemies away,
Build a circle-wall to shut
Night out and shut in day.)

We will not live in fear, in petty fear,
Nor shelter with an arm
Angled in terror; shock her innocent ear
With this insane alarm.

Now all the world will nod to her,
Nothing ever snatch
At her in evil —
          Something flew
Slant on the window!
            Fear is in my kiss.
And if you suffer it will be for this,
(O innocent and brave and grave and small).

Monologue for Mothers (Aside), New York:
Random House, 1929.

114

Command from a Hammock

Whale-cloud, go off, a mile an hour
On your slow busness with the air,
Getting ingredients for a shower
Until you reach the sky-scape where

My love, not styled a little man,
Looks like a black twig in the sea,
Under, in shadow, smaller than
He ever seems when seen by me;

And on your way contrive some weird,
Arresting form; make yourself so
Peculiar, cumulous, elephant-eared, —
Leave off the whale shape as you go....

And loom so queerly as you put
Your twilight on him while he swims,
His eyes will open first, — then shut,
Salt-water silver, round the rims,

That he will say to someone else, —
Half to himself and half aloud, —
As one child always sees and tells
Another, pointing, *See the cloud!*

Travelling Standing Still, p.50

Going Somewhere

Travelling standing still, I took
Years to do a piece
Of one Pacific Island. Now
Everywhere I look —
As if I stood on top the Pole
And saw surrounding how
The horizon was travelling
While I was standing still —
The world goes round and round and I
Am pure content to be
Its tiny axis toward a sky
That points and centers, spinning by,
In an earth that is, with me,
From root's depth, into tree,
By tiny atoms, back and forth,
Shaken, a round trip out of earth,
To earth's depth as before.
I could not travel more.

One circle out of earth and back
Takes seventy years at least;
The other goes with mental speed
Around to the level east.
The atom of my mind can look
While it is being taken
Upon an arc the plumed trees took,
Shaken and unshaken.
So the two circles. Momentary
The horizontal one.
And the tall circle, too, the airy
Flight to the flowing sun,
Converge on this, my standing still,
My travelling through space,

Going somewhere, until
I arrive at no place.

Travelling Standing Still, p.55
Previously published *The Nation* (June 1928)

Doomsday Morning

Deaf to God who calls and walks
Until the earth aches with his tread,
Summoning the sulky dead,
We'll wedge and stiffen under rocks,
Or be mistaken for a stone,
And signal as children do, "Lie low,"
Wait and wait for God to go.
The risen will think we slumber on
Like slug-a-beds. When they have gone
Trooped up before the Judgment Throne, —
We in the vacant earth alone —
Abandoned by ambitious souls,
And deaf to God who calls and walks
Like an engine overhead
Driving the disheveled dead,—
We will rise and crack the ground
Tear the roots and heave the rocks,
And billow the surface where God walks,
And God will listen to the sound
And know that lovers are below
Working havoc till they creep
Together from their sundered sleep.

Then end, world! Let your final darkness fall!
And God may call and call and call.

Words for the Chisel, p.45

Legend

My friends who come up for weekends think of the Willskys as a case — one of hundreds I cannot. We share snow-storms, garden-blight and telephone troubles. The struggle to live on the Berkshire hillside keeps me from the detachment of my week-ending guests. They do not see how strangely significant the story becomes with some pondering.

The literary legend, started by Glaspell and Frost and O'Neil, needs revising. These housewives do not run out into a blizzard, or leap into a mountain torrent, mad with the tedium of farm existence. In our community all the puritans who were at all inclined to go mad have done so long ago. Those who remain are flinty-sane. It is the foreign women now. They live in the houses where the American women had their tragedies, and strangely enough, they too are beginning to break and weaken. Tough Mrs. Willsky, for instance, the Polish peasant woman who worked like a man in the fields in the old country, acting over here as if she had three hundred years of thin blue Yankee blood in her veins.

Tap the underground river of misery by taking up the receiver. At any moment in the day, you may hear it.

"What are you doing now?"

"Oh, cooking dinner. I got the men to feed."

Pause

"Well don't do no good to complain."

Pause

"No I can't stand it here very long, though."

Mrs. Willsky solved that problem. When her eighth baby began she went to a doctor and cried; he scolded her and told her to go home and be a good mother. Month after month the problem got worse. There were six children living. In the New England kitchen there were howlings and screechings and scoldings, eternally. There was so much work.

The children had to be beaten regularly to get them to work in the fields, to plant, weed and strip tobacco. Or they got sick, or ran pitchforks into their feet. And now the oldest, Helen, wanted to leave home and earn money. There was one way to keep Helen, and that was to get sick, too.

The sickness was indefinite. Nerves, Mrs. Willsky called it. Doctors said it was nothing. Then Mrs. Willsky found that she had no stomach. Her food went into her legs and arms. She grew very ill. Helen nursed her seven months, until the baby came. After that, everybody, including Helen, expected her to get well. She turned her ravished face to me and said

"One baby a year. Better die."

And the resolution held. She was only thirty, but the resolution held. The countryside is marvellously beautiful. Her husband owns two farms. The baby is very sweet. It hurt her that we should want her to live. She turned her back in disgust on this life-enamoured community. Four different doctors told her that she was playing sick. But it was much more intense than playing. The devil came, and ghosts, and obscure Polish furies and horrors. When the baby cried, she wept that Helen would have to be its mother, but her resolution held.

It took five months, in the end she had her own way – the first time I suppose that she had ever hammered with her will and made a fact of desire. My suggestion that she rebel at another point did not appeal to her — refusing to have any more children was too mild a sin. She defied God and died. On the night of the first snow. The snow sent her far beyond her wits, and it was not easy to return.

Fourteen year-old Helen, who has the place of wife and mother now, finds the whole thing hard. She believed all the horrors her mother saw in the air. She has vowed never to marry. The neighbors say she is pretty hysterical, and once they thought she had gone out of her head. Lately she has turned a deaf ear to the baby – simply sits at the telephone. All day long she wails out the recital of her troubles. The girl used to look like a Botticelli, with flax hair. Lately she is queer and ugly. If you take up the receiver there is the voice

"—but anyway, I don't see how I can stand it —".

Birth Control Review (July 1925), p.199

The Plague

One evening my father came in late to supper just as we had lighted the kerosene lamp and put it in the middle of the cleared dining table. He had been off seeing the superintendent about building the new school.

"Hayashida is sick," said my mother, "and wants to see you before you go to bed."

My father took a little hand lamp and went out into the tropic blackness, down the latticed walk to Hayashida's little whitewashed house, where he lived with Kiko. The screen door banged after him, and he was gone a long time, while I watched the mealy damp baby moths who came under the lamp shade and got cooked on the kerosene surface of the silver lamp. Then the screen door closed lightly, and my father came back holding his lamp up.

"Mama," he said as he blew out the light and stood some distance from us, "Hayashida has a bubo under his arm as big as an egg."

He washed himself with kerosene and called up the doctor on the telephone, sitting down as he waited for a connection. Mother sent us to bed. We didn't know what a bubo was.

The next day the doctors — about four of them and seven health officials — came to see Hayashida. They told my father to say that Hayashida had measles and dismiss the school indefinitely. This is what my father did, because he had to, although he hated to stand up before all his schoolchildren and tell a lie. Hayashida besides being our Japanese boy was the janitor of the school. He had swept it out on Monday afternoon just before he was taken sick.

The neighbors knew what they knew — the measles story wasn't very convincing. The doctors went in and out of the little whitewashed house where Hayashida lived, and Kiko could be seen standing limp against one window — all her lovely oiled hair pressed against the glass. We children loved Hayashida and Kiko. He was a big rawboned Japanese, gaunt and yellow, and very merry. He had come to us right off the plantation when he couldn't speak any English. Only Kiko could speak, because she had been a silkworm girl in Tokyo. Under the lattice of the passion vine over our door they stood beside each other and wished to come and work for us. Hayashida took care of our huge garden and the lawn; he clipped the hedges and swept the walks, and all afternoon long, while he ran the sprinklers and changed them, he kept our swings going too, and carried us around on his shoulders. Once a centipede crawled up inside his blue denim pants and he caught hold of the cloth and called to us to look while he squeezed it to death so that it wouldn't bite him. He also sang very sweet songs to himself in a high silly voice all the time he worked.

Now, with a great bang, we were overridden with doctors who tramped into our house and brushed past us children as if we didn't even exist.

124

"You've got to fumigate," said one. "How solid is this house anyway?" and he poked at the new wallpaper and made a hole. "I thought so — built out of sticks," he said.

I wanted to yell at him for that; to bang him on the head; to tell him to get out of my house. While some of the strange men were talking to my mother, the same one who had broken the paper went over and yanked down the curtains. "Take down all the hangings," he ordered my father.

Then the death wagon came for Hayashida. They carried him out with masks over their own faces and gloves on, and little Kiko walked sorrowfully after him in a kimono which she had ceased to wear since she lived with us. Now she reverted to kimono, and carried a few belongings in a little handkerchief. She sat at his head in the wagon, and a few children were there to see what was happening. My father tried not to cry; so did we all. Hayashida was going for good. No one ever got well of the plague.

"Good-by, Hayashida," said my father, "you have been a good boy with us."

Hayashida sat up in the wagon.

"Will you take care of Kiko if I die, Mr. Taggard?"

So he went away. The doctors hurried him off to the receiving station and he was put in quarantine. Now two health officials fastened on us.

"Take your children and go away for three or four days while we fumigate. Go anywhere. There is no danger. You haven't been exposed. Go visit friends. Don't let anybody know. There mustn't be a scare. This is only the sixth case. We must keep it quiet."

"I won't go to a friend's house," replied my indignant mother. "Where shall we go? There isn't a place in the world."

"You've got to get out for about four days," they said savagely, wishing she wouldn't quibble with them.

I started to take down some dresses.

"Little girl," one of the bawled at me. "Don't touch those

things. Get out of the house in the fresh air. You can't take anything with you."

So we went, headachy and driven, forlorn in our old clothes about four o'clock, knowing that all the neighbors down the long road to the streetcar were looking out from behind the doors and whispering that there was Plague in our family.

The streetcars go very fast in the islands, because there are such long stretches. They are open — a row of seats and a roof. On these flying platforms you go across rice fields and wait at switches for the other car; you climb a hill with a drone and then branch off into Palama where the Japanese live.

At four o'clock on a school day it seemed strange to be riding through Palama. Dimly, the reason for this ride — the distinction of having Plague in the family, the awful importance of an event that seizes you the way a cat does a rat, the very great satisfaction of having something happen that is huge and terrible, that may end in darker, grimmer events — all this was in our minds as we went through Palama, looking at the Japanese and Chinese, the children, the withered women in their flat-chested black sateen coats and earringed ears. On all the faces that turned up to our car as it danged its bell through the crowded streets and down across the bridge, I extended the now gently painful knowledge that Hayashida would die, that our house would be fumigated and that my head ached and my feet were cold.

On we went through Honolulu, past the hardware store where Sherwin Williams paint folders were tucked into little boxes – (we always helped ourselves to the little booklets with their shiny inches of blue and tan); past our little church looking brown and dusty on a weekday with the shutters closed and the bougainvillea vine next it blooming cerise in the heat; past the Palace, the Opera House, the statue of Kamehameha where the idiot Portuguese boy stood all say, worshipping and rubbing his hands; past the rich people's houses on the way to Waikiki.

Waikiki was our heaven always. It was always reserved for the greatest occasions of joy. A sharp turn — our car was running wildly over the swamp in the stiff breeze from the sea, with Diamond Head lifted up, brown as a niggertoe nut, running parallel with our track. Another curve and wind and a switch, and the smell of salt, and the first turn of a wave, between two hedges as we started up again, running headlong into Diamond Head – headlong for the place where the water came into the arm of the old brown-purple mountain.

(Oh, the sea, the sea, the sea, the sea, the waves; the high clouds; the bright water, the crazy foam on the surf away out, the blue limpid lovely empty water. Oh the sea.) So I cried to myself, and got up to stand on the seat.

"Sit down," said my mother wearily. She had a headache, I could tell.

We sat fixed, waiting for the great joy of seeing it suddenly, as we knew we would – the mountain, the surf running in with its arched neck and blowing mane, the dizzy blue water level on the sand. There it was. Oh, sea, sea. My brother and sister wouldn't sit still. My father cheered up, lifted his head and his dreamy gaze to focus on it; my mother sat dully, because her head ached so. I could tell, by the narrowed slits of her eyes. She didn't look. The sun hit the water and the sunlight hit you as it shot off the surface. Black things danced in the air. It hurt between the eyes to look at it.

We got off at the Waikiki Inn and my mother and father hurried ahead. We ran for the sand.

They came out of the office in a minute, looking very embarrassed and troubled and trying to look untroubled. A Japanese boy led them to a little cottage under some vines and unlocked the door. My mother looked in and then came down to us.

"You can't go in the water today. I'm sorry. Get out right away. You look like little wild children. You mustn't get wet," she said in a lower tone when we came, holding up our skirts to our waists, all wet-legged from the first tumbled wave. "Mother doesn't dare let you get in the water. One of us may have it."

With that her face looked so terrified and in such dull pain that we came limping in, letting down our dresses, and picking up our shoes and stockings. As we walked away from sand to grass lawn, the sea talked and roared and mumbled and swished at our backs. We didn't dare even turn around.

That night I was sick. The black dots in the air turned to balls of fire; the terrible sunlight on the water, the terrible water we couldn't go in, that became noisy torment, throbbing like the heart in illness; fever that took the bones and broke them and wrenched the stomach. My mother was sick too. We were sick together. The others slept. I lay under the thick mosquito net as if I were as wide as the Pacific Ocean and the fever took one arm off to the east, the other to the west; my legs stretched into dimness I gazed flat upward, fixed, at some immensity — I immense, and facing immensity. The kerosene lamp purred on the table, a yellow torment. My mother sat retching with a sick headache. Now and then she would come and bow her head on the bed outside the mosquito net and say, "Oh, Genevieve, will this night never be over?" and then she would vomit again.

The sea rose outside in a great wind. A hard tropic tree scratched and clanged on the iron roof of the cottage. It was utterly black except for the torment of the little flame in the lamp. The ocean broke outside so near, the same wave sounds as in daylight, but so interminable at night, and no one to hear it, but us, me and my mother. The waves hit the shore like a blow on a wound; the lamp burned in its chimney stifling the air, never wiggling, just burning. Horror, the black death!

She fanned me and called out that I was her first born, and rubbed the wet hair from my head and chafed my feet. Her hand on my legs made them limited again at the bottom of the bed, not so long that they had no feet as a moment before. "Oh mother, will this night never end?"

It ended — fear and a sick headache and a little fever — that was all. And I did not die except in some experience of the mind.

transition (Paris), no.5 (August 1927), pp.77-83

The Creative Woman: The Problem of Marriage

Editor's Note: Genevieve Taggard, a brilliant young writer, has made a reputation among American poets. The author of several volumes of poems, she is also the Editor of May Days, *an anthology of radical verse from the* Masses *and the* Liberator. *She is an ardent worker in the Socialist Movement. Her article is rather away from our usual subjects, but raises an important economic issue.*

"Women and children first." That is, women put children first, and men are inclined, in turn, to put first woman. Except when the men are artists. Then, if they are good artists, they refuse to put anything but their work first. But women bear a closer relation to children than men do to women.

When a man becomes an artist, the chief problem which he carries over as a man into the artist's life is the old primary necessity of earning a living. The problem has gone unsolved; or has been solved badly in innumerable ways, but whether the solution is less or more of a solution in all the varieties of cases, it always remains — significantly for the psychologist, not to speak of the man — the solution to something external to his being.

In the future, where women are likely to be artists as often as men (I do not mean contributors to the *Saturday Evening Post*), a new subjective problem will have to be solved, or at least experienced and endured, as part of the lot of a creative existence.

Just at present women have skilfully dodged the problem. They have not had an accounting with themselves. And they are being applauded for being as good as the world thinks they can be — not as good as they know they might be. In this generation women are released and men enormously hampered by the economic pressure of modern life. For although a certain percentage of women artists do have to earn their livings just as men do, if they unite with another person the burden slips from woman to man. More women are allowed to devote themselves to "art" and a non-lucrative "career" with the tolerance of a paternal bank account. One man has always stood economically for the support of more than himself. A single woman is not ordinarily required to take care of a number of others. She is doing very well, in the world's eyes, if she takes care of herself.

In the future, the inner and difficult dilemma of the woman artist will involve this economic world and make grievous trouble for her. Not because she herself will require food, clothing and a place to live of another person; but because she will want children, who must in turn have all these things and many costly others. And children will make of her a slave and a parasite – two beings she cannot very well afford to revert to, since they have been for thousands of dark years the very things that kept her in abominable silence.

Why, if so inevitably she becomes a dependent as soon as she bears a child, will she insist, nevertheless, on having one? That is the battleground of the woman artist. The man's struggle for a chance to live long enough to get words on paper, for all its overtones and tangles, is a simple matter compared with this will divided against itself that will wreck women as individuals and call out of them repeatedly a mindless desire to create — not poems, pictures, music — but new human beings.

For women believe (because life takes care that they shall) in the blind philosophy that life itself — the white light — is more important than any refracted colour. Rather scornfully and cruelly they understand that art, from one angle, is only a plaything, quite sterile as compared with the power in themselves. The greatest we have accomplished matters little to dead men, or stones. This women do not forget.

Because they are fashioned to bear children, and because children must be born, women are fatally inclined to fail as individuals and console themselves for failure in the fresh start of children. This is the cowardice men never indulge in. Their failures are in the open; called failures and nothing else.

This hidden and extremely unintellectual belief latent in women — this negating the importance of fulfilled expression — will come to the surface in time. Those women will express it who are possessed of the problem. Those who refuse to meet it will not count greatly except as decorative artists — a thing women have always managed to be with much effect. The woman who tampers with the wholeness of her nature will pay a high price for her evasion. A man may either want children, father and support them; or decide that he will not be so burdened. As an artist, either decision will not enter as deeply into his point of view as a similar decision by a woman.

This will be the case for many reasons, too confused for me to unravel, one very natural one being curiosity.

Whilst a woman knows that her body has not had the experience for which she is primarily fashioned, she will have the timidity of a novice in her work. The authority of experience lacking, she will either attempt to follow a man's pattern in her life and work, or remain throughout her thirties and forties an artist of adolescent griefs.

And the other way? The familiar status of life — dependent on a man for more than a mere good living.

An artist needs the authority of experience as well as the prompting of emotion. A woman artist wants to bear a child if for no other reason than to discover that it will not do as a substitute for her work. That it hinders her in a hundred ways, she will be certain after it is born. That it develops a new set of functions and emotions as well, she will see clearly. If she is an artist, and not just an idle and restless lady of quality, a child will in no way appease her initial craving. But having acquired this necessary knowledge, she will also have acquired a child, perilously high in her affections.

She will have the choice of supporting herself and her child — meanwhile creating Great Art — or becoming that double and cumbersome entity – a married woman.

The New Leader (London), (7 January 1927), p.10
Previously published in *Birth Control Review* (1925),
and *Equal Rights* (8 May 1926), pp.77-83

Collected Poems
of Robert Frost

The humanists have been trying to pigeonhole Robert Frost. Long, long shall our humanists sit with their rubber bands in their hands ready and waiting to snap them around the quotations they want from his works. The rest of Frost they would undoubtedly discard. Texts from this book laid neatly on four sides of him may serve the two-dimensional critic and the literal-minded reader; but not even his own texts nicely dove-tailed, can box the intelligence expressed here so sure of its goings-out and its comings-in. Frost is too cussedly non-conformist to trust even his own words as texts five minutes after he has uttered them. His mind is too seasoned, to humorous, to relish the owlish solemnity of dicta and dictations. He trusts his poems as poems, as metaphors spread to catch meaning, as words that have become deeds. He has given them speech that suggests not one meaning but many. Any effort, therefore, to strip Frost down to singleness of meaning in the interests of propaganda must be opposed. The wisest and most mature poet of our time should not be hacked and shaved down to suit a pigeonhole. If, in their text-gathering, the humanists had paid more attention to Frost's behavior with his poems, if they had understood the meaning of tone and intention — if, in other words, they had known how to read poetry and not merely how to collect texts, they would have abandoned the attempt.

If they had not claimed, but rather praised Frost, some similarity might have been noted; for Frost embodies virtues the humanists extol. It is only natural that they should covet the aphorisms — pithy phrases, culled here and there from his work, which would help plead their case.

Those who have read each of Frost's books over a period of fifteen years have observed certain traits of character in his poetry. Frost detests seeing an idea used past its strength, or a metaphor with wobbly knees urged to a gallop. In this he is like a farmer who will not over-tax his horse's capacity as surely as he knows it management. Frost flogs no emotions up hills too steep. This instinct of delicate judgment about the weight and value, fitness and right use of materials is the sign of a master. The humanists who study masters have found this virtue outstanding. They call it a humanist virtue, and claim Frost because he possesses it. "The Lockless Door" should have given sufficient warning:

> It went many years,
> But at last came a knock,
> And I thought of the door
> With no lock to lock.
>
> I blew out the light,
> I tiptoed the floor
> And raised both hands
> In prayer to the door.
>
> But the knock came again.
> My window was wide;

I climbed on the sill
And descended outside.

Back over the sill –
I bade a "come in"
To whatever the knock
At the door may have been.

So at a knock
I emptied my cage
To hide in the world
And alter with age.

There is always an empty room and a just-opened window when you knock imperiously on Robert Frost's door.

In this collected edition of his poems we may study, with especial profit, the prevailing meditation which runs, from the first poem written thirty years ago, on and on in, and out and through and under the facts and faiths of our contemporary life, down to the last poems written yesterday. Here is a mind that grows but never changes, that understands, with each poem accomplished, more and more about the mastery of form, storing much observation and illustration from experience, handling actualities with assurance, but a mind, nevertheless, that does not change, because it gives to experience something more spiritual, more creative than the things it takes away. This is a mind that unfolds, but never learns; it is that old phenomenon, the poet's mind, first described by Plato when he said that all knowledge was recollection. "Into My Own," which opens this collection, gives the key to the entire book. With the dark forest of life before him, with the ache for exploring it within him, the poet says, of his return:

They would not find me changed from him I knew —
Only more sure of all I thought was true.

Experience is merely the test and discipline for intuition and insight. Such inner certainty needs no texts and rules as outer props.

This inner certainty which is akin to Emerson's self-reliance and Thoreau's self-sufficiency, is the mental vantage point for Frost, about which he wrote while he was still a young man:

> If tired of trees I seek again mankind,
>   Well I know where to hie me — in the dawn,
>   To a slope where the cattle keep the lawn.
> There amid lolling juniper reclined,
> Myself unseen, I see in white defined
>   Far off the homes of men, and farther still,
>   The graves of men on an opposing hill,
> Living or dead, whichever are to mind.
>
> And if by noon I have too much of these,
>   I have but to turn on my arm and lo,
>   The sun-burned hillside sets my face aglow,
> My breathing shakes the bluet like a breeze,
>   I smell the earth, I smell the bruised plant,
> I look into the crater of an ant.

This ability to look at man, and then at an ant or a star and then back again, gives Frost a point of view from which he may criticize our life even while he participates in it. He is a thoroughgoing critic of all our thought. His wisdom which is self-made carries him past many of our jumping-off places. He goes on after we stop. Often Frost seems to be saying to himself: "No, no, that won't quite do." Examined, this system works just so far. One more step and it breaks down. It is plausible, perhaps; but as a system, it won't do. The strength of a poem or a metaphor lies in the fact that it need only be plausible. A system must be water tight; it guaranties, it advertises itself as water right. Frost disbelieves in guaranties and systems. He insists, for instance, that science is merely an extended metaphor — that is, that science is attempting to describe the unknown in terms of the known. It is then a kind of poetry, and should be treated as plausible material — not as cold fact. When Einstein's theory of relativity was mentioned in conversation, Frost countered, "Wonderful, yes, wonderful; but no better as a metaphor than you or I might make for ourselves before 4 o'clock."

If a pigeonhole wishes to include a poem like "Sitting by a Bush in Broad Sunlight," which says of God that,

> One impulse persists as our breath;
> The other persists as our faith.

it must make room, too, for the same subject-in-hand, found in "The Bear." Man

> ... sits back on his fundamental butt
> With lifted snout and eyes (if any) shut,
> (He almost looks religious but he's not).
> And back and forth he sways from cheek to cheek,
> At one extreme agreeing with one Greek,
> At the other agreeing with another Greek
> Which may be thought, but only so to speak.

It the pacifists seize on "The Peaceful Shepherd" they must remember, too, the profound comment on the virtue of the hero, in "The Soldier." "Acquainted With the Night" identifies itself with all the night cries of woe; a few pages over another reflection on the same night-grief is ironic:

> We may as well go patiently on with our life
> And look elsewhere than to stars and moon and sun
> For the shocks and changes we need to keep us sane.

The humor of true proportion dominates this ending — individual trouble with the background of impervious stars:

> Still it wouldn't reward the watcher to stay awake
> In hopes of seeing the calm of heaven break
> On his particular time and personal sight.
> That calm seems certainly safe to last tonight.

Man with his limitations; man with his possibilities beyond limitation, are the themes, I think, in these poems. In other words, toil and creation. The men who made New England and Robert Frost used their hands and their minds. On a bare new continent Old World equipment was often unsuitable. These experiences of toil and creation — for the first years chiefly toil — have culminated in Frost and they make him the large man of our time. He knows his universe of stubble-field, barn-lot and orchard; he knows what day-labor it exacts, and by what co-operation man may eke out his days. He is, like every true worker, full of the lore of his tools and his materials, "gear, tackle and trim." He records fatigue, the battle with the soils and the seasons. He writes down the comedies of this life – for instance, "The Cow In Apple Time." He records a community of interest between men at work together (see "The Tuft of Flowers") and a responsibility, a love for the animals which share man's toil. Toil has dignity in this poetry; it is universal human experience portrayed concretely, in locality, in Yankee accent.

Then lest toil become a doctrine, Frost abandons it. Like Thoreau, he revelled in his life, and he here and there rebels in his verse, from the morality of work-for-its-own-sake. He loafs. We see him insisting on leisure for meditation — rejecting toil for something better and more active — creation. In insisting on leisure, he made himself master of life and his thought. Either our contemporary poets manage an enervating leisure in which they wilt for lack of contact with the life of the rest of the world or they work to small purpose at pointless tasks in which they do not believe, saving a bit of themselves for fragments of half thought or they waste themselves entirely as rebels or slaves. Frost accompanied the swing of his scythe with the ease of his thought for many years. When the time came he knocked off work and called it a day.

In a talk at Wesleyan University in 1926, Frost said: "I think what I'm after is free meditation. I don't think anybody gets it when he's in anybody's company — only when his soul's alone.... The person who has the freedom of his material is the person who puts two and two together, and the two and two are anywhere out of space and time, brought together."

And again: "There are two types of realists: the one who offers a good deal of dirt with his potato to show that it is a real one, and the one who is satisfied with the potato brushed clean. I'm inclined to the second kind. To me, the thing that art does for life is to clean it, to strip it to form."

The rejection slips that came back to Dartmouth, Derry, Lawrence, Cambridge and Plymouth all said for fifteen years that Robert Lee Frost, college student, mill hand, shoemaker, farmer and school teacher was no poet on the side. Some of the poems in this collection date back to 1898; recognition came in 1913. Between these two dates Frost schooled himself — he learned to write by writing and to think by thinking. The rejection slips fluttered about him. The outside world gave him a series of occupational names while he continued to perfect himself as a poet. "A Late Walk," written in 1897, contains this stanza:

> A tree beside the wall stands bare,
> But a leaf that lingered brown
> Disturbed, I doubt not, by my thought
> Came softly rattling down.

Eventually the whole of New England felt the touch of the thought that brought down the leaf in 1897.

Frost is a mature artist in a society of clever mechanical youngsters.

New York Herald Tribune Books (21 December 1930), pp.5-6

A Woman's Anatomy of Love

Review of Fatal Interview,
Edna St. Vincent Millay

This is the first of Miss Millay's six volumes of verse to be composed entirely of sonnets. Each previous volume has carried a good number, however, for ballast. In "Renascence" we read in 1917 her "Bluebeard" and Sonnet V; in "Figs from Thistles" those flawless examples, II, III and IV; in "Second April" came the unexcelled (I mean unexcelled by any sonneteer), Sonnet XII, "Cherish you then the hope"; in "The Harp Weaver," that marvel of serene arrangement, "I know I am but summer to your heart"; in "The Buck in the Snow," "On Hearing a Symphony of Beethoven." All together Miss Millay has published, when we count the fifty-two of this collection, something like one hundred and twenty sonnets, and as those who read *Reedy's Mirror* in 1920 or those who possess *Mr. Houston Peterson's Book of Sequences* know, the original twenty published then together which have been broken up and used to steady the freight of the five previous books form the true beginning of this ever-growing sequence.

This impressive series is an anatomy of love written by a woman from a woman's point of view. Even in the sequence entitled "Sonnets from an Ungrafted Tree," which drops the pronoun I, and tells the story of a farm woman who tends a dying man she cannot love, we come in roundabout way to this theme. In this exposition of the light and shade of emotion we see, especially in the publication of this last group, a long contest between surrender and refusal to surrender, with the conception of the mind's integrity and the soul's chastity uppermost. Miss Millay has built up her most splendid sonnets upon this struggle and has given their extended argument something as central to turn upon as a life-experience. It is the artist who withdraws from

> ... the puny fever and frail sweet
> Of human love ...

But the sustaining faith in Beauty's "massive sandal set on stone" is an emotion which is permissible to those who cannot write verse.

Fittingly enough, in 1920 Miss Millay stressed the volatile, evanescent aspect of human love. In the midst of her passionate exposition as to its duration — "only until this cigarette is ended," "whence flee forever a woman and a man," "longing alone is singer to the lute," "Oh think not I am faithful to a vow" — (the lines are numerous, unforgettable and apposite) — comes the poet's discovery of a permanence within or beneath change. This gives the sequence an austerity which accents the bitter gaiety, the witty and incorrigible spirit of her best work. Her instruction to her generation heretofore was this: live passionately; expect the worst; be reconciled to the death of all that is moral; cherish the fragments of all that is immortal; and when the fatal hour comes as it must, go on in the spirit of that shepherd who sang grieving for dead Lycidas, in the spirit of his sorrowful and healthy wisdom, "to fresh woods, and pastures new."

Now, as "Fatal Interview" suggests, this *a priori* knowledge, this conviction-from-the-first of the brevity and tragic dissolution of love is uppermost — but with this difference: that heretofore it was recognized as in the nature of love, but here it has unmistakably happened, and here the poet asserts and re-asserts her own fidelity to a mortal person, a fidelity not felt before because her sure theory prevented. And here, coincidental with the experience which contradicted all her premonitions, is the verification of her wisdom, for with the expression of a durable love is mixed the bitter admission that the relationship itself is at an end.

> Nay, learned doctor, these fine leeches fresh
> From the pond's edge my cause cannot remove ...
> ...
> Yet should you bid me name him, I am dumb;
> For though you summon him, he would not come.

This new experience brings the long and splendid train of the sonnets not to a close, perhaps, but to some kind of temporary conclusion; in the end we find again an avowal of the old symbols in the worship of immortal things, this time phrased as "Sparrow-drawn and her arrowy child"; but this conclusion, although it echoes the younger devotion, is on higher ground and bears all the marks of tragic experience. Nowhere has Miss Millay expressed her self-knowledge better than in Sonnet XLVI of this volume:

> Too season-wise am I, being country-bred,
> To tilt at autumn or defy the frost.

Edna St. Vincent Millay is one of the few poets in our whole tradition who handles the sonnet with mastery. She knows not only its surface laws, the mechanics of its management, the possibilities, advantages, limitations and black abuses of the form, but she knows, because she is exceedingly intelligent in the pursuit of her craft, all the subtleties of the form as well. She can lighten a line, throw accent where she desires, model a phrase to contour, turn a phrase in anticipation of phrases to come in chime, set an apt word in a tone of old color, run in a conversational aside, startle, delight and overwhelm by the adroit use of language — language often quite divorced from image, precise color or concrete detail.

But there is a deeper reason, I think, for her pre-eminence in this form. First of all, Miss Millay's thought and all her references are everywhere traditional. Book-lore is her reality. "The lively chronicles of the past" is her phrase. Queens, knights, princes — Isolde, Guinevere, Francesca, Lesbia, Persephone — the list is very long. High-syllabled words from books, touched with the tang of actual speech, traditional conceptions and old stories are Miss Millay's materials, added to her own very active sense of life. She illustrates by her book-lore, her metaphors have the colors and the textures of old embroideries, jewels, weapons, pictures. She is uninterested (except in her fondness for New England countryside) in new sights, new forms, fresh images or the discoveries of simple meditation. She does not write to tell the world what it does not know already, but to announce a truth the poets have voiced for ages, of which the world has always been aware. Only in the adroit power, zest, and spirit of her utterances are we aroused. Is it not natural, then that her happiest form should be the one used by the noblest poets of the tradition?

Then, too, Miss Millay is constantly musing on the doctrines of the one and the many; theories of permanence and change underlie her metaphors of the seasons; brief varied life and long, uniform death are her antitheses. The sonnets are elegantly and lightly metaphysical, and this fugue becomes a play of opposites. Is it not fitting, then, that the poet should choose the sonnet form instinctively and find it flexible to her touch when it suits so well her mind — a form as highly designed as life, and as limited?

It seems to me that Miss Millay worships only one thing — perfection. Such a worship throws difficulties in the path of human love, but it suits the ardors of the sonnet-writer and the lover of beauty alike. She does not value uniqueness, she has no patience with rebel esthetics, new forms, strange or oblique insights, or any kind of naturalism which loves irregularity, which everywhere opposes logic and the almost machine-like perfection of detached art. Odd insights are awkward to her. Her preferences are for those elegiac and harmonious gestures of the greatest Greek sculptures. I should even dare to push the statement further and say that Miss Millay is interested in perfection, not people, in art, not in life — her courage and self-scorn testify to her own self-rejection for the sake of her first principle. Is it not natural then that Miss Millay should choose the sonnet form which demands in the very act of writing, this attitude?

Astute and experimental thinkers, poets who temper an acknowledgment to "innate ideas" by the realization that much that appears innate is only the conventional in thought, tend to warp and distort form, using it for an end and not for itself. Never is there any such impulse to be found in Miss Millay's thought or her work. She aims only to fulfil the sonnet form, just as she aims only to re-say what is true — never to find new meaning or to burst old form, or to transcend either. Her form, like Euclid's outline, and like the course of love, is something, to her inevitable, inherent in life and love, written in the heavens and in the human brain.

The conviction forever at work beneath the bright variety of her speech is a highly simplified view of life; in extended work the danger of monotony increases with each re-affirmation. Miss Millay's critics have evidently felt, while objecting to this or that in her work, that life as we are forced to face it today seems to be too brutal, too disintegrated, too complex and too full of unexplored possibility to be interpreted by a set of pastoral or medieval symbols. That her attitude is too literary, even too academic, her emotions too idyllic and slender for the first rank in poetry. In her work Miss Millay has an excellent answer to such criticism. She might say, I fancy, that one should not read poetry as one reads a newspaper for the brief news of the chaotic day; that in a sense simplicity Is immortality; that we read a bit of Sappho and Horace and the lyrical ancients for the inescapable simplicities, the perennial emotional truths, such as are found in this work of hers.

Indeed, in criticism and in the business of limitation, the worst that can be said of Miss Millay's work is that sometimes — and sometimes oftener than sometimes — we wish to read some more manifold, less eloquent or more angular poet. That at her worst she is pseudo-classic, as Keats was, and for the same reason, for worshipping the classic gods and verities with an ardor not really classic at all — pseudo-classic. That at times this perfection seems arid. That there is too little meditation and reverie in her work, too much care for geometric simplification. Miss Millay leads one of the three important contemporary schools of poetry. By the members of the two other schools her influence is deplored, as she was deplored by Amy Lowell, who saw her rise to power in the early 1920s. Miss Millay is a far better poet than Miss Lowell. My own adherence is to a line of poets who seem to me less philosophical, that is to say, more subtle, less abstract. Since I do not in any way adhere to Miss Millay's school, my praise is all the more fervent for what she has done. We remember always a poet's best, his high-water mark — his poorest vanishes like mortal speech. Her best is in the world of Shakespeare's sonnets and, in her own field, for the reasons I have given, she cannot be excelled. Immortality here is defined, served and achieved.

New York Herald Tribune Books (19 April 1931), p.xi

Poet Out of Pioneer

My mother and father were the two most remarkable young people in a very small Western town: my mother, a pioneer extravert, a hard-working, high-handed, generous, and handsome girl. She never set limits to what she could do. She believed in miracles made by her own hands. When my father came, she was in rebellion against small-town sterility, determined to go to college and become, not a raw country girl with the limit of grammar-school learning, but a cultured Christian gentlewoman, who could paint, sing, write, and testify to God's glory. My father had come West from Missouri for his health. He looked like Abraham Lincoln, but delicate and Quixotic. My mother's strength fascinated him and, I suppose, scared him to death. Church and school linked them — he, the principal of the grammar school; in a crude community, a man of learning (six months in a church college); the superintendent of the Sunday school and leader of Christian Endeavor. She was his first-grade teacher and a very good one. Not for nothing had she been mother to eleven brothers and sisters

149

on the old ranch. Children were happy with her. She furnished them a firm foundation.

My father, of course, felt the charge of vitality. They married and for two years lived in a state of enforced chastity, I suppose, determined to save money and go to college. They saved $2,000 and were departing for a higher life when my uncle, my father's brother, came penniless from the East and married a shrew. My father loved my uncle with an unnatural simplicity. Brother John and the shrew wanted the two thousand to buy an apple-farm. My mother saw an older love in my tender father about to swamp her ambitions. In this emotional tangle I was conceived and it was I, finally, not my father or my uncle, who defeated my mother. The money went of course to John, college plunged into inaccessibility, and my mother was in the usual trap and, I am sure, as bitter as any modern woman about it.

Suddenly came a chance to go to a tropic country – another way out. Romanticists they both were, although they called themselves missionaries. And so when I was still a baby my mother gave the rest of her possessions to my uncle, packed up me and her baffled desires, and set off with her Shelleyesque husband to the heathen. The story is a complicated one; I shall follow only the trends of the two temperaments. My mother, with ultimately three children and a passive husband, still had her old ambitions in this new land. But with us she did not encourage the freedom she gave her little school-children. At home she was a major domo. The family became a highly efficient organization — it had to be, when she gave most of her day to teaching. Although she took care of us all, there was never any ease or leisure; we were not permitted happiness. In the public school and the missionary chapel these two labored, giving their crowded time free for Jesus. My father was the principal, a flexible glove on my mother's strong, stubby hand. She was still his "primary" teacher, his wife, cook, housekeeper, refuge, and intelligence. And so complete was her domination over her man that she expected to mold and use me as she had used him.

But I, of course, began before I can remember silently and consistently to oppose her; to defend my father and to rebel at her steam-roller tactics. I was lonely and excitable. Fairy-tales were denied me — no reading but the Bible — so I made Bible stories into fairy-tales and she found me very difficult about them. She believed in authority. I would not submit to it. She drove me to music lessons and housework — all done to the moral precept: *there is only one right way.* I should have been a musician or a composer; but she blocked the path, hemmed in with her vigilance all creation. Music, made hideous in the guise of duty, I abandoned and took another way out — with words, where no one could give me orders. I dreamed and made fantasies, and soon I lied habitually, to escape her, and went underground in all my desires. I was my father again, but a girl this time, and enough like herself to match her mettle. I had a good childhood in spite of the fact that we lived in a state of nervous tension at home and, as missionaries and school people, in a superior and controlled fashion in public, upholding the just, the good, the true. That was easy because we had the advantage of our less educated native neighbors. My father, as the years went by, became a vague sort of scientist, fleeing away from my mother's pressure. She, passionate and unfulfilled, lived in her three children.

Her objective was this cultural life she had never reached herself, and toward it our faces were always directed. But there was a division in my mother's own mind which she had never faced. Our religion was the religion of the small town, based on a fear of the big world, on a fear of the rational, the progressive, and the huge bugaboo of "Darwinism" and Higher Criticism. And yet however my mother fought against the liberal Congregationalists and the damned Unitarians, and however fanatical was her matter-of-fact mysticism, she wanted her children to live in that intellectual world and, I suppose, to solve, in a Christian fashion, its problem for her.

Twice my father collapsed and was told to his immense relief that he had tuberculosis and that he need no longer inhabit our world. His ailment was undoubtedly psychological. Twice we starved, and adored our mother for her gorgeous strength, and pitied and averted our faces from our father. And then the old theme reentered.

My mother demanded of my now wealthy Uncle John the $2,000 that had made him a comfortable apple-grower, and had kept her in bondage. We lived on canned salmon and rice and wild tomatoes for several months, in a shack where the tropic rains poured on our beds; and John wrote evasively with no inclosures. My father loved him still and would do nothing about it. My mother went as nearly insane with rage as she could permit herself, but only on Saturday mornings, when she could safely compute compound interest on an outlawed loan. The story spins out and out. We returned to the small town in an attempt to collect the two thousand, after a letter from my uncle offering us an old farmhouse near him. There, used as my uncle's hired help and wearing his family's cast-off clothing, we integrated ourselves into the single struggle to exist – without him. At length we returned to our tropics, penniless still, but to decent poverty and our own way of life. And my mother and father took up their teaching where they had begun fourteen years before, in a three-room school on a sugar plantation. This was a little too ironic for my frail father who had just managed to complete before his return to the States a twelve-room modern school for his beloved natives. He fell ill again and again we existed — I teaching in his place to get the $25 a month allotted a substitute.

I was ready for college. On two hundred borrowed dollars we came to a Western university town and there as servants in a boarding-house began again the struggle that included our whole story.

Am I the Christian gentlewoman my mother slaved to make me? No indeed. I am a poet, a wine-bibber, a radical; a non-churchgoer who will no longer sing in the choir or lead prayer-meeting with a testimonial. (Although I will write anonymous confessions for *The Nation.*) That is her story — and her second defeat. She thinks I owed her a Christian gentlewoman, for all she did for me. We quarrel. After I escaped, she snapped the iron trap around my brother and sister. That is their story. I do not know if they will ever be free of her. She keeps Eddie Guest on the parlor table beside the books I have written — a silent protest against me. She is not pleased.

I cannot pretend to be entirely frank in telling the story that results from this story; or to apply to it any such perspective. Let my daughter tell it later on. She will see outlines I cannot.

I think I have not been as wasted as my mother was — or as wasteful. I have made worse mistakes, which might have been more fatal than hers and yet have not been, at least for me. My chief improvement on her past was the man I chose to marry. I did not want a one-way street of a marriage, like hers. I married a poet and novelist, gifted and difficult, who refused defeat as often as I did. Hard as it is to live with an equal, it is at least not degrading. We have starved, too; struggled as hard as ever my folks did. But the struggle has not been empty; I have no grudges. Intellectually as well as emotionally my husband had as much to give that was new and strange as I had. In marriage I learned, rather tardily, the profound truth that contradicts Jesus when he said, "Bear ye one another's burdens." I am a better person when I bear my own burdens. I am happiest with people who can bear their own, too. I remember my mother's weariness and contempt for a man who could never take up her challenges. Seven years with a real person is better than her thirty with a helpless, newspaper-reading gentleman.

The pioneer woman was a dynamo – and her man nearly always ran out on her. From the bitterness in such women many of us were born. Where was her mate? Did she destroy him? Did he hate her for her strength? Was he weaker because she was strong? Where is the equilibrium, anyway? I do not know, for sure, although I spend much time wondering.

Marriage is the only profound human experience; all other human angles are its mere rehearsal. Like every one else I have wanted it. And yet having it, it is not all I want. It is more often, I think, a final experience than a way of life. But I am a poet — love and mutual living are not nearly enough. It is better to work hard than to be married hard. If, at the beginning of middle age, we have not learned some of the perils of the soul, in this double-selved life, we are pure fools. Self-sufficiency is a myth, of course, but after thirty, if one is a serious-minded egoist (i.e., artist) it becomes more and more necessary. And I think it can be approximated.

Lucinda Matlock, in the *Spoon River Anthology*, says:

> We were married and lived together for seventy years,
> Enjoying, working, raising the twelve children,
> Eight of whom we lost,
> Ere I had reached the age of sixty.
> I spun, I wove, I kept the house, I nursed the sick,
> Rambling over the fields where sang the larks,
> And by Spoon River gathering many a shell,
> And many a flower and medicinal weed,
> Shouting to the wooded hills, singing to the green valleys.
> At ninety-six I had lived enough, that is all,
> And passed to a sweet repose.
> What is this I hear of sorrow and weariness,
> Anger, discontent, and drooping hopes?
> Degenerate sons and daughters,
> Life is too strong for you —
> It takes life to love Life.

My mother was not this woman, nor am I, but we are both some way kin to her.

Nation (19 January 1927), pp.63-64

Circumference

"My business is circumference."
Emily Dickinson in a letter to Colonel Higginson, July 1862.

For some centuries English critics have been at work to revise or apply the term metaphysical given John Donne and his school. The word does very well, I think, if we use it of poetry, to describe a state of mind, not to designate a system of thought with the exactitude of the philosopher or the scientist.[1] "Dryden gave the term metaphysical to the odd terminology of Donne's poetic philosophy," says Gosse, "and Johnson borrowing the suggestion,

---

[1] "The poet is a valued member of the community, for he is known to be a poet; his value will increase as he grows to recognize the deeper insight into nature with which modern science provides him. The metaphysician is a poet, often a very great one, but unfortunately he is not known to be a poet, because he strives to clothe his glory in the language of reason, and hence it follows that he is liable to be a dangerous member of the community." Karl Pearson, *Grammar of Science*, Part 1, p.17.

defined the school to describe not Donne only, but all the amorous and philosophical poets who succeeded him, and who employed a similarly fantastic language, and who affected odd figurative inversions. The influence of Donne upon the literature of England," Mr. Gosse concludes, "was singularly wide and deep, although almost wholly malign."

I have been attempting to collect into a book what may be considered the most malignant of Donne's verses, together with others since his time, down to the present, which seem to bear them a good comparison, not merely from the school commonly supposed to be metaphysical, but from English and American poets generally. There are more poems of this genre than poets; with many lyric and dramatic minds the metaphysical is a mood assumed for the moment, or one manner of approach, not a constant quality. Unless we agree to use Donne as the measure of the metaphysical poet, and draw all others to scale, we must admit to begin with, that in searching for the Metaphysical Poem we are only after an abstraction. A long search, however, among many approximations, and repeated varieties, gives a reader a certain knack at imagining the purest possibility of treatment, of which the poems one encounters are only less acute designs.

I must state at the outset that I find only two genuinely metaphysical poets of the first order of clarity in the entire span of our poetry. So far as an unscholarly knowledge can contend, with the use of a definition that comes from a study of forms and habitual choices of material, I find this kind of mind perfectly exampled only in John Donne and Emily Dickinson. Dante, Goethe and Lucretius live in other languages.

"Metaphysical poetry," says Grierson, in his excellent introduction to *Metaphysical Lyrics and Poems of the Seventeenth Century*, "in the full sense of the term, is a poetry which, like that of the *Divina Commedia*, the *De Natura Rerum* and perhaps Goethe's *Faust*, has been inspired by a philosophical conception of the universe and the role assigned to the human spirit in the great drama of existence. These poems were written because a definite interpretation of the riddle, the atoms of Epicurus rushing through infinite empty space, the theology of the schoolmen as elaborated in the catechetical disquisitions of St. Thomas, Spinoza's vision of life *sub specie aeternitatis*, beyond good and evil, laid hold on the mind and the imagination of a great poet, unified and illumined his comprehension of life, intensified and heightened his personal consciousness of joy and sorrow, of hope and fear, by broadening their significance, revealing to him in the history of his own soul, a brief abstract of the drama of human destiny. 'Poetry is the first and last of all knowledge – it is as immortal as the heart of man.' Its themes are the simplest experiences of the surface of life, sorrow and joy, love and battle, the peace of the country, the bustle and stir of towns, but equally the boldest conceptions, the profoundest intuitions, the subtlest and most complex classifications and 'discourse of reason,' if into these, too, the poet can 'carry sensation,' make of them passionate experiences communicable in vivid and moving imagery, in rich and varied harmonies."

Johnson and Dryden described the seventeenth century poet as a man of learning who drew on his knowledge for his phrases, symbols and comparisons, and who treated of matters "beyond physics." The eighteenth century being unable when it made its definition to know the work of Shelley, Wordsworth, Coleridge, Browning, and Blake, should be pardoned for covering them all, and leaving, still, room for another kind of poet — in no way defining a temperament that marks John Donne from John Keats. However, the eighteenth century does have in mind something it has not defined. Taking Donne as an example, it wished to describe a scientific sharpness and an angularity; a saltiness of phrase designated by them as "wit"; and a coldness that made it possible for the mind to probe itself, as it writes of itself, lavishly and unmercifully. All this was concealed under the large word, *learning.* "Beyond physics" involved God, the universe, and the soul's torments – psychological poetry.

Such a poet is born with a salty sanity in his bones. He will take neither (Keatsian) sensuous assurance of life, nor (Miltonic) moral glory, nor a Poesque exit into madness. What he needs to find is a thoughtful pattern for the universe — a need in him so pressing that he is inclined to himself present the universe with that pattern when it is lacking. Ideas being for this temperament as real as grass blades or locomotives, the poet's imagination is always riding the two horses in the circus, Idea and Fact; they gallop neck and neck in his work, he has a genius for both the concrete word and the dazzling concept. In Donne's case the two horses got to galloping apart after a time — he saw that he finally must take to one or the other. Religion and Philosophy fascinated his mediaevalism — a grave-yard of ideas that might be dissected or shown to have a functioning structure. But Science fascinated him too, Gallileo and Copernicus gave him the food his imagination craved; from them, for a time, she constructed his new philosophies — having played at paste till qualified for pearl — until the labor of putting raw science in relation to the world's cultural knowledge got to be too difficult. Such a labor is not the work of one man; a poet may only perform it with some group to pick and cull for him. And because Donne had to have a coherent universe, even though a fictitious one, he went over to God.

Perhaps my definition will seem to my readers to cover a large number of poets still. Shakespeare's mind lived in a metaphysical country and the image of its bigness casts a shadow over all who have written since. But his dramatic and human gifts enrich on one hand where his lyricism etherializes on the other, this faculty, so that we have it only best expressed in speeches in the plays, in single ejaculations, unexcelled and unravelled; and in the less musical sonnets. Milton, who had learning, and who did his best in his mammoth fashion, to construct a scheme worthy of God and Man, lacks the wit and the impudence and has none of the subjective sense that makes the dilemma of the metaphysical mind. Pope and Dryden used metaphysical material. Pope delighted in changing the shape of an idea into a metal ribbon. Dryden built a word cathedral of regular, formal prosody. Keats is the clearest possible example of what a metaphysical poet is not. His truth is in essence, not in pattern; he knows the substance of life to be sufficient; any scheme was to Keats, extraneous. Whether this belief would have continued in him is a matter for speculation — as he grew into his forties and fifties, the romantic philosophy might have beaten itself out into a hardness and the meaning of design. The eve of St. Agnes is sensuous in the highest possible fulfilment.

> Beyond a mortal man impassioned far
> At these voluptuous accents, he arose

Beside this Donne's

> Then since that I may know
> As liberally, as to a Midwife, shew
> Thy selfe: cast all, yea this white linnen hence....

is cold and mental, however human; curiosity is its deepest impulse.

Coleridge and Poe, with Swinburne, Rossetti and the rest of the noisy, windy, wild young poets abandon the world of metaphysical exactitude for made splendors — their poetry is a kind of projected psychology; they show what the mind may feel and imagine if inflated and elongated. The true metaphysician is subjective, but he wants his mental stuff unstimulated; the complete abnormal does not interest him. Blake, fierce and tender, who saw visions of English greens, made a lamb and a tiger with a simplicity and an insight one step beyond the mind. Science, for him was a hellish invention against the spirit of man. He says "Go winged thought, widen his forehead," of the negro — and means what he says. Metaphysicians do not mean what they say: they propose possibilities; their world is all hypothesis and compact. Making mind and emotion one, as no one else but Keats has approximated, Blake says: "A tear is an intellectual thing." The metaphysician is neither fierce nor tender, as was Blake. He is a stoic, and has small joy in even that attitude.

Wordsworth and Shelley both meditate continually on man's destiny, the universe's destiny, and cover much, with Tennyson, that Donne (our metaphysical measure) if a modern, would attempt. But they separate themselves off by an attitude of worship; a lack of saltiness and homeliness. When Wordsworth tried to be homely he wrote the "Idiot Boy"; when Tennyson tried to be terse, he wrote "In Memoriam" which succeeds now and then in being simple. When Shelley wrote the "Hymn to Intellectual Beauty" he filled it with vague hues, full of desire, but as removed from the earth as a blowing cloud. Vague nobility is not the metaphysician's favorite note. Wordsworth, Shelley and Tennyson were all a little too bright and good for human nature's daily food. Donne's frank eroticism which they lack makes a good beginning for the whole self – unities are essential – the whole universe, the whole man. In the end God becomes his unity and to Him he speaks curtly, as to an honored inescapable fact, with his own antagonistic majesty:

> Wilt thou forgive that sin where I begun,
> Which was my sin, though it was done before?
> Wilt thou forgive that sin; through which I run,
> And do run still; though still I do deplore?
> When thou hast done, thou hast not done,
>> For I have more.

Browning most clearly has characteristics that link him with Shakespeare and Donne, and give him the task of taking up the actual world as where they put it down. He has a rich human variety, and an ability to ponder in all sanity the unravellings of the mind. He wants his people dynamic, not anatomies, however: — *She had a heart somehow too soon made glad*, is too alive when taken in its context. Donne, or Shakespeare, only, of all English poets, might have written, in Browning's place, "The Light Woman." Splendid and broad as Browning's blade is, at times it lacks the keen edge of the lightly acid gentlemen, his two forbears. His dramatic monologues desert the nicety of metaphysical tracing; first and last, (with noble exceptions) he runs to God a little too swiftly, because of a lack of subtlety, I think, or a love of benignity.

For all these swift judgments exceptions abound; in the poet most foreign to this as a constant state of mind, there are moods when the metaphysical comes uppermost. Blake, Wordsworth, Browning all write approximates of what I would call the pure metaphysical poem; and of their many poems I hope I have chosen the best for my collection.

But in either the welltrodden or the ragged by-paths of English-American poetry I can only discover one mind whose predominant flavor is in Donne's world. Emily Dickinson, nineteenth-century recluse, and the seventeenth-century Dean of St. Paul's were both attempting a revolutionary technique, and a plain homely grandeur. Neither quality has been very well understood. That angularity complained of by Johnson and Dryden in Donne, became the snare of Colonel Higginson's platitudes when he tried to give Emily Dickinson helpful criticism. What these critics could not see was that both these poets were deserting formal composition for the subtlest of all techniques — the form of an idea. Critics have demanded an external lyric gloss of many poets who should have gone on eliminating to the metaphysical extent. Ideas are irregular; they are beautiful in their entire uniqueness as pure form when simply revealed as idea, not as some form of expression. To give an idea no form but itself, to show it as organic by an inner music, as if the bones of a skeleton were singing in their own rhythm — that is the technical obsession of

161

the metaphysical poet. Beside him every other poet becomes a little diffuse and decorative.

Emily confessed her desire when she wrote to "scalp the naked soul." Few poets would pretend to so little, or do so much. Where Donne allows his cerebral fancy and his pedantry to spin out, past his climax (which so often comes in one line or two, followed by a larger climax, not so acute) Emily says, making of one thought the design of a poem:

> The heart asks pleasure first,
> And then excuse from pain;
> And then those little anodynes
> That deaden suffering;
> And then, to go to sleep,
> And then, if it should be
> The will of its Inquisitor
> The liberty to die.

Such a sharp knife has rarely flashed in literature. In the same world of the mind's comment on the mind, find:

> What fortitude that soul contains
> That it can so endure
> The accent of a coming foot
> The opening of a door

Donne, if anyone might have conceived:

> Pain has an element of blank

or:

> The brain within its groove
> Runs evenly and true.

The wit, the power to make an epigram which Donne's age so loved, is all in Emily Dickinson. A poem made into a prose sentence reads as follows:

> Surgeons must be very careful when they take the
> knife. Underneath their fine incisions, stirs the Culprit,
> Life!

It is the same colloquial downright phrase that Donne so used,
to say:

> I am too fools I know
> For loving and for saying so
>   In whining poetry;

And:

> If the unborn
> Must learn, by my being cut up and torn
> Kill and dissect me love; for this
> Torture against thine own end is,
> Racked carcasses make ill anatomies.

The mind of Emily Dickinson has the power of a microscope. To
the small facts that fall so well within a woman's knowledge she
applies the enlarging gift of her imagination — with the result
that she does just what Blake wanted himself to do: She sees the
world in a grain of sand. She gives us universe in atoms, makes a
death in eight line wild and gigantic as a dramatist of pure terror:

> We noticed smallest things –
> Things overlooked before,
> By this great light upon our minds
> Italicized, as 'twere.

The last stanza of this poem is perhaps the most purely majestic
writing done in our country.

Donne does not inspect Dickinson's minutiae — he tries to get
the seen and the unseen into one scope. He complains of science:

> The new philosophy calls all in doubt,
> The Element of Fire is quite put out;
> The Sun is lost, and the earth, and no man's wit
> Can well direct him where to look for it.
> And freely men confess that this world's spent
> When in the Planets and the Firmament
> They seek so many new; they see that this
> Is crumbled out again to his atomies.

The mass of science, hinted by the half discoveries of his age, was so enormous that Donne's mind could not put it in order. He needed order:

> Poor soul, in this thy flesh what dost thou know?
> Thou know'st thy self so little, as thou know'st not
> How thou did'st die, nor how thou was't begot.

***

> We see in Authors, too stiff to recant
> A hundred controversies of an Ant
> And yet one watches, starves, freezes and sweats,
> To know but Catechisms and Alphabets.

So we have Donne — a mind, said De Quincy, which gives us "thoughts and descriptions which have the fervent and gloomy sublimity of Ezekiel or Aeschylus." A mind religious because cosmological with neither real awe nor love for the God who was so necessary to it; — irreverent, racy, actual and at times pedantic and fragmentary in the extreme.

Donne's collapse as a rebellious and worldly intellect — when by the voltage of his work we are forced to conclude that he had more intensity, and cut of us a bolder facet than Emily Dickinson — makes the significant suggestion for us that it was less possible to follow the bent of such a mind in his day than it was in 1850, or than it is today. Science is lamented and deplored by contemporary romanticists. For the metaphysical poet, Science is the freedom of the universe — and in the future our greatest poets may well be poets of this mind. Some Moses striking a rock on the desert Mr. Eliot describes as the wasteland and with his touch liberating a vast unused mentality; the excitement of enormous sweeps, the dizziness of looking in all directions at the surrounding fact.

Introduction, *Circumference: Varieties of Metaphysical Verse*, New York: Covici Fried Publishers, 1929, pp.3-13

A Pattern for the Universe

Despite their tumultuous relationship, Taggard and Wolf had many years of happiness and mutual creative support,[1] and she dedicated both *For Eager Lovers* (1922) and *Words for the Chisel* (1926) to him. After their return from the West Coast, they rented a farmhouse in New Preston, Connecticut and worked together on a collection of their critical articles which, though never published, was to be titled "Forgive Us Our Debts." But insufficient income, Robert's mental instability, and the frustrations of two ambitious young creative writers trying to make their careers and maintain a family life was putting heavy pressures on their marriage.

By 1926, Robert was staying at his studio in the barn at New Preston while Genevieve lived in New York City and worked as librarian for the New School for Social Research. That August, they vacationed in the Adirondacks with Kenneth Durant and his

---

1   Taggard to Josephine Herbst, 1922-23, Josephine Herbst Papers, Beinecke Library, Yale University.

wife Ernestine Evans.[2] The following year, Robert set off on a trip to Moscow to try to persuade Sergei Eisenstein to accept his new film script.[3] Having recently joined the newly-founded radical journal *New Masses* as contributing editor along with Taggard, Wolf would also be delivering lectures in Moscow on proletarian writing in the US and sending the texts back to be published in the magazine. On his way to Russia, he wrote to Genevieve from Paris about the problems of gender roles conflicting with the needs of creative writers trying at the same time to be spouses: "It seems to me that a man has to be primarily creative in his work and a woman in her love." It may have been this statement (fairly chauvinist even in those times) that prompted her to reply with her article, "The Creative Woman: The Problem of Marriage," published in *Equal Rights* that year (p.131).[4]

In that essay, Taggard expressed her belief that female physiology and male dominance continued to make women of her era subject to psychological pressures for childbearing and family life. This led to a larger problem, society's failure to recognise "the importance of fulfilled expression" for women, thus undermining women's ability to express their own creativity. She acknowledged the biological urge to produce offspring — she had heeded it herself — but warned that if women ignored their need for equal creative status with men they would remain immature "artists of adolescent griefs," unable to address wider human and universal issues with "the authority of experience." This was the public

---

2   Wolf to Ernest Hemingway, 24 August 1926. Ernest Hemingway Papers, John F. Kennedy Presidential Library, Boston, MA.

3   Possibly the anti-capitalist political satire, "Loony", for which a scenario was published in *Nation* (9 September 1925), p.270.

4   It was also printed in the London radical magazine *The New Leader* (7 January 1927), where she was described by the editors as "an ardent worker in the Socialist Movement."

declaration of a commitment to women's rights which Taggard had held from the early days of her marriage, when she realised that she was not prepared, as her own mother had been, to settle for the role of mother, wife, and housekeeper.

This issue was alluded to in a series of three poems she wrote during the early Twenties, variations on the theme of the Pygmalion and Galatea myth. The first iteration of this poem, "The Girl Galatea," was written as a sonnet in a letter to her husband Robert in June 1923.[5] A near variant, "Galatea's Prayer," was published in the *New York Evening Post* (29 Nov 1924) and the *Montreal Star* (28 Feb 1925). The character of Galatea presented in her final version, "Galatea Again" (p.100), published in *Words for the Chisel*, no longer girlish or supplicating, adopts a serious and experienced voice, decisive and unyielding, and the original sonnet structure is abandoned for a much more concentrated expression, hardened and polished.

The use of classical myth as a metaphor for the psychological state of the artist was widely employed by the post-Romantic and post-Symbolist poets, particularly Pound and Eliot, the great exemplars in the previous generation for the younger poets writing just after the Great War. Re-narrations of the Pygmalion and Galatea myth have a distinguished genealogy, having been employed by W.S. Gilbert in his play of 1872, in poetry by Robert Browning (one of Taggard's acknowledged favourite writers), and in the ground-breaking play *Pygmalion* (1913) by George Bernard Shaw, socialist hero to many in the post war generation, including Wolf.[6]

In "Galatea Again," the voice is that of a woman who has undergone a psychic transformation which she now — awakened to her

---

5 Taggard to Wolf, 19 June 1923, Genevieve Taggard Papers, New York Public Library.

6 Wolf, upon demobilization after WWI, returned from Europe via London in order to meet Shaw and interview him for *The Liberator* 21 (December 1919), pp.22-23.

vulnerability — wishes to reverse. "Great mortal feuds" refers both to the gender conflicts within the relationship and also perhaps to the struggle of the physical self against death. Becoming mortal, after the safety of immortality in stone, has disadvantages she is unprepared for. In the second stanza, the man appeals to her maternal instinct, "clutching" at her dress, but she vows to remain impassive, invulnerable to emotional blackmail. This is a poem about the tension between real physical passion and the woman's need for an independent life of the intellect, of the sort Taggard called for in her essay "The Creative Woman."

Stimulated by reading Dickinson's poetry with Sara Bard Field early in the 1920s, Taggard embarked on a critical biography of the poet, writing it alongside the creation of *Words for the Chisel*. When Taggard wrote about Dickinson's style, she may have had in mind a review by Field of her own work in *Words for the Chisel*. Field suggested Taggard carved her poems "with sharp tools" for a "sculpturesque technique." Dickinson, Taggard wrote, laboured not "on granite or even on marble; rather, she "employed gem-tactics; her poetry had flash, had facet."[7] Taggard's own approach in this period was one of classical excision and a carefully considered economy of expression.

Several years earlier, Floyd Dell pointed in an essay in *Liberator* to the late-symbolist aestheticism of Théophile Gautier, whose concern with "mere artistic preoccupation as such" Dell thought supported a morality of technical excellence above all else. Dell quoted Gautier's *Émaux et Camées* [*Enamels and Cameos*]: "Carve! paint! chisel!/ That thy fluctuant dream/ Be sealed/ In the resisting block," and warned against holding the aesthetic so sacred that "it is then of no consequence whether the old commandments

---

7   Taggard, *The Life and Mind of Emily Dickinson*, New York and London: Alfred A. Knopf, 1930, p.236.

are kept or broken."[8] Knowing Gautier's book herself may have led Taggard to call her book of poems *Words for the Chisel*, accepting the challenge to create works through precise technique that would cut through technical perfection to deal with the deepest concerns of ordinary men and women, revealing psychological and social truths.[9]

Enamels and cameos are respectively built up and carved out, but both are manmade jewels. In Taggard's "Enamel Girl" (p.104), the subject of the poem is related to the figure of Galatea in the sense that she too is a created being, transformed from a normal psychological state into something made impervious to emotional risks, but unlike Galatea, she is self-created. In the third stanza, "Careful not to care" is a paradox which makes the line turn on its own axis; it catches the reader up short, then turns and focuses on the meaning, a rejection of the risk of "caring." The object of that turning-away is "burning beauty in blue air," an image of the sun, Dickinsonian in its replacement of an abstract noun (beauty) for the very real physical event of the brightness of sunlight. To not care for beauty that burns in "blue air," is to avoid the spiritual realm where blue air and burning beauty exist as one.

The couplet in stanza ten, "You faded. I never knew/ How to unfold as flowers do," offers another paradox, a reversal of natural process in the relationship: a full blossom that fades, alongside a bud that cannot bloom. The realization comes to the speaker that she has hardened herself to the point that her fearfulness has become self-destructive, even as the vulnerabilities of betrayal and mortality are avoided. This awareness, rather than turning her toward life, makes her even more fearful of real contact: the "caress" is desire,

---

8   Floyd Dell, "Literature and the Machine Age", *Liberator* 7:9 (September 1924), pp.28-30.

9   A copy of *Émaux et Camées* with Taggard's bookplate was offered for sale by a French bookseller in 2017.

which may wound; and the kiss is the full expression of the "fragile ecstasies," brittle expectations that may crack, if the desire for connection is conditional upon preserving and protecting the ego, perhaps indicated by the stress on the word "I" in the final stanza: "Now terror touches me when I/ Seem to be touching a butterfly."

During Wolf's absence in Paris and Moscow in 1927, Taggard was hard at work. She was assembling her next collection of poems, *Travelling Standing Still* (1928). She was writing for *New Masses* contributing to pieces such as "Are Artists People?" and producing reviews of Sandburg, D.H. Lawrence, Robinson Jeffers, *American Caravan*, and Laura Riding and Robert Graves' *Survey of Modernist Poetry*. And she was completing the manuscript of her Dickinson book. As she worked on *The Life and Mind of Emily Dickinson* (1930), she began to explore the potentially parallel states of mind between Dickinson and the Metaphysical poets, particularly John Donne, which also provided a rich resource for the introductory essay for her anthology *Circumference: Varieties of Metaphysical Poetry* (1930) (p.155).

Herbert Grierson's book, *Metaphysical Lyrics and Poems of the Seventeenth Century* (1921) brought the Metaphysical poets to public appreciation, peaking with Donne's tercentenary in 1931. Taggard's *Circumference* was the only other anthology of this school of poetry besides Grierson's to be published between 1900 and 1930. Taggard may have been first drawn to the Metaphysicals because she recognised some of their tendencies in the work of Emily Dickinson. "Only John Donne, two hundred years before," she wrote, could write with such compression of meaning, and could propose "such multitudinous possibilities in line after line of rapid sketch."[10] But perhaps it was also because she was personally inclined to a terseness of style and a unified sensibility

---

10   Taggard, *The Life and Mind of Emily Dickinson*, p.232.

(of the abstract with the real, of thought with feeling) in her own work. In her 1934 article in *Scholastic* magazine, "John Donne: A Link Between the 17th and the 20th Centuries" (p.235), she was introduced as "a metaphysical poet herself."

Grierson placed at the top of the seventeenth-century poets' achievements their "peculiar blend of passion and thought, feeling and ratiocination,"[11] and for him, Henry Vaughan encapsulated these qualities and was a greater mystic than either Donne or George Herbert. As if to test herself against the Metaphysicals' standards, or to use their best tools for her own purposes, and also perhaps to declare herself by contrast as anti-mystical, Taggard wrote the poem "Remembering Vaughan in New England" (p.182). First published in *The Nation* in October 1928, it remained a favourite of hers, appearing as a broadside with an illustration by J .J. Lankes in 1933, then included in her book *Not Mine to Finish* (1934), as well as in her 1945 collection *A Part of Vermont*.

Taggard begins with a quotation from Henry Vaughan's poem "The World": "I saw Eternity the other night/ Like a great Ring of pure and endless light...", and she contrasts this transcendent vision with her own first lines: "I saw reality the other night,/ By New England moon-light," exchanging Vaughan's idealism for a more concrete, and Americanist, objectivity. The "great Ring" of endless light in Vaughan's poem approaches the mystical transcendentalism of Ralph Waldo Emerson, with whose writings Dickinson was familiar. In his essay on "Circles", he referred to St. Augustine's idea of the nature of God as "a circle whose centre was everywhere, and its circumference nowhere".[12] When Taggard used Dickinson's "My business is Circumference" as the epigraph

---

11   Herbert J. C. Grierson, *Metaphysical Lyrics and Poems of the Seventeenth Century*, Oxford: Clarendon Press, 1921, p.xv.

12   R.W. Emerson, *Essays: First Series* (1841).

to her book *Circumference: Varieties of Metaphysical Poetry*,[13] there was an echo of Emerson's definition, not simply of the furthest extent of the rational mind, but of an unbounded and immeasurable abstraction, a metaphor for the Absolute.

But in "Remembering Vaughan", Taggard rejects the transcendent dream for the clarity and sharp-edged tactility of real things seen in the direct, unmediated light of the intellect. The first paradox, one of the primary characteristics of Metaphysical poetry, is offered in "the substance of moon-beams", in an effort to objectify moonlight, to give it colour, and tactile qualities such as "texture", with adjectives like "rough", and "coarse". Substance is a surprising quality to attribute to moon beams, but by the end of the poem Taggard has confounded the reader even further by calling for the moon to take on entirely the role of the sun: "O pure moon-beam, / Let it be day." Her supplication is paradoxical, asking the moon, associated with the subjective mind, the dream and the unconscious, to act as its opposite, the sun, symbol of the intellect and clear seeing.

A few years later, Joan Bennett in her *Four Metaphysical Poets* (1934) defined the work of the seventeenth century poets as analytical in their abstract thinking and in their extremes of ideas – the macrocosmic and microcosmic, the sublime and commonplace – producing what is known as the "conceit', the conceptual surprise that marked their works, that shock of the clash between ideas. Taggard used just such a technique in "Remembering Vaughan in New England", forcing the dream-like character of the moon into sudden juxtaposition with the sharp brilliance of sunlight, images usually kept far apart in the mind. Vaughan, Bennett thought, was particularly sensitive to the textures of nature and

13   Taggard, in her book on Dickinson, cites Martha Dickinson Bianchi's *Life and Letters of Emily Dickinson*, Cambridge: The Riverside Press, 1924. Taggard's quote appears on page 242.

the qualities of light in everyday experience, but his poems were forged in the cosmic-personal relationship between the soul and God. In Vaughan's poetry these two vastly different parts of human experience could be suddenly seen as aspects of an ultimate unity.[14]

The poet's search for a pattern for the universe figured large in Taggard's mind as she was writing the text for *Circumference*. Both Dickinson and Donne sought meaning in a relationship with God, but Taggard's selection in her anthology avoided an exclusive identification with a specifically religious concern. Within her definition of Metaphysical poetry as "psychological", too wide-ranging for many critics, she included not only "the soul's torments" and the self-consciousness of the modern poet, but "learning" and "the universe" — the world of science. Although she herself had been raised in the full confidence of Christianity, in the church of the Disciples of Christ, by her thirties she needed an alternative faith. As she wrote in her introduction to *Circumference*, "because Donne had to have a coherent universe, even though a fictitious one, he went over to God." And, under the pressures of the Depression in the 1930s, Taggard went over, as did so many of her fellow liberal poets, to Marx.

<hr />

14   Joan Bennett, *Four Metaphysical Poets: Donne, Herbert, Vaughan, Crashaw*, Cambridge: Cambridge University Press, 1934, p.77, p.80, pp.90-91.

III
Marvelous Now is Man

Lark

O, lark, from great dark, arise!
O, lark of light,
O, lightness like a spark,
Shock ears and stun our eyes
Singing the day-rise, the day-rise, the great day-rise.

O Believer, Rejoicer, say
Before Evidence of Day
The Sun is Risen.
                              Where
No sun is, come loudly in the air;
Let ear and eye prepare
To see and hear, truly to see and hear;
To hear thy three-fold welcome in the air,
To see all dazzle after long despair,
To see what none may see now, singer, singer fair, so fair.

O, lark alert, O, lark alive,
O lovely, lovely changing arrow-lark,
Sprung like an arrow from the bow of dark,
O, lark arise
Sing the day-rise.
                         The great day-rise.

Not Mine to Finish, p.6

To the Natural World: at 37

Exquisite world, powerful, joyous, splendid,
Where, almost when we learn to live, our life is ended,
Where, when we gather our trophy errors in,
And face the array and cannot again begin
To make another life less fatal, less
Like a poor travesty of some greatness,
World, you rebuke us calmly, ceaselessly,
With mute round of rising sun and mimicking sea,
With flood and ebb and taciturn refrain
In round diurnal rings, waxing to wane.
Our mortal life runs through you its swift line
Closing no circle, marking its scratch design,
Fusiform, the spindle, this is its mortal shape;—
O lovely world, midway in large landscape
I pause, look forward. Weakness with wisdom lie
Ahead with nodding age; error and energy
Behind, dim in regret and chaos where
I left my early self and got the despair
That seizes all who see how folly gone
Is their sweet youth with darkness sudden on.
World deign, for one moment, O deign to culminate
One wave in me; O in me consummate
Your surge with all beholding happy power.
So, overlapping once, here in the midway hour,
Let me watch outward splendor solemnly for
Life's brief in all this bigness, O sun's calm, O

Sea's roar.

Not Mine to Finish, p.91

Try Tropic
Of the Properties of Nature for Healing an Illness

Try tropic for your balm,
Try storm,
And after storm, calm.
Try snow of heaven, heavy, soft and slow,
Brilliant and warm.
Nothing will help, and nothing do much harm.

Drink iron from rare springs; follow the sun;
Go far
To get the beam of some medicinal star;
Or in your anguish run
The gauntlet of all zones to an ultimate one.
Fever and chill
Punish you still,
Earth has no zone to work against your ill.

Burn in the jewelled desert with the toad.
Catch lace
Of evening mist across your haunted face;
Or walk in upper air, the slanted road.
It will not lift that load;
Nor will large seas undo your subtle ill.

Nothing can cure and nothing kill
What ails your eyes, what cuts your pulse in two
And not kill you.

Not Mine to Finish, p.10

Remembering Vaughan in New England

I saw Eternity the other night
Like a great Ring of pure and endless light....
— Henry Vaughan, The World.

I saw reality the other night,
By New England moon-light.

All of my life, living had been
One or another kind of dream.

Now, nothing festooned itself between
Me and the substance of moon-beam.

The land is honest, small and swept
Bare as a barn-yard floor

In winter. And no third thing crept
As it had, times before.

No feeling, its mist to intervene,
No inner thought to warp....

I stood: and behold, the trees were lean,
And lo! the hills were sharp.

Moon's no ephemeral faint stuff
First seen, painted upon

Windows and walls — it is yellow as dawn,
After dream, it is marvelous rough,

Coarse as hoar-frost — texture no dream
Can invent.
        Cut my vague dreams away!

Moon in New England, O pure moon-beam,

Let it be day.

Not Mine to Finish, p.9

Blame Them

With the first pang, she knew the whole:
The loom's behaviour: how the edge
Once the thread pulled, ravelled the mutual soul,
And how each night, with the night's pledge

How to set, herself, the mutual task again.
He wove his piece with troubled eyes,
Astonished at the strands of pain
Until with practice he grew clumsy-wise.

She like an adept, quarreled and sang;
You might have joyed to see her face;
Lit by such zest from the first pang,
So poison-sure from the first embrace.

But both were broken-hearted — she
With a deadly touch she could not quit
Worked the design to the end, and he
Thought only he was to blame for it.

While she, so poison-ardent and so deft
Traced in their love a fair picture of his pain;
Right hand the subtle assassin to her left:
Told all the mean geometry of her brain.

Judge here, you, lyric and imitative lovers,
Who take emotions from a book by rote,

What brand of poison this was. Let who first discovers
Name for this evil, plan an antidote.

Not Mine to Finish, p.78

Metaphysical Exercise

"After great pain a formal feeling comes."

A feigned death will I die.
So found I, once before,
In death's great alchemy
How I
Grew strange, resplendent, more
Marvellous at heart, learning the reason why
All must die and also I.

All must die once, but more than once will I
Copy death's state.
Throng of the dead, throng not for long create,
I join your hosts, — slowly I go
Beyond the zone of pain and pleasure, my
Self so released, and learned, and passionate.

...feigned death, that copies so
The posture of cold woe that is not woe;
Feigned death, our healthy lie...
...feigned death, rehearsed in quiet, try
The nerve reluctant, until I
Learn by such fractions, what it is to die...

Trance, all reconciled,
This is death's art;
This will I teach my heart
For practice, by and by,
When from this trial death, I come to try
Life once again by whose great power we die.

We die:
A grim death, life-in-death, we die.

Not Mine to Finish, p.69

The Four Songs

Four songs I'll sing to you
From the four seasons taken,
Each of them partly true;...
Showing you how once-shaken
Like autumn; like winter, stoic, sad;
Elated like early spring
I am; like summer, equally laden
With fruit of matron-mind and maiden.
Four songs I'll sing
To you, — flute voices anyone
Might, from all nature fancy and seize on;
Since it is well in singing songs to you
I should select those clear and general
Moods-in-the-earth mankind has known so well,
Four songs I'll sing to you,
And amply sing.

But to these affirmations will you add
— Nothing you see in nature, no, nothing —
Something no summer mirrors, an outline
No moon will stamp with her official shine,
Something not sung by me, but mine;
Added, if added, by its like in you.

Four songs I'll sing to you.
False, candid art!
So much of me as is not me
I give to you, re-worded, with all my heart.
Then, done with seasons, sun and moon and sea,
Knowing their symbols no more than little-true,
I wait the sure rejoinder, — monody
That comes when I am done, from listening you.

What else I am you are implored to sense
At your own pains. Our odd identity
Cannot be sung. In us, this difference
No metaphor from nature can supply.
So if I would, I could not further, I,
Whose words past this monotony are all mistaken;
Four songs I'll sing to you, never to die
From the four seasons taken.

Not Mine to Finish, p.15

Words Property of the People

By me used hopefully to stammer
What cannot except by miracle be said;
Anxious to show that a poet's mind
Is as useful as a carpenter's hammer,
As real for plain people as the color red.

Not Mine to Finish, p.21

The Trance

In middle life, that time of highest light,
When under every object clings its shade
I fell into an apathy of sight
From looking at the pattern overlaid

Across the earth, the dazzling bright and dark
Complexity, the strange elaborate braid,
The tattoo, good and evil, heavy mark
Like that long twist the Snake in Eden made

When he through pure pale leaves ran mazy lines.
The diamond back of evil in all things
Copies that mark, its multiple designs,
and still he falls along our earth in rings.

Such webby tangle in all earth's array!
My apathy like any shadow clings
To all the happy objects of high day.
Before the snake the bird shuts down its wings.

Only declining sun or hazy eye
Can help indelible lines to shift or fade.
Then can the rigid bird come to and fly
Into the wave of the oncoming shade.

Himself, he has no shadow — belly tight
He skims our land and under him no shade.
It is the sun, the very bliss of light
That gives the shadow out of dazzle made.

His coils are melancholy. Heavy snake
Crawl off a little way a little while!
When shall I from this reptile slumber wake,
Move, salute the sun and smile.

Not Mine to Finish, p.18

Life of the Mind, 1934

*(The words in the books are not true
If they never act in you.)*

Fret fools the days away
Best sellers for their food.
And bad philosophy.
Fret fools. But we,
We dare not read for long,
But snatch our thought, our song,
As soldiers do their meat.
Necessity to eat,
Necessity to act,
And act aright renews
The mind's link with the arm.
Imperative to choose,
Imperative to do,
This time's dynamic form.

Once we were students. Then
Grave faces hours pored
Over the activity stored,
The energy of great men.

That time must come again.
If not for us for those
We will endow once more
With tested word-in-deed.
All poetry and the great prose
Born in a like uproar
Where someone had to bleed.

The battle of the mind,
Tranquillity, too, the kind
Quick teachers face, the jest,
Keen argument with a friend,
That sport and the sweet zest,
All fall, must fall, behind.
That time is at an end.

Now action like a sword.
Now to redeem the word.
Now blood for stubborn proof
No one may cut apart
Word from the living deed,
Or live this life aloof.

Fear is a flimsy creed.
"I believe with all my heart"
In the one way to believe.
"This thing is good — I give
My living to see it live."

Bleak thought and bastard art,
How easy to relinquish both!
So to be wise, so learned
If never more returned
To temporary peace!
So not to die of sloth,
Or live best-seller's ease.
But to stand upon our oath.

Calling Western Union, p.56

Definition of Song

Singing is best, it gives right joy to speech.
Six years I squandered, studying to teach,
Expounding language. Singing it is better,
Teaching the joy of the song, not teaching the letter.

And of all forms of song surely the least
Is solo. Only lark in the east
Can say — what no other lone singer can say —
The glory, the glory of the arriving ray.

Singing is the work of many voices.
Only so when choral mass rejoices
Is the lock sprung on human isolation
And all the many welded into one.

Body sings best when feet beat out the time.
Translated song, order of bold rhyme, —
Swing the great stanza on the pavement, — use
The public street for publishing good news.

Deepest of all, essential to the song
Is common good, grave dogma of the throng;
Well-spring of affirmation in accord
Beneath the chanting utterance, the word.

Song is not static — joy becomes a dance.
In step, vast unison, in step advance.
This is the life of song: that it mean, and move,
And state the massive power of our love.

Calling Western Union, p.7

Flute in Late Summer

The dandelion is frayed
And puffed on pipe.
Summer is delicately made
And the season ripe.
See the sun on the grass fade
From gold to green stripe.

Summer is delicately made.
While it is, it is ceasing.
At first we are a touch afraid
At summer's teasing,
And move from sun to shade
Fear shadow-increasing.

At first we are a touch afraid.
We start, we take care.
We delay, or we evade,
We wait or we stare
To see ripeness decayed
And the bright earth bare.

We delay and we evade.
But by degrees, relenting,
Color-timbre, grade on grade
The dimming eye inventing,
Until even the pale and the half-shed
Blow clean with calm consenting....

The dandelion is frayed
And puffed on pipe.
Summer is delicately made,
And the season ripe.
See the sun on the grass fade
From gold to green stripe.

Calling Western Union, p.45

Return of the Native

Now, after years serving demonic excess,
Exalting those whose god-passions send them mad,
I am stranded on a simpler shore, much less
Sumptuous, — a land permanently sad,

Bearing a somber harvest — an old island,
With cactus and asphodel and olive on
The rock itself. This oddly, is my land.
Here a moderate joy yellows the sky each dawn.

We toil — here toil has lost its hectic haste.
The outrageous wrongs men do lessen, diminish.
We are frugal, we share, we despise waste.
The work I have is good. It is not mine to finish.

Not Mine to Finish, p.13

O People Misshapen

O people misshapen, hugging bones in old coats,
Wavering as you walk, hurrying on mean streets
    and stairs,
Poor eaters, with bodies the clinics hastily patch
And push out into dark, dirt, roar and lack again...

Come close-up, faces, showing sunk eyes and
    skull forehead,
Blinking with light and the horror of being seen.
Brothers, Comrades, pool the last strength of men
In party, in mass, boil into form, and strike.

We will see you change, — shoulders swing broad
    and slow.
Your coats will not change this winter, no. But you
In ranks no distant day, clad and alert,
As resolute as storm, born of this bad extreme.

Calling Western Union, p.28

Real, Over Rock and Stubble

Sometimes it is the shadow that we see
More clearly than the substance — then the real
Is where the mind and the emotion move
Over our rock and stubble — watch the mark!
Sun's shadow, if of me, I can control
A little; if I sit, my shadow crouches;
I rise — it answers. If I contemplate,
Back to the sun, this print of quiet me,
I'm the philosopher, flattened.
                    Oh, but the sun
Who is the shadow-maker, consummate,
And will allow a play of attitudes,
When I grow rigid in real meditation,
Enviously moves, moves, moves. He pulls my shadow
                    down
Into all-shade. He goes, to leave me single.

Substance and shadow, walk the maudlin earth,
And laughter, laughter, laughter, light us down
To the last mimicry and the same doom.

Not Mine to Finish, p.59

Platform for Poets

The lavish words we write
Need a base on level stone.
Architecture of height
Perpendicular, alone,

Needs horizonal fact.
Oh Poetry-To-Come
Lay what is most exact
For the door-sill of your home.

Proportions not in dream,
And order, such as care
Cuts from a stony seam
And sets with shafts of air.

O poet, learn the trade,
The blithe, the sturdy toil.
How lovely what is made
Of stone, mortar and soil!

Blue-print, rivet, beam,
Propose our house in space.
We have seen the huts of dream
Squalid, in a waste place.

Calling Western Union, p.24

Image

Mask-face of old grief, death-mask, massive
Visage uttering Joy; Joy sputtering; glorious oracle!
Joy, red on tongue with wind on frozen forehead;
Mouth open, Joy just-spoken, grief just-broken;
Clarion throat eloquent, quenching cries; eyes
Wide, soul of Hallelujah, Ah,
Fury of song and drum and gong; fury
For the color of flags snapping on broomsticks,
Screw it in chromium on motor-cars,
Put the medallion on money,
Let it shake large and quiet in star-water.

Calling Western Union, p.27

Proud Day

(Marian Anderson on the steps of the Lincoln Memorial)

Our sister sang on the Lincoln steps. Proud day.
We came to hear our sister sing. Proud day.
Voice out of depths, poise with memory,
What goodness, what splendor lay long under foot!
Our sister with a lasso of sorrow and triumph
Caught America, made it listen. Proud day.

The peaceful Lincoln sat so still. Proud day.
Waiting the Republic to be born again. Proud day.
Never, never forget how the dark people rewarded us
Giving out of their want and their little freedom
This blazing star. This blazing star.
Something spoke in my patriot heart. Proud day.

Long View, p.54

Eye of the Beholder

The external world is slowly wronged
When Nature is centered in one breast.
This modern nerve, enduring, strung
A little laxer with the heavier years,
Makes dual and discrepant worlds.
— O agitation so prolonged
Past sweet fatigue and healthy rest! —
Anxious and inadequate
We face the natural world, we try
To see with modern, with accurate eye
What only the heroic and passionate,
The healthy and whole and wise can see.
Glance through the window — plain picket fence,
And tall, and glittering with life, a tree.
Ah! Outline shaken by the sense
By sick nerve shaken, wavers so,
Diminishes in blurs, is hung,
Crude picture of our partial woe,
Like a flat curtain, horrid with scrawls.
It flaps and doubles, suddenly nears,
Mountain and tree, warped and immense...

The real tree lives. The wrong tree falls.

Calling Western Union, p.20

Long View

Never heard happier laughter.
            Where did you hear it?
Somewhere in the future.
            Very far in the future?
Oh no. It was natural. It sounded
Just like our own, American, sweet and easy.
People were talking together. They sat on the ground.
It was
      summer.
And the old told stories of struggle.
The young listened. I overheard
Our own story, retold. They looked up at the stars
Hearing the serious words. Someone sang.
They loved us who had passed away.
They forgot all our errors. Our names were mixed.
The story
      was long.
The young people danced. They brought down
New boughs for the flame. They said, Go on with
the story
      now.
What happened next?
            For us there was silence,
Something like pain or tears. But they took us with them.
Their laughter was peace. I never heard happier.
Their children large and beautiful. Like us, but
new-born.
This was in the mountains of the west.
They were resting. They knew each other well.
The trees and rivers are on the map, but the time
Is not yet. I listened again. Their talk was ours
With many favorite words. I heard us all speaking.

But they spoke of better things, soberly. They were wise
And learned. They sang not only of us.
They remembered thousands, and many countries,
far away.
One poet who sat there with them began to talk of
the future.
Then they were silent again. And they looked at the sky.
And then in the light of the stars they banked their fire as
        we do
Scuffing the ground, and said goodnight.

                    This poem I bring back to you
Knowing that you wonder often, that you want
Word of these people.

Long View, p.14
First published *New Republic* (11 October 1939)

Poems of the American Tradition

Review of The People, Yes,
Carl Sandburg

The reactionaries won't like this book — of course. Here is a poet who sings softy and mockingly just out of reach, strumming on a simple instrument, cracking jokes, gently insulting those people who resolve to run the world to their own advantage, and now and then, in a sure and warning voice saying distinctly, in accents of an old wrath:

> The people have come far and can look back and say
> 'We will go farther yet'
> The people is a plucked goosed and a shorn sheep
>   of legalized fraud
> And the people is one of those mountain slopes
>   holding a volcano of retribution,
> Slow in all things, slow in its gathered wrath,
>   slow in its onward heave,
> Slow in its asking: 'Where are we now? What time is it?'

Carl Sandburg is closer to the heart of the American tradition than any writing man living — that we all know. And teachers can bind him close in the minds of their pupils to Emerson, Whitman and Twain, Dickinson and Thoreau. Sandburg has never forgotten John Brown and the revolutionary meaning of Lincoln. Americans, drunk on dreams of barren empire came close to forgetting. Who remembered? The immigrants remembered, and the dirty aliens, the wops and the kikes; those who came over steerage, and worked with their hands, and dreamed of sending their children to college. The dangerous radicals did not forget. Sandburg comes out of the reborn tradition, once Yankee and Anglo Saxon; later the passionate possession of the people who came from Europe and believed what the prosperous forgot.

Here is a hangover from the hopeful middle-class handicraft world. Sandburg writes about today — about steel puddlers, and the unemployed and the buyers of wire mops in the ten cent stores. But he loves and remembers in the manner of his speech, the folk talk of a past day — the corner-grocery, cracker-barrel philosopher world. He himself talks this lingo.

He does not talk about the exploited and the exploiters in those words. "The People" is a fluid term. The people, it seems, is 98 percent. The two percent left over he calls "pooh bahs": the bankers, the rich, the crafty, the powerful. This may not suit the analysis most of us make. It is too misty, too mystic, too fluid.

If the people had no one but Sandburg to tell them the way out of darkness, they would remain in it forever, lulled by their far off revolutionary destiny, content to be "The grand canyon of humanity, Pandora's box, a clock of doom and an avalanche" — someday. This hymn to the people is not enough, we may say, and we may go on to say what follows this general love. The hard-headed specific science of the way out will not be sung by Carl Sandburg in poetry. He stops with the affirmation, memorable and moving to all of us now, memorable, I believe in a time long distance, too, when we have a new world. His is the first affirmation, "The People, Yes."

The American Teacher XXI:3 (January-February 1937), pp.33-34

Not Mine to Finish

Melancholy and despair are the most persistent themes in modern poetry. Poe's Raven croaks in Eliot's Waste Land. Most of the manuscript poems that come to college teachers, editors, and judges are dictated by sincere despair and disillusion. I think this is the natural expression of the times in which we live, of course. But it indicates something else, also — something with which we as teachers and lovers of poetry have to do.

At Bennington, now and then, I read this poem to my students in the hope that it will strike home to them. It is by Carl Sandburg and is entitled "Joy."

> Let a joy keep you.
> Reach out your hands
> And take it when it runs by,
> As the Apache dancer
> Clutches his woman.
> I have seen them
> Live long and laugh loud,

> Sent on singing, singing,
> Smashed to the heart
> Under the ribs
> With a terrible love.
> Joy always,
> Joy everywhere —
> Let joy kill you!
> Keep away from little deaths.[1]

Every year in our schools a new wave of talented children come up smiling — so talented, often, that they make us feel very humble, even when their verses are immature and faulty. Wonderful talent! A richly gifted country! And they grow quickly, and show more promise. And then they stop growing. As soon as they throw off their childish illusions and begin to grow out of the child state, the period of unnatural gloom closes in on them.

For the past ten years I have worked with young poets — generation after generation of them. Where are they now? They have lost faith in themselves. Why has the crop failed?

Our society is destroying talent. The worst of it is that we as teachers, with the best intentions in the world, are partly responsible. We ourselves were raised on a curious set of dogmas about the artist. We pass these dogmas on to the children we teach. Today these beliefs are not valid, and the talents die.

We were raised to believe about the artist that he must be aloof from life, keep himself unspotted from the world, et cetera. Poetry is too spiritual for contact with brute fact — poetry is of a superhuman order. This is a poisonous fallacy.

We were raised to believe that the artist should not over-develop his intellectual powers — that the growth of his mind would kill his emotional drive. This is a stupid fallacy.

We were raised to believe that the young artist should cultivate

---

1   From *Chicago Poems*

his own originality in a kind of narcissistic dream, that he should create a wilful sensibility and drive it to violent extremes, that he should spontaneously "express himself". This is dangerous.

We were led to believe that the artist need not be a good craftsman if he have enough *inspiration*.

Because of these beliefs, we direct our young writers to turn away from the only source of all art — the raw material of life. We allow them to grow soft intellectually, and we participate in that vulgar Philistinism, "self-expression." We turn them inward on barren little selves, deflect their healthy energy from its true objective – the outside world. We give them the feeling that artists are better than the common run of human being; and we do not even require of them that they master the craft of writing, so that in the end they are not even honest workers. That is why, I think, so many wither up and come to nothing. To be sure, a few find influences and manage to survive. And some become commercial successes.

The point of view we have sincerely taught our young people has been nothing more than a provincial hang-over from a dead literary movement — the Romanticism of the last hundred and thirty years. I think we live now in a time that marks a great change – change as great as the one in 1798 when Wordsworth and Coleridge published the *Lyrical Ballads*. There are many signs that literature will leap to a new level, just as it did then.

The best justification for our attitude toward the young artist can be found in the natural parental instinct to protect what is fine and sensitive from a world that has grown so chaotic and complex and brutal that we tremble to see our young people of talent shattered by it. We act like fearful parents. In this we are not wise. We must prepare them to live and act in the world. And this applies emphatically to our young writers because writing properly understood is a *kind of action*.

Do you know a poem by Elinor Wylie called "Sanctuary"?

> This is the brick layer; hear the thud
> Of his heavy load dumped down on stone
> His lustrous bricks are brighter than blood
> His smoking mortar whiter than bone.
>
> Set each sharp-edged, fire-bitten brick
> Straight by the plumb-line's shivery length;
> Make my marvellous wall so thick
> Dead nor living may shake its strength.
>
> Full as a crystal cup with drink
> Is my cell with dreams, and quiet, and cool ...
> Stop, old man! You must leave a chink;
> How can I breathe? *You can't, you fool!*[2]

The only escape justified in art is the escape, like sleep or like refreshment, that brings us back stronger and better-equipped for the business of life. The moral of the greatest escapist poem in our language written by the greatest escapist, is very simply this — *we must come back to the world of flesh and blood in the end*. Those who make our children analyze and memorize "The Ancient Mariner" and permit them to overlook this passionate experience are not fitted to teach young people how to read poetry.

Waste and starvation in our cultural life are the inevitable accompaniment of waste and starvation in our social economy. Robert Frost's definition of poetry fills in the gap between the poet and the world. He says, "If I were forced to make a definition of poetry it would be this: 'Poetry is words that have become deeds.'"

Progressive Education XII:6 (October 1935), pp.371-72

---

2 From *Nets to Catch the Wind*

Mallorcan Memory

In 1931 when I was living on a Guggenheim Fellowship in Puerto Pollensa, a fishing village on the northeast coast of the island of Mallorca, I scribbled down the first lines of a poem. It was early morning, and the water of the bay was edged with crystal. My hands shook. I was enormously excited:

> I met an angel walking in Mallorca,
> A sunflower striding, petaled with rays, a broad visage,
> Who spoke sternly and with joy; "Hurry, hurry;
> America, Revolution, Go home," he said in Spanish.

I was not thinking about America. I was thinking about Blake's angel of revolution and Van Gogh's sunflowers. I was also thinking of a young priest I had just seen walking by the edge of the water, coming away from mass, kicking up the back of his dusty gown with his large feet. The angel agitator took his place. I was also thinking of the recent coup that had sent Alfonso scurrying to Paris. I was thinking of the faces I had seen in Barcelona; and the way people hunched together over the tables of the cafes in Madrid; and the bookstores, displaying pictures of Karl Marx. I was thinking of the crowds on the bull-fighting Sundays — the Solemnedad, they called it — people, lean, intent, and ardent. And with the poverty of workers and peasants vividly evident all around us, I thought naturally of the great force hidden beneath the surface of the quiet tourist life we were living.

I was in love with Spain, it seemed a country charged with a power as yet latent. And I felt this keenly because I was in need of change, after ten years in New England. When I wrote, groping for this new reality, I could not keep the angel and the sunflower of the two anarchist artists, Van Gogh and Blake, out of my sun-drenched mind, much as I disapproved of anarchism. Anarchism was in the air. It is now too late to get the facts of that world; but I know now that I saw the inscrutable edge of something that has become history.

Sense Images

That year in Mallorcan Spain piled up thousands of little pictures, trifles, fragments. I did not understand what was going on. But I go back in memory now, drawn by the intense, knife-edged excitements of that life. Now every news story is infused with the sense images of that year. A blind man becomes hypersensitive to touch, to smell, and to tone of voice. Because I could not talk directly to the people with whom we lived, I began to dwell on facial expression as if I were a painter; on tone of voice and accent, as if I were a dog who wished to guess the mood of a master. This led me to feel that we were living with a people about whom the usual tourist sentimentalities were taboo, a people of great dignity, capable of freedom.

We heard wild and beautiful melodies hundreds of years old. Poverty and superstition had not destroyed the voice that spoke in them. We heard street songs, work songs — lamentations and serene, joyous meditation. There were special melodies for each kind of work, but given the set form, each worker might ad lib the words, speaking his thoughts with the movements of his hands. There was a song for whitewashing a house, another for mending a boat; a song for washing clothes, a song for ironing. If you knew the songs you could tell as you went down by the edge of the sea what each person in the Puerto was doing; the chant of occupations blended into the peace of the hour. Spain, magnificent in cathedrals, upheld by the landlords, the crown, and the church, was never so impressive to me as in this intangible music.... The landlords drove the Moors out of Spain but the workers' music held an echo of the Arab cry.... Then the republic came and the workers grew hopeful of a better world. They had no warning of the gigantic betrayal to come. The landlords feared the infringement of the old absolute power, based as it was on authority and superstition. Even in 1931 it was possible to see that the rich landed class would organize in some way against the young democracy.

But to return to the songs, where the voice of the people was resonant. On the bay we heard the moonlight song for spearing fish, a song that mingled with the put-put of the little boats; in the rock mountains echoed the song for cutting palmetto.

We came down the mountain one afternoon late, after a trip through the pass to Formentor. Pure faint lemon sky, ruffled iridescent sea, and mountains behind us, in lines like those on a graph, sharp and eroded; rock bristling nearby with the palmetto fans. And flat on the little rim of the bay, a bit of fertile soil, where a few squares of trees and bean grew, behind the white cubes of huts. A bell jingled in the wilderness of rocks where sheep and goats ate spiny moss. We thought we were alone except for the sheep-tinkle. We looked down from our height on the village where smoke puffed up thin blue from evening fires. Fragrant smoke we knew it to be; and the air, radiant still, was the sea-clean air of islands. Then we heard the first bar of song and saw that a boy was cutting palmetto far off to the left, singing as he bent with his sharp knife. He hacked and sang a wild minor phrase. We walked on, the soft lifting wind of evening on our faces; we walked, tired and elated, sensing the loneliness of that afternoon toil. Then away to the right came the answer of his comrade, far off, invisible to us. I have never heard such tender melancholy music since, and never will. All afternoon they had been conversing back and forth, with the mountain for soundboard.

Today those boys are being bullied by Italian fascists. If they are not dead.

"Hor-nay"

But to get down to familiar things, and into the company of flesh and blood: the early morning voice of the bread boy crying "Hor-nay, hor-nay," is equally vivid. The mouse-colored donkey of the dainty hoofs and the large tender eye ambled in the cart; and the cart where the boy sat above blue wheels bristled with sticks and slabs of bread, and *enciamadas*, a mushroom-like breakfast bun. Hor-nay, hor-nay, he would cry, delivering bread and messages. Slowly he progressed, impeded by pretty girls who held him in conference, sticking geraniums into the donkey's bridle, and offering water-cress. We called the boy Hor-nay. I hope Hor-nay does not wear a blue shirt and beat anti-fascist fishermen with the butt of his gun.

We came to Mallorca because it was cheap. The franc and the lira were up — the peseta down. Spain's poverty was an advantage. Many others came for the same reason — blond German boys and girls who had seen the starvation years in Germany came, driven from home by what seemed to us then an unfounded fear of a little Munich demagogue. Famous German intellectuals came, and rented the cheapest rooms and read newspapers from home with agonized faces, and went for long desperate walks by themselves, looking as if the end of the world had come. The riffraff came, riffraff of all varieties, elegant and seedy. Scholars arrived, padded in shawls, and caught cold, and went away. One young American who was getting his doctor's degree in geology at

Heidelberg was run off the nearby island of Minorca by the Civil Guard, who grew suspicious of his notes on strategic formations – his geologist's hammer, authorities felt, was the camouflage of a German spy. The English, of course, had been there for twenty years, living quietly in superb isolation, indifferent to the life of the "natives," bowing only to gentry and Spanish titles. Retired English colonels sipped aperitifs with cold reserve while the first Americans floundered in the mud of the new territory.

We all grumbled at first about the lack of comfort, and remembered the French beds and the plumbing at home. But after a bit this humble fishing place became quite chic, and newcomers who could not see the archaic charm for the mud and the flies were made to feel very gross indeed, very provincial. Only grumpy Babbitts held out in the hotels, sputtering about the amount of oil in the food. One by one they left, humiliated by simplicity. Formentor, where speed boats tied and yachts put in, where you could get a manicure, remained a lonely Monte Carlo.

Peacetime Mallorca

We set up housekeeping. We gardened, we wrote, we swam, we sailed, we learned a little of the language, and much, by long observation, of the people. We had yards and yards of imperfect conversation with the inhabitants of the Puerto about the groceries we bought, the mail we wanted, the schools we needed for our young, the tennis court — because the untethered goats were fond of eating the stray balls — and finally a great deal of talk when we wanted to rent a rowboat. On festive occasions we ate at the Fonda. There we got rice tinged with saffron, cooled with bits of squid — *calamaris*, a much prettier word, it was called. There we came for a glimpse of itinerant Spain; smugglers, guitarists, and circus people. The people of early Picasso. There we liked to pass the time of day with Manuel, who always wore a white coat, a white cloth on his arm. There we were invited to see dances as old as the Phoenicians. Then we sat in the sun to dry our muddy feet, watching the life of the village — the wharf, the church, and the fishermen's cooperative.

Pollensa, of which our village was the Puerto, lay six miles inland. We found a café where we could sit while waiting for the bus, a dark and poverty-stricken place, but agreeable. Here we could spell out the contents of Spanish newspapers, socialist newspapers, full of columns of poetry, exquisitely rhymed. We called the proprietor of this café El Greco because of his striking resemblance to the painter's portrait of himself as an old man. In the cave of the dark café we could sit in the long waits for the bus, and look at the town as it went by to market, while El Greco, in a dark corner, stared at us.

Two miles from the Puerto, on a bit of fertile land under rock mountain, was our house, Can Cingala. We rented it in a babble of tongues from a sad-faced spinster daughter, who made inventories many yards long. She went off to Palma very fearful of her dishes, horrified of our bare ankles and our *espadre*, shuddering into a black coat and gloves on a hot September day. It took time to learn how to live in this shabby-genteel house, designed for the strictest kind of dolorous family life. A fisherman's sunny house, immaculate with whitewash, would have been nicer. A house with fewer rocking chairs, and no piano out of tune, and no mended cut-glass. Bit by bit we dared to put away the splotched brocades with ball trimming, and the framed chromos.

Doing business with fishermen was something quite different. Painter friends came, and got themselves a white cube on the shore of the bay. In the mornings they sun-bathed in the boats drawn up on the sand, and played with the children, and swam with them, and painted the old men, and fed the donkeys. Soon they had many friends up and down the line, and especially among the old women who mended nets or shelled almonds. Then, presently, our friends wished to move to the Canaries. They had paid three months' rent; we were given the keys to keep while they wandered. Out of the next complication we learned something about the ethics of the workers.

Another painter arrived full of determination to paint, and paint immediately — no house was to be had, no room; everything was full. Could he live in the house of his friends, the other painters? We thought he could; why not? But no, we must write a letter, said the woman who had rented to the Canary friends. She must be assured of the consent of the original lessee. No number of pesetas could bribe that woman. Why? Because the first tenants had left two shirts, a pair of bathing trunks, and three books in the house. For a week our incumbent painter fretted and tried to paint in the wind. The key in our possession could not be used. And when the letter arrived from the Canary friends, the fisherwoman feared that it was a forgery. It took several telegrams and endless talk before we succeeded in the simple act of unlocking the door. Then, with solemnity, the fisherwoman bore off the property of our absent friends to her own house where it was guarded and delivered to its owners when they returned. We came to admire that woman. She stuck like a barnacle to her conception of honesty.

Centuries of poverty had made this honest honor of hers. What does a Spanish peasant, worker, fisherman, *own?* The clothes on his back, and if he is married, a bed, or a pallet, a chair or two, or a stool, a few clay pots, a coil of rope, a basket, and maybe a goat. Nets, perhaps; and part of a boat. The peasants of the Middle Ages had more.

Maria took us under her wing when we moved out of somber Can Cingala down to the small white house on the water; Maria had a sense of humor. Of all the Spaniards I knew, she is in memory the best example of those who fight and work today. The women of Spain are sad now — they have lost children in air raids, and husbands and brothers in the mud of the trenches. But they are determined. Their faces on the screen resemble Maria's. How to describe Maria? That is hard. But I can imagine Maria sitting in a congress of workers' deputies.

221

I remember best how she sat on the floor and played the phonograph; also how she brought twin kids for us to see, when they were born next door; and how she ran in and out, picking flowers for all the glassware in the house. We went to parties at Maria's house and sat in rocking chairs placed in double rows and rocked and tried to talk to the old people politely. Before we left, Maria and her friends, the masons and carpenters building a house nearby, gave my sister a party, impromptu. It was for her and the full moon; they brought along a decanter of wine; they poured out their friendship. Good luck in "Nueva Yorka." They danced all their dances and sang their very best songs.

Maria and her friends and children will live out their lives under Italian fascists, friends of Franco, invaders of Mallorca and our little Puerto, unless some very heroic fighting and dying ultimately succeeds. When will Franco fall? Defeated in the first battles we must prepare for sterner struggle.

Now and then a little news trickles out of Mallorca. The violence is past — now terror reigns. The fondas are full of uniforms; and the people work in silence.

No Poems About Angels

I heard their voices; their faces look straight at you in the newsreels. I predict a change. And I must try to write a poem, but not about an angel as before.

Those millions of Marias, Manuels, and Juans who put their bodies up as a barricade to defend liberty and a decent wage don't need poems about angels. They want new forces, the release of new forces, and some hope for future victory. Remember their songs and their faces.

New Masses (16 May 1939), pp.7-10

Romanticism and Communism

Mr. Burgum's article, *Three English Radical Poets*, published in the last quarterly number of *The New Masses*, interested me not only because it discussed Auden, C. Day Lewis and Spender, but because in discussing them Mr. Burgum wrote the kind of criticism we must have for a new literature. It seemed to me to be solid and brilliant work, a cantilever bridge (to quote Lewis) between poetry and social fact; a good bridge, firmly planted at the right points on either shore. I should like to comment on what Burgum says about the tradition of the modern radical poet.

My comment runs in the following direction: Should the poetry about to be born belong to the Romantic Family? Should Shelley and Whitman and the "revolutionary" Swinburne come to the christening? It is a bourgeois family, let us be sure of that. At least let us get some of the values, some of the characteristics of this Romantic family out on the table where we can see them; let us describe them with accuracy; and let us see if the Romantic type set up by this family is the whole definition of the artist, the poet, the genius.

Radical readers who look on the poet as a soldier in the ranks of the class war should examine the doctrine of their poets as carefully as they would examine some candidate for the party. It is hard to pin a poet down to doctrine, but good criticism can do it. The off-hand judgments of some radicals have been based on mere texts lifted from a writer's work. But if poetry is to do its work, it is more than a matter of texts and right words. I want to offer one general idea which may help to get at the essentials in this more serious test of poetry's significance.

It is doubtless true, as Mr. Burgum says, that C. Day Lewis' Marxian conviction grows in some way out of the English version of Rousseau's Romanticism, which took belief in the perfectibility of man for its central tenet. But to me these two doctrines are opposed and cannot be glossed over, modified, or reconciled. I cannot see how anyone nourished in the older set of dogmas — on assumptions held implicitly and unconsciously from childhood — can become the poet of revolutionary significance today without a change in attitude that amounts to the destruction of his older belief. It is not as easy a growth as we seem to assume when talking of romantic poets and Communism. And yet our criticism is still uncritical, that is to say, lacking in insight, when it attempts to interpret either writers of 1830 or writers of 1930.

If you have read nineteenth century poetry with open eyes, you have seen the degradation of that great dogma from Rousseau, expressed with sublime energy by Blake in 1800, ending in all the decadence of the 1890's and prolonged with blood-transfusion of various sorts, into our own time. I say that this faith is finished. And I say that it is worse than no tradition. It is only of value now if understood as a phenomenon of the past; it has something to teach us of course. But so long as it is tinkered with and doctored, in the hope that it may be joined to Communism, it represents the blind-alley that will catch a great deal of good talent.

Communism implies a faith that cannot be reconciled to the truths of the Declaration of Independence and Rousseau's *Social Contract* and Shelley's poetry. My claim is that what I call the "faith" implied in Communism is based on a much deeper understanding of man. We are so much a part of Romantic ideology — all of us, with few exceptions — that we find it very hard to realize that all the Romantic dogmas are mere half-truths; and what is more, that they have not always been valid — something we continually assume. If we had more critics who were not bound to serve middle-class ends, we would be aware of the very significant fact that in general all literature, and for that matter all art, before the rise of the middle class to power in the nineteenth century, proceeded from another set of assumptions. In general, these assumptions are sounder for art than the creed of romanticism and can be interpreted in perfect accordance with the theory of Communism.

Romantic faith decayed seventy years ago in the light of the facts. People have tried to perpetuate it; every conceivable change has been rung on the scale, but the tone gets weaker and weaker, although often more shrill and much more violent. Certain of our poets have been forced to testify — Swinburne, Wilde and T.S. Eliot, for instance — that we live in a flea-bitten world mostly peopled with straw men. Our society is degenerate, they say; weariness and melancholy are almost the only emotions proper to the poet of sensibility. All affirmation is crudity and springs of lack of experience. Capitalism could not be more roundly damned by its most severe critic than by the children of its last phase. The dogma of democratic, individualistic, and finally anarchistic realities cannot be received. But these dogmas are full of threat for us as entrenched counter-revolution. The simpler souls among the reactionaries believe these dogmas as God's truth. A total change of view must come. The poets should be the first to see it coming.

Historically the Marxian theory follows in time those beliefs that resulted in the establishment of democratic institutions. But Marxian theory, as I hope I am understanding it, is a principle that contradicts the spirit of nineteenth century romanticism. The doctrine that man is essentially good and potentially perfectible has been fully exploited by capitalism. See what it leads to: anarchy, lack of form, lack of order and objectivity. This doctrine said: "Destroy institutions and give men freedom and Eden will result." The hatred of institutions, and in recent literature, the hatred of the "soul-less machine" is always to be found in the Romantic. Communism, which knows that man needs organization, needs institutions, needs machinery, cannot be served by any modification of the Romantic spirit. Our literature confirms this. The Romantics are false now as they were not in 1800, because they assume as their natural rights, the fruits of machinery, the benefits of civilization and the joys of culture, without being willing to pay for them.

When the first Romantics wrote they were reacting against a bad society; and also they were inspired to some degree with a hope which the greatest of them felt for humanity as a whole. This humanity was an abstraction, to be sure — an abstraction of their own class interest, if you like. As soon as the value of this idea had exhausted itself as reaction it lost nearly all of its virtue and was ready to be used for sentimental and egotistical ends. Now and in years past, it can only lead the artist who takes it seriously to the jumping off place. We bourgeois poets were bred on chaff. If we look beyond the bounds of middle-class art, we see that no other culture has every lived on such saw-dust. Before the little interim of the last hundred years, the best wisdom of all poets of all cultures has seen the individual in his relationship to something bigger than himself. In fact, the anarchism inherent in Romanticism, if taken quite seriously by its followers, would destroy art and all communication. Meaning implies audience, implies society. The Romanticist who makes himself and his subjective universe the only reality must nevertheless use words, a common possession, a social tool. But if the Romanticist, the extreme individualist, denies the reality of society, the mind of his audience, the community of agreement, the experience and mutual understanding behind words and symbols, how can he do anything but abuse and pervert his medium? And this is, of course, what he does.

When we look beyond these writers we see another use of words and meaning, which is right and proper. We see meanings in perfect accordance with society; we see symbols that have the large simplicity of universal recognition. That is, we see the poet using symbols not out of his private store of free associations, irresponsibility; but with perfect regard for the prevailing meaning the symbol had for the audience. This regard was once the test of a good poet — his ability to divine the emotional and intellectual power of words when released in the mind of an audience was his power. Words have no meaning except in context – that is, in relation to each other. But a truth such as this is not understood by the Romantics, who transfer their individualistic absolutism to their use of words; they think of themselves standing alone in a chaotic universe, mysterious to all but themselves; and so their words must stand. Such behavior runs exactly counter to the temper of the good artist, who knows that all meanings lie in the relationship of artist to audience, of one word to another, of one meaning in relationship to another meaning. And so the Romanticist when he writes well proves that he does not really believe what he professes — first, he communicates, which means that he is not self-sufficient and unlike all other people, and second, he does pay attention to relationship, to form. But he cannot see that this is also necessary in society, and that he cannot live, a law unto himself, either inside it or outside of it.

Only after the false principle of the individual, a little universe sealed away from all the rest of life, has been ridiculed to death, can the proper function of poetry be understood. This meaning cannot come back until we have a classless society.

All this is A.B.C., tiresome and trite to those who have gone far beyond me, I know. It sounds too theoretical for practical people. I hope not too theoretical when it is applied. I would apply it at this point: too many radicals have joined in the bourgeois worship of the Romantic poet — treating him as a possession of radicalism. To do this is to be a gull. It is quite possible to read and relish poets who express attitudes foreign and contradictory to our own; in fact this is natural if you are seriously interested in literature. But to imagine that Whitman, or Shelley, or Victor Hugo expresses our revolutionary meaning today is nonsense. Now it is time to say that what we find in them is a spirit of the bourgeois revolution, deceptive to our ends. We cannot be like the poets of a revolutionary democracy and should not imagine that we can learn how to write from them. It is time to point to a very deep difference between their passion for social change and ours. Is there any room in Communism for the eternal rebel, the Shelleyesque protagonist, the ethereal creature who flies forever in an azure mist away from reality? Shelley's motivation was a pathetic one; but that is no argument for breeding him a thousand little imitators. And Whitman is all right, too, in his place; but I don't want to be told that either his ideas or his technique are the be-all and end-all of good radical writing. I can't use these humanitarian nineteenth century writers. Let me try to say why this is so.

The Romantic notion that the individual was capable of godlike perfection and expansion leads directly away from the central and vital truth of Communism. This godlike type, this poet who is a law unto himself, who is above life, in his opinion, and above material limitation, this person who pretends to be free of human limitation and free of the need to accomplish realities with his fellows, can only feed his audience with the fiction of personality, the decay of those convictions that once fought for a free market, free competition, laissez-faire, and all the rest of it. The theme in these poets is some disguised form of individual grandeur – and since the individual can only achieve grandeur *in scale*, he must gain it by some form of deprecation of his fellows and society. In other words, if you like, this is a completely immoral doctrine. And Communism is moral in the only true sense — it insists that the individual find himself in relation to the people with whom he lives.

This artist, this Romantic poet, does consistent things with ideas, emotions and words. He destroys humor; humor has something to do with a sense of proportion. He cannot tolerate a sense of proportion. Laughter goes, personal grievances multiply. He destroys objectivity. Objectivity has something to do with sanity. He is the enemy of objectivity, since it breaks down his subjective world and his godhood. Eventually he destroys meaning. He pretends to scorn his audience; but his chief desire is to have his audience concur in his own self-opinion. Because this has happened in the cases of the greatest geniuses long after they are dead he demands that it happen to him. A strange dilemma is then invented — the poet begins to talk about two worlds, about the world of dream where he is a god in fantasy, and the world where he is just John Jones, *i.e.,* the world of reality. Observe what the Romantic poet does — he takes the reality of dream and illusion out of life where they belong and where they are a common experience, and he makes this experience into an anti-life principle, a weapon against the rest of life and all who live in it. He so destroys the validity of dream that like an abused thing or a worn-out word, poets of the new literature will probably regard it as an old whore attached to the dead order. This Romanticist has a way of destroying much that he touches. It all comes from the impulse to give himself an importance in defiance of what is true — a wish-importance. And this can grow very tiresome indeed — tiresome even to its practitioner. The strain is really too much for human nerves; and the dope type, the suicide type, and the type that glorifies madness as an index of genius, multiply. The audience a good poet should have cannot concern itself with these maladies — only a sick leisure class can fasten, in self-justification, to the chronicle of the sick artist. His other audience, busy with the problems within life and living with the discipline of material limitation, has no one to write the story of its struggle.

Now our mistake has been in accepting these types as inevitable artist types. We should have been told by our students of literature that the attitude called Classical did not foster such types. It is agreed that at the core of the Classical view is the sanity of viewing man as a very limited and imperfect animal. We call to mind most easily those writers tagged Classical who have done very little else than to record the evidence to prove how silly, how knavish, how ignorant, and vain, in other words, how un-godlike, man is. Others have been able to show the value of the imperfect animal when he is engaged in a struggle for something good outside himself. You are going to ask me what this has to do with Communism. I say that a social theory that aims to build a society that will make it impossible for one class of men to exploit other men, is clearly based on a realistic and sane acceptance of man, the imperfect animal. At one stroke the "Evil" the Romanticist finds so difficult to diagnose, is handled and objectified. No Romanticist can do anything so acute.

This is how the two literary schools fall into formation. I quote from T.E. Hulme, who says that the Classical writer feels: "Only by tradition and organization [can] anything decent be gotten out of him [Man].... The Romantic, because he thinks man infinite, must always be talking about the infinite; and as there is always the bitter contrast between what you think you ought to be able to do and what man actually can. [Romanticism] tends, in its later stages at any rate, to be gloomy."

The Romanticist tends, we should say, to end in futilities and in melancholia, in philosophic defeatism. Whereas this other type, depending on his nearness to a full acceptance of Communism, tends to sobriety and action; he does not go in for gloom, since that is a form of self-indulgence; he is interested in the world even when what he sees is intensely gloomy.

We see that Communism faces the first fact of man's imperfection and weakness with the only possible moral and realistic plan of action; whereas the Romantic is never hard enough, nor clear enough really to espouse Communism — he may try, but press him, and he will deviate inevitably. He is more at home with anarchism, or Utopian schemes, at first requiring men and women to act from a series of noble instincts; then turning defeatist and using the citations of failure for personal excuses. A poet who has ventured outside the narrow range of Romanticism is much more quickly at home with the aims of Communism, since, if he knows the Classical view, he sees the necessity for discipline, and more important than anything else, he accepts without spiritual prudery, all the facts of human nature. He is one up on the Classical poet who accepts and resigns himself to a fixed human nature. He is far ahead of the Romantic poet who is in love with the impossible because it is impossible, in love with non-human qualities (i.e., Shelley); hating mankind for its lack of dream-perfection. Let us say that the new poet is in love with human beings as Lenin was in love with them — knowing faults and virtues with accuracy, unsurprised at even the strangest things in human behavior, capable of laughter, capable of action with others; totally incapable of anything so wasteful as reproaches, wailing grievances, or preachments.

In these realities the new literature can find its themes. How will the new artist who is a thorough Communist differ from the writers of the great past? In this, that he will not see the weakness in men fixed and absolute, or use its incidence to advocate passivity. This is the great power of Communism, that it uses self-interest with human idealism, making the two work together, harnessing this energy as it would an energy in nature to make a machine, incorporating both self-interest and idealism in forms that will last.

Only in this fashion can the ideal of social good become a reality; in a form so invincible that it makes the environment of future generations. Only in this fashion — (the silly old argument) — change human nature; in a form where the good of the individual and the good of society coincide proving that the futile dilemma of the liberal and the Romanticist — Individual versus Society — is a false, a manufactured, not an inevitable problem. This great wisdom has no corrosion of cynicism or defeatism about it; neither is it a vain hope.

How can the Romantic child, the poet fed on another set of values, treat Communism as anything but his arch-enemy? He loves chaos — chaos has been glorified by his masters. Until he loves order, discipline, form, and proportion in both society and literature, he finds every fact of the new order a threat to his happiness. He desires to be above his fellowman; he will not admit his human limitation; he indulges himself in attitudes that show him as non-moral as a god, himself his own law. Being a self-lover, he hates society, fears the bugaboo, Authority, and babbles about his freedom. How comic you say? Comic here; but read cheap biography of popular genius and see how seriously author and reader brood over this non-existent freedom. The good artist knows that he needs society, that he works best with right authority, and that freedom is a word. The Romantics augment the cult of genius and inflate all values until they have no meaning, except the pull on the readers' infantile self. We see these types all around us — bitter, weak, violent, suicidal, ridiculously vain, hysterical, the prisoners of egotism. We are supposed to adore them. In an age where the other set of values were taken for granted, these people would never be indulged; they would become the butt of jokes, the Malvolios of drama. But they are pitiful even in their foolishness; they are starving to death for lack of connection with life. We see them distorting language, straining for effect, play-acting greatness. At their best, they express our sick era. At their worst — adolescent art, it's a great bore!

Where is the genial, sober, salty, level-headed, profound type of the older literatures — no gods and giants, but men, grown to full capacity? Communism will produce them; we shall never read their works.

At this point I check myself and remember that Marx saw the value in neurotic Heine (who might stand as the epitome of all I am attacking), when several radical factions condemned him. So I confine myself to attacking the type. I enjoy Heine! It is too late to change the poets of a contemporary generation — you cannot return them to oblivion, like a dun, unopened. If he is ninety-percent tosh, it's just too bad. A better tradition and he might have been – but that's not the point. I return to my thesis: the best art is the work of society, the artist is only the efficient cause; poetry's only vitality, like the vitality of society, lies in Communism.

A Note from the Editors of New Masses

Miss Taggard's article is so provocative that it is certain to arouse considerable discussion. Her article, however, contains certain assumptions regarding Communist ideology which are unclear and somewhat mistaken. This is because Miss Taggard uses certain terms without clearly defining them. In the beginning of her discussion she makes a contrast between Romanticism and Communism without defining the term Romanticism. Obviously she means bourgeois Romanticism, and it is necessary to bear in mind her restricted references. We can imagine, for example, a "revolutionary romanticism" — a poem, story or play projecting a vision of a socialist society: an outgrowth of the dialectical forces perceived in the present breakdown of capitalism.

In contrasting Communism and Romanticism she leaves an implication which is not corrected until nearly the end of her discussion:

that Communism rejects the concept of man's perfectibility. This is a misstatement since it is precisely because Communism believes in the perfectibility of man, that it works for a system in which, through discipline and socialized institutions, man can perfect himself. The contrast is rather between the anarchic anti-social individualist idea generated by Capitalism, which exalts the ego, and the socially-motivated institutions of Communism which adjust the relationship of the individual to society.

Miss Taggard's position can be considerably fortified by specific references to those final literary stages of bourgeois Romanticism, such as Dadasim, Stream of consciousness, the Revolution of the Word, Objectivism, Futurism, and so on, together with their outstanding practitioners. Even if in a sense these writers are committing and have committed literary suicide, in that very suicide they destroy within capitalist society some of the impediments to a new social order. Those who can go no further than the act of destruction nevertheless fulfil a revolutionary function, for it is such destruction which paves the way to new creation. The individualist rebel – the bourgeois romantic – is the potential ally of either reaction or revolution. In Italy the Futurists have gone with the Fascists; in the Soviet Union the Futurists became part of the proletarian revolution. The fate of the bourgeois romantic is fundamentally dependent on his historical milieu.

New Masses (25 September 1934), pp.18-20

John Donne:

A Link Between the 17ᵗʰ
and the 20ᵗʰ Centuries

Who was John Donne? Why does he haunt modern poetry? Yes, he wrote a song beginning, "Go and catch a falling star." That does not sound very modern. The new school in England would write, "Go and catch a falling cricket-ball." Why is he called "modern" by so many commentators? Why do our poets take titles from his work — as if to ask his approval of their own verse — as if they thought of him as their master? *Fatal Interview*, title of Edna Millay's last book is taken from one poem which the moderns love. *Newfoundland*, which entitled a group of poems in which Archibald MacLeish announced his return to his native land, holds the memory of Donne's line:

> Oh, my America, my Newfoundland!

Elinor Wylie's *Angels and Earthly Creatures* was delved out of Donne's sermons. T.S. Eliot says, in *Whispers of Immortality*:

> Donne, I suppose, was such another
> Who found no substitute for sense....

And the other day when I was re-reading *Stalky and Company*, I came on a passage where one of the boys mutters:

> Then you have done a braver thing,
>   Than all the Worthies did;
> And a braver thence will spring,
>   Which is, to keep it hid.

The poets, including Kipling, love this poet. The writers of text-books scold him. They mark him down to C minus because he so loved and expanded what they call *"the conceit"*. He started a new school of writing, they say, which led poetry toward artificiality. And they quote Ben Jonson who wrote that "Donne, for wrenching of accent should have been hung." This wrenching of accent delights us now. But Dr. Samuel Johnson condemned him again, in the next chapter of our literature. And so on, to the late Edmund Gosse, that Victorian law-maker of critical rights and wrongs, who said: "Donne's influence on English literature has been singularly wide and deep, but almost wholly malign."

Critics, even the best of them, tend to emphasize one quality in a writer out of all proportion to his balancing or compensating other qualities. It is very true that Donne is witty to the point of artifice; but it is also true that he is astonishingly, refreshingly direct. There never was a poet who began poems with swifter attack:

> I long to talk to some old lover's ghost,

he says, speaking right out of himself. Virginia Woolf in her essay on Donne quotes this line to illustrate this quality.

> For God's sake hold your tongue and let me love!

he says again. Such personal, direct and vital exclamations run through all the devious patterns of his work. Here is a poem called "The Expiration," which I think you will enjoy. Notice that Donne makes a very original pattern on the word *Go*, at the end and the beginning of the verses; putting *So, so*, at the very up-take of his poem, to chime with the three exclamations:

> So, so break off this last lamenting kiss,
>   Which sucks two souls, and vapors both away,
> Turn thou ghost that way, and let me turn this,
>   And let ourselves benight our happiest day,
> We asked none leave to love; nor will we owe
>   Any, so cheap a death, as saying Go;
>
> Go, and if that word had not quite killed thee,
>   Ease me with death, by bidding me go, too.
> Oh, if it have, let my word work on me,
>   And a just office on a murderer do.
> Except it be too late, to kill me so,
>   Being double dead, going, and bidding, go.

Do you know Drayton's sonnet which describes a leave-taking much like this? It, too, is very direct. The lovers are not alien dead people who wore gay costumes and behaved like people in a story book. They are very real, indeed. Great writing out-wits Time and Death in this fashion.

Here is another sample of the attractive Donne who comes close to us by means of his peculiar literary power. Sir Phillip Sidney tells how he struggled to write; after many failures, he concludes:

> Fool, said my Muse to me, Look in thy heart and write.

Donne seems to be following this advice with himself. But he looks not only into the heart, which he finds full of astonishing feelings, but he looks as well into his mind. And so he is something of a psychologist; and he says:

> I am two fools, I know,
> For loving, and for saying so
> In whining poetry.

He goes on to say that he did say so, "in whining poetry," because he had hoped that he might ease his pain in love. And here Donne uses a grand metaphor and proves that he knows a lot about human behavior:

> Then as the earth's inward narrow crooked lanes
> Do purge sea-water's fretful salt away,
>   I thought, if I could draw my pains
> Through Rhymes's vexation, I should them allay.
> Grief brought to numbers cannot be so fierce,
> For, he tames it, that fetters it in verse.

Read the rest of the poem. It is called the "Triple Fool." In the next verse, Donne tells how "some man, his art and voice to show," sets music to his poem and sings it. And this, he says, makes him three fools. The best ironists are those who use themselves in sport. "Isn't my behavior ridiculous?" Donne asks over and over. That attitude is close to our time. But no one living has been so passionate nor so bantering with himself.

I open my Random House edition of Donne's work in preparation for this article for *Scholastic* readers. Is it the twentieth time I have read him clear through? He is better each time. I read this poet carefully first in 1926 when I was preparing *Circumference*, an anthology of metaphysical poetry. Then I read Professor Grierson's editions. If you like what you read here, get either the Random House edition edited by John Hayward or Professor Grierson's edition, which Oxford has recently issued in a cheaper format. This time I come at Donne from a slightly different angle. I saw Charles Laughton in his winning role as Henry VIII in the movies. I picked up Francis Hackett's *Private Life of Henry the VIIIth*, to supplement that picture-impression. Then I read Lytton Strachey's

Elizabeth and Essex. I remember bits from *Orlando*. I fancy that I can see Donne, the young blade, on a London street in the confusion of his day. He had a stormy life. His early poems suggest a very debonaire young courtier and wit, the flatterer of noble ladies, adventuring in and out of love as a boy might climb in and out of windows, just because of high spirits. His own heart, which would be called "hard-boiled," "sophisticated," "smooth," by the young people who cultivate such indifference today, affords him a subject. And the fickleness of the young women he makes love to, becomes a companion subject. And so you will read a great many poems about women's constancy. Sometimes Donne begs his lady not to love him sincerely, sometimes he scolds her for her infidelity, sometimes he boasts, about his own ability to love all sorts and conditions of women — and sometimes it is perfectly clear that Donne writes on this subject because it is a favorite with all the young poets of his day. Then we catch the accent of improvisation, of pure fancy and jest.

We know that Donne was an ambitious young person whose only chance to rise in the world lay in allying himself with the right people, the right party; — in other words, Donne could only get on by being a henchman of some sort of other. All this wit and ambition might easily have put him where he deserved to be, except — and here we grow interested that Donne was a passionate, a disastrously forthright person. He was a Catholic when it was unfashionable, nay, even dangerous to be Catholic. And to make matters worse, this gay young rake fell in love! With exactly the wrong woman. Wrong that is, from the point of view of the ambitious. He fell in love with a member of his patron's household and eloped with her.

> John Donne,
> Anne Donne,
> Undone.

he wrote shortly afterward. It is succinct. It was too bitterly accurate then. But for our purposes John Donne's undoing is our gain. For the erstwhile young rake, the Don Juan of little 17th Century London began to write the noblest of love poetry; the poetry of mature love that has burned its bridges without real regret. It finds tongue all the way through the poetry, picturing human love as both a wonder of the body and of the spirit and mind. In an early verse, in the midst of many statements that women are mere toys for men's pleasure, he had made a discovery:

> If, as I have, you also do
> Virtue attired in women see,
>
> And dare love that, and say so, too,
> And forget the He and She....

This discovery never left Donne. He had some trouble in finding God, later in life, even after he became Dean of St. Pauls, but he knew the fullness of love, as you will see if you read "The Sun Rising"; the song beginning, "Sweetest Love I Do Not Go for Weariness of Thee"; "A Feaver"; "The Anniversarie"; "A Valediction of Weeping"; or the "Extasie."

This last poem is one of Donne's greatest. Do not read it in the *Oxford Book of English Verse*, for there Quiller Couch has cut off the last and greatest lines. There is a passage so superb that I hesitate to lift lines from it. Donne is saying that love is a matter of souls, but, he says:

> So, soul into the soul may flow
>   Though it to body first repaire....

and again:

> Love's mysteries in souls do grow
> But yet the body is his book.

I have not even begun to tell you about Donne's reading of the young Gongorist school that flourished in Spain; or of his interest in the new science. My space is all gone. If you like Donne you can know him by yourself. I have talked about the young passionate Donne. There was an old passionate Donne who wrote great religious poetry. Read the young Donne when you are young; and remember to read the old Donne when you are old.

Senior Scholastic (March 24, 1934), pp.11-12

Collected Poems (1938)
Author's Note

The reader will misunderstand my poems if he thinks I have been trying to write about myself (as if I were in any way unique) as a biographer might — or as a romantic poet would, to map his own individuality. Since the earliest attempts at verse I have tried to use the 'I' in a poem only as a means for transferring feeling to identification with anyone who takes the poem, momentarily, for his own. 'I' is then adjusted to the voice of the reader.

Many poems in this collection are about the experiences of women. I hope these express all types of candid and sturdy women.... All those who try to live richly and intelligently. I have refused to write out of a decorative impulse because I conceive it to be the dead-end of much feminine talent. A kind of literary needlework.

I think that the later poems — and some of the early ones — hold a wider consciousness than that coloured by the feminine half of the race. I hope they are written not by a poetess, but by a poet. I think, I hope I have written poetry that relates to general experience, and the realities of our time. A poet never says two percent of what he wishes to say, but that endless realization is his business. I hope my poetry is full of joy and affirmation; the 'dark' poems are there, but only to test the joy.

Statement printed on dust jacket of *Collected Poems* (1938)

Hawaii, Washington, Vermont: A Frame for the Verse

When my grandparents were young, you pulled up stakes and went west if you couldn't stand things as they were. You did not stop to find out why; you were sure that it would be better beyond the horizon. Those pioneers, by beginning all over again and again with a new lay of land and a new set of neighbors, delayed solving a problem that had to be solved some day. They took heart every time they subdued the land and lost heart very shortly after. Patiently, they repeated the toil of the body, only to throw it all away for the mad conviction that a promised land lay waiting ahead. This stepping westward had been going on in my family ever since the Taggards and the Bensons and the Arnolds and the Hollands had left the first farmsteads in Vermont and Virginia; over the Daniel Boone Trail to the Ozarks, down the Hudson River Valley to Illinois, they went, looking eagerly around them for something they never found. They stopped only when the land ended in the Pacific.

I wish I knew more about them. Their behaviour is so human and so unphilosophical. I wonder how they put their desire and their discontent — how did they talk to their wives when they resolved to abandon home for uncertainty? Did they think about free land when they meant free life? Did they convince themselves that their neighbors were a rotten lot, and assume that people were made out of different clay in the new country? Was it greed; or a determination to be a ruling class, to come out on top; or a fear of civilized ways of living?

When I watch children who toil at building dams and bridges and play-houses with superhuman zest, to conquer an almost impossible piece of work, and then see them droop over the finishing half of the job, I think of these people of mine. They dwelt in

> Possibility,
> A fairer house than Prose....

They had no knack for the prose of plain living that comes after giving up splendid possibility – after you settle down and say: "These are my acres; here I live until I die."

In the little western town I came to know, this devil-take-the-hindmost individualism bore a poisonous crop. The extremities of life on the frontier forced pioneers en route to join forces temporarily, for the sake of survival. But when at last they had to form a moderately honest and enduring community, they made a sterile job of it because they were people with no community feeling. Their individualism was disappointed; they had less sense for the arts of group living than those grandfathers who left the east. Social good will was quite dead in them; the only thing that could unite them temporarily was hatred of an outsider.

Eastern Washington, the land of the Nez Percé Indians in 1867, was the stopping-place of my grandfather; there he raised his nine children and was killed mysteriously in a feud; there my mother married my father when he came west from Missouri in the 1890's. By this time the young people who were my mother's friends had ceased to look westward with the long look of hope.

They counted their acres and dug in, settled to the routine of town and farm.

The ration of those who went west had decreased with every stop; thousands left the east for the hundreds who arrived in the far west. And of those hundreds only a very few found this digging in impossible. Some turned around and went back east. Others moved like chessmen from town to town perpetually. Out of the community my grandfather helped to establish, only my mother and father discovered in 1890 that they did not want to stay to share that life. They resigned their jobs as school teachers, gave away their household goods and took a tramp steamer from Portland to the Hawaiian Islands. There they met much that was unfamiliar and there they stayed.

Stayed until the doctors said that my father had worn out the climate and could not live any longer with the chalk dust of schoolrooms; it was "lung trouble." He had been building a little community and a large school. He and my mother were teacher-parents to scores of children of several nationalities; but now he was done for and must retreat. He had saved no money; his only resource was a sum which he had lent to one uncle who lived in the home town. Now he and my mother must return to the life they had rejected. The line westward was to turn back on itself. And we children were to see our America with the eyes of outsiders.

Everything conspired to make the return painful. Island life had changed my parents' minds and their tastes. They had lived with dark people; they had got out of the fatal chain of self-interest; they had seen a life that touched the Orient. At twenty-five they had rejected the small town and all its values; now as middle-aged people they knew how right they had been to reject it. The Island life, for all its faults, offered a liberal and amiable existence. My parents hardly knew that they had become mild internationalists in their labor of fourteen years; they spoke no jargon of international theory; but they knew the natives, person by person, and in many small and humble experiences they had changed.

As if to advertise this change they were to take back with them their three children, who were as brown as natives and as happy-go-lucky. My sister had a Hawaiian middle name; our talk was full of Hawaiian expressions; we had seen a great many American tourists and we did not think much of them. We dressed as children dress now in the summer, as children did not dress in 1910. And we were accustomed to an immense enjoyment in every day of life. All these things had very little to do with money, because we were poor; but it did not matter very much, in the Islands.

This was our garden of Eden; our newfound-land; and we were being driven out. The tropics had spoiled us for grim living on six acres set out to pear saplings between two railroad tracks. Intensive farming, my uncle wrote. I think my father hated farming, extensive or intensive, as only the son of generations of gnarled old farmers can. The graciousness of a Hawaiian garden suited him better. My father went round that garden, pollenizing the papias for the last time, selecting a perfect mango with a pink-freckled cheek, leaving many to hang between the shining leaves. There was a certain look on his face; but he said nothing. My mother was very busy packing and saying *good-bye – good-bye*; but she remarked over and over as if in her sleep that she would miss the sea. We gave away our starched white clothes; nobody wore white in the wheat country. With many small finalities we were leaving this delightful, unusual, and hybrid life, going back to be merged, grafted, initiated into the common environment of American children.

So we packed our books, ate the last mango and the last alligator pear and said good-bye to the Portuguese, the Filipinos, the Puerto Ricans, the Japanese, the Chinese, the Hawaiian-Chinese, and the hap-a-haoles. Stefnotice and maile and plumeria dripped from us on our way to the boat. My father opened a trunk and slipped in a calabash and a lahalla fan. We got the Australian boat to Vancouver.

Hot stubble faces met us at the train window. I ducked down and took a quick look at the hot face of the town, with the feeling of a person about to enter a jail. Dust, ankle-deep, paved the main street. Broken wooden sidewalks bordered by dusty weeds led to a block of ramshackle stores. A drooping horse and a spring wagon stood hitched in front of the post office. No trees in sight; just stubble-covered hills through which we had come for hours.

We children found even the first day in the new home town as dull as ditch, or rather dish, water. Houses had the blinds down to protect carpets. Houses were tight and smelled of dust. Kitchens were hot with wood stoves. Parlors were not to sit in. Flies swarmed around doorways. Outside there was stubble or dust, no grass. Children must not play in the orchards. If little girls were bored they could hem dish towels or swat flies.

It began like that. We saw it very clearly and with astonishment! These people, these white people, were barbarians! They thought it was a lark to go down to see the noon train come in! They waited with great tension in a room full of tobacco spit for the mail that consisted of another mail-order catalog. They screamed out the news if a neighbor had a haircut. They told each other how many overalls they had in their washtubs last Monday. They didn't know how to live at all. At first we were sorry for them.

Our parents looked strangely humbled. Our father chewed on a straw. He was trying to be jaunty, to put on the airs of a farmer. Our mother, our clever, intelligent mother, was a worried woman in a prosaic apron smelling strongly of laundry soap. We began to see why she had chosen the outlandish tropics for herself and her family; and to connect the oil pictures she painted and discarded, with red hibiscus and pink cane fields, and lavish festoons of fruit we had not prized till now. In our homesickness we saw our mother and father on the outgoing track that we had just reversed; and our dejection was increased by the effort they had made and the delayed unhappy ending. We hauled our trunks and boxes out to the unpainted cube of a house on the six-acre intensive farm. The pear saplings looked like twigs in the earth; the rest was weeds and dust. And on the back stoop we were confronted by an iron pump, unprimed, handle high in the air.

The light of an August sun is a pitiless thing on the face of an ugly small town. The first frost, the first snow, the first shy spring day gave that town a momentary loveliness, the charm and sweetness that a bath and a clean dress give to a dirty orphan child. But it was August — weeds, litter, dung, flies; dust-covered snowball bushes. Dust-covered gardens made August the month of suffocation. The body could not breathe; the farmers feared rain as much as they feared greater heat. Dust storms blew over the wheat hills. There was no place to go swimming; there was no ice and very little water. There were no ice-cream cones, no cold lemonade, and no soda pop. What queer people! If you walked to town in the heat hoping for some goody or treat, adventure or calamity, you saw nothing promising — store people dozing behind counters, and a farmer or two, a crying baby, a farm woman in a faded dress walking on run-over heels as stiff as if she were on stilts. I tell you we saw it as clear as day because we had not seen it always — it did not seem so forlorn to them....

And then we found that this was the lazy loafing ground of those who were not "in harvest." These were the fortunate. The others were out with the crews. The women, some of them my aunts, were cooking for forty ravenous hands, peeling tubfuls of potatoes and baking pies in batches. The men behaved like men in war time; they slept in their dirt-caked clothes; they went unwashed and unshaved for weeks at a time. Their eyes were blood-shot from chaff, their tempers ragged with the misfortunes of the machinery and the horses that had to co-ordinate to make an efficient combine. They staggered and snarled and gulped their food. If the thermometer rose, the wheat would cook on the stem and a year's desperate work and a year's credit would be lost. And even while they cut and threshed the stuff, the market might go down — if the thermometer did not rise.

The wheat hills were around us; we would never get out. We were buried inland. We were buried in the fact we didn't like to face — that it took a great deal of sodden work just to produce bread. We had escaped that horrid fact in our fruit-bowered Island. Bread was prose, and we had been raised on juicier fare. We liked fruit, not bread, and games and leisure and flowers and blue water. The life of the town was not complicated by such tastes. The town worked in a frenzy or rested in a stupor. The town was divided between the haves and the have-nots — there were those who owed money to the store, borrowed money from the bank and lived on their mortgaged wheat crop; and those who owned the store, the bank and the wheat crop. Half of the town was sold to the other half. The exploitation was an inch by inch battle extending over years. It was a battle of wheat, blood, sweat, and cunning, and it was not pretty.

Many of these matters were hidden from our childish eyes. But soon enough we saw where our family stood. We were in the owned half. The stalwart American who owned us was our uncle who still owed us money. Because long ago we had lent him some money he was soon a jump ahead of his fellow townsmen and then soon possessed several of them. That gave him a taste for the thing — he was a realistic man; he never signed papers unless they were in his favor. We had no papers to show for what he owed to us. When in all good time we returned to the wheat country he let us live in the unfinished house he had acquired, and we became his hired help. So very slowly it became clear.

That August I packed apples in my uncle's warehouse. He paid about six cents a box if I remember rightly; it took some time before I could pack correctly. After I grew skilful I packed about six boxes a day. There was nothing to see outside the door of the warehouse but a railroad siding, two box-cars, and rows of dusty apple trees. The girls who packed with me were pink-faced and yellow-necked from cheap powder; they talked in thin disguises of who lay under railroad bridges when it got dark; and what she said to him. I didn't understand why they lay there. They soon found out I had never played kissing games.

The day of rest was stultification. Best bib and tucker did not help. The preacher was not eloquent; the music did not lift our eyes up to any hills for the psalmist's help. The church service was like a stream in summer — a thin trickle of religiosity, the drone of singing a little off key, and a grim comment by the most pious on those who stayed away. There was neither refreshment nor change in the tempo. It was just a dusty church and a hot preacher in broadcloth. Sunday had one bright spot. At one o'clock the train from Spokane passed like a streak and the mail clerk threw off my uncle's Sunday paper as it passed. If we children would hunt for it in the weeds we might keep the funnies. The Katzenjammer kids!

Our homesickness waited a few weeks to take complete stock of our situation — and then in that tight little unpainted house came the most violent attack. I woke up one night thinking that I had heard the retreating and advancing whirr of the lawn mower; and I dreamed of the sound of the water sprinklers jetting as they whirled circles of silver on the ferns by the house. The smell of fresh-cut grass was the odor of home. That persisted as something right and natural after all the exotic perfumes of white flowers faded from memory. We thought of the wide cool home in Hawaii, with its clean matting floors and the verandah where the passion vine curled. And there were sudden brilliant recollections of little pictures framed by a pleasant relief — the water then ran every evening in fresh rivulets down the garden side, the freshly swept coral walks sprinkled with the light pollen of algaroba bloom. How we missed the sea we had taken for granted! How brilliantly we saw the waves, rolling at that very moment in to shore — the great blue combers racing, necks arched, the surf blowing back like manes in the wind of their own making. We had been poor in Hawaii, too.

We lived with people owned by a system; but our poverty and theirs had not been abject. It had not cut us off from human exchange. We were not a community armed to the teeth with suspicion and envy. Flowers and a sky were amiable and so were we.

And conversely there seemed now to be some connection between the quality of the land outside the fly-specked window and the people who lived with us in this mysterious knot we called the town. The dry rustle of corn in the hot wind had an unfriendly sound. Would the land and the people always reject us? When we were quarantined in the Islands under suspicion of the black plague, our neighbors put a pot of tea and a plate of cakes through the picket fence. We were always finding a pile of sugar cane, or a heap of mangoes, on the kitchen porch, impersonal thanks for bandaged feet and medicine. We were always being thanked in delicate ways for things we did as a matter of course, since only we had the doctor book, and the drug supply of the little community. If we went to the mountains to pick guavas, the Portuguese children trooped beside us to help fill our pails, and we came home with the leis they made for us, just for fun. The Chinaman who sold his truck to my mother made jokes in pidgin English every morning, as a matter of sheer politeness. My parents worked and we children played in a community of dark faces that always smiled.

Here with our own people it was harder to be human. Our boss uncle dealt with us, and the town watched. He wanted discipline; he wanted to see us knuckle down. We had been away in a lazy pagan paradise. Luck had caught us off guard. That situation the town enjoyed. Gradually we found how they felt about us: *We told you so. You couldn't settle down and work with your hands like the rest of us. You wanted travel and book learning. You were stuck up and you raised your kids to be stuck up. Well, now look at you. A sick man, wife and three kids! You'll just have to take your medicine.*

When fall came and frosty days, school began. My uncle couldn't find it in his heart to pay us what he owed, but my aunt announced to her sewing circle that she wasn't one to see us go ragged that winter. And so we went to school in the made-over woollens of her charity basket. When we needed groceries and fuel we were allowed to charge on my uncle's bill at the general store. Soon the town passed the word from mouth to mouth that we were living on our relatives.

The first day at high school I was painfully conscious of my short pleated skirt and my braids. The school was a desolate place. I gave up the hope of finding girls for friends who were like Jo and Polly in Louisa May Alcott's books. The prettiest girl there slapped her belted waist and boasted that she had gotten herself down to sixteen inches that morning by putting her corset strings around the bed post. The girls were all ready for marriage; most of them were paired off and treated as married people. The hectic love making in that high school was as premature and as brief as the spring that came early to those hills and died after a breath. When I tried to make friends with the girls near me snubs and snickers told me where I stood. My clothes were funny; my talk was funny; and it was whispered that I had lived in a grass hut with cannibals.

The principal looked like a nice young man. He had come west from a college near St. Louis. He was not like the rest. I hoped for a time when he would help me out — say something gentle to me. He seemed even colder than the rest. He was trying to culture these boys and girls, read them Wendell Phillips's orations and Poe's poems in assembly. They guffawed. He bought Millais' picture of Isabella weeping over the Pot of Basil and hung it behind the platform where a map had been. I began to read Keats's poems; like a famished child I began to read poetry that would make me dizzy with delicious sensations, something to vary the stale diet of plain days. But the principal who stood for so much in my eyes seemed colder and more distant to me than to any of the others. For two years I did not know why I worked under his displeasure. Then he told one of my aunts who told my mother. It seemed that on the second day of school I had been reading and he was interested to see what engrossed me so. I remembered then what I had done; yes, I had borrowed a detective story called *In the Bishop's Carriage* and had read it during all the chilly recesses when no one would speak to me. It was the first sexy thriller I had ever read. When my possible friend, the principal, gum-shoed up behind me and saw the title, he shut down on me forever. Nothing I could ever do in that school would convince him that I was a decent girl.

A few funny things happened. My mother used to be called in as a substitute teacher now and then. In the Islands her work had been with the smallest children; what we would call a nursery school now. Well, one day she drove in to take the place of the sick teacher and she faced for the first time in many years a room full of white faces. The school routine went well enough until the late afternoon when the children grew restless and noisy. For relaxation my mother thought she would let them sing. She stood up and put out her hand to quiet them. "*Pau*," she said, "*Pau, children*." It was her old phrase that meant *stop, hush, attention*, in the Islands. She burst into laughter to see the blank amazement on the faces upturned to her. We all kept doing things like that. But now that I try to remember the other funny things we said and did, I find that they have gone out of memory. My brother and sister told many funny stories on themselves to try to cheer my mother and father at home. But my mother and father did not always think them funny.

I have never written about that town in my prose stories or used images from its life in poetry — except once when I addressed the town as a foul bitch and then decided I'd better quit. But somehow everything I have done since I escaped it has remembered its existence. It seems to be the active source of many convictions. It told me what to work against and what to work for. To escape it seemed necessary. Still mine was only a partial escape. Grant Wood draws those faces now; he knows those people. Sinclair

Lewis told a story familiar to my adolescent rebellion in *Main Street*; Sherwood Anderson, Dreiser, and Edgar Lee Masters put some more of it down in their books. Still, it does not do to escape, if you leave your own people behind. A lonely, unsatisfactory performance, getting free of the plain folks, who speak the vernacular and tell the stories you used to hear at bedtime. If that's the American reality – and it seems by many testimonies to be – then how futile to leave and walk off into another dream, the dream of beyond-the-horizon, the delusion of pioneers!

The broken finger nails on the stubby hands of those people! The envy and scorn for all trades that differed from their kind of toil; the disgust for all other skills; the malignant hatred of all desire that did not have money for its object! Was it for this that the intrepid crossed the plains and the Rockies? To make this life! What a sorry life! Based on mass panic and fear of a whole complex of things in a civilized world. Foreigners, first and foremost: Chinks, Wops, Polacks, Swedes, Huns, Frogs — ridicule at one end, lynching at the other. City people, smart folks, gentle folks, stuck-up people — freeze 'em out. Book learning, scientific ideas, the higher criticism — down with it, it's immoral. Innocent pleasures, beauty, joy of life, wine, pictures, music. So you're getting too good for us plain folks, are you!

What if they had read Tolstoy's *What Is Art?* Were they condemning the pastimes of the bourgeois, the parasitic? Don't you believe it! They hated arts and sciences and culture because even the meanest examples of them imply group life. They were a deadish lot; individualism, the creed of their fathers, had starved them.

I think of my uncle as a representative of the extreme case. Individual greed was so justified in that small world that it permitted exploitation inside the family. There was no frontier of hope; no one took for granted natural love of his fellows. "This," they said as they slopped slop for their hogs, "this is life! Damn anybody who gets away."

When I read *Winesburg, Ohio*, and *Main Street* and *Spoon River* years later I saw a clearer pattern. When I lived in that town I was sixteen years old; and I had never played kissing games. I could not see what went on beneath the surface. I could not make sense of what I saw. An older person is less baffled in a small town. He sees deep enough into the human heart to give him some life story. The lives that fill *Spoon River* and *Winesburg* have enough violence to destroy the passive blank of what I witnessed. My mother and father had lost their taste for small-town poison. And so I was denied even that reality with which to cut the surface. If you have no other quickening, and you take drops of gossip for years, your appetite grows. You love crumbs of the truth, even if it is hideous and distorted. And you run to meet gossip. It will cut down the massive pretense in which you live. But if you have not needed it for your daily diet you develop an aversion for thinking the darkest things of your fellows. They were indifferent and stuck up.

And very poor. My father grafted pear sprouts onto twigs and waxed them, working at home in the kitchen, coughing and drooping, an old man suddenly. Once during our darkest time, our uncle prayed as he stood at the communion table for those who had had to be brought low because of their pride. Our faces burned. He was praying for us in public.

It was a beautiful snowy morning, perfect for sleigh-riding. We had no sleigh and the horse had died of old age. Suddenly we heard sleigh bells jingling over the hard white earth. How joyous! How unlike this place! But when the sleigh came near we saw our pious uncle. And what do you think he had come for? In his brand new cutter with his team of beautiful blacks, my uncle had come to take the three children of his poor sick brother out sleigh-riding! Ah, but we had learned passive resistance. *No*, we said, poking at snow with the toes of our shoes. *No*. And he jingled away, softly, over the snow.

We had some relatives who deserved a better name. There was a whimsical uncle who told Paul Bunyan stories. The town whispered that he belonged to the I.W.W. Once I remember he got drunk. That was after forty days on a harvester. He was utterly lovable. The town said with satisfaction that he would go to the dogs. We had two other uncles, very nice ones who did not run with the town. One had gone to the Philippines as a soldier and came home sick with tropical dysentery. He had a beautiful, gentle wife named Barbara and two beautiful children and a Saint Bernard dog. The town said he would never amount to shucks and he never did. He was a nice man, resigned to failure. The other uncle was a vast creature as hearty as the day — extravagant. He had six sons. He made jokes and filled a room with pleasure whenever he walked in. He bought horses for his sons to ride; and trained them to be hard with themselves and gentle with people; but he borrowed money on his next wheat crop and got all mixed up with the bank, buying linoleum and a modern sink for his wife, who was extravagant, too. The town got him, but his sons went to college.

"Sis," he told my mother, driving his spanking pair out to the debt-clouded farm, "I tell you, you'll never get it. You didn't ask for his name on paper and it's an outlawed debt. Don't you suppose he knew?"

We made a few friends, slowly. After a while the brightest boy in town gave me a copy of Shakespeare and Ruskin's *Sesame and Lilies*. It was spring at last. The town was sweet with locust bloom; thorny trees snowing blossoms where bees in vast armies worked for harvest! For lo! the long winter is past and the spring is come, we all seemed to sing. And the meadow larks carolled down the railroad track on our way to school. If that hill that could be seen from the kitchen window had not been planted to winter wheat, had not stayed green all winter, my mother said, in a moment of confidence, if it had not — she could not have kept from going crazy. The swift, brief spring deluded us and told us lies about our little world. My admirer was going to college. When he came up the railroad track one spring night to call on me, the town hoodlums chased him back with blank cartridge shots. "How he ran!" they laughed the next day, slapping their thighs, wild with spring lust. And my boss-uncle warned my stooping father that I would go the way of all the girls in that town if he let me out walking with my admirer.

I have a farm in Vermont now which I do not farm. For a time I earned my living in Vermont as a teacher, like my parents. The farm is a wild place; I bought it because it had a western look — not the west of the wheat hills, but the west of timber and rushing water which I continue to love. It lies about fifteen miles from Londonderry where some of my people were buried more than a hundred years ago. The best that my people went west for could have been found fifteen miles from their doorsteps, I think.

I have been looking for a good community for many years, in my own country. I found it in New York for a while. Then I found it in Connecticut where I lived after I was married; and I saw it spoiled by a writer or two who cheated our neighbors and wrote them up as country bumpkins. I knew when that happened that I did not agree with my group of fellow-writers that it was all right to out-wit and exploit farmers who shared with them. But this was the doctrine of writers returned from Paris in the dark ages, the 1920's.

I love that Vermont acreage even if it is only worth a few dollars an acre. They say owning land makes one conservative. I am not conservative. I would rather lose my land than give up my ideas. I am not a true member of my Vermont community, of course, because I do not live as my neighbors do, by work on the land. This article is its only crop to date; if I sell it I can make the next payment.

I wonder if that little town near Walla Walla has changed? Gas stations, radios, ten-cent stores, of course. But has it changed?

How do the farmers talk? Have the banks taken the best land? Do the farmers ever strike? Do the children read poetry?

Winter, 1933-1934.

Two years later. 1936. Now as my book goes to press I must say in the clearest and simplest manner possible that I was wrong about Vermont. At first it looked to me the way it looks to the summer visitor who goes up there to get a rest. And then the facts contradicted my hope. I saw canned wood-chuck in the farmers' cellars. I saw slums in Brattleboro and Burlington. I knew children who picked ferns for a few cents a day. I knew a man who worked in a furniture factory for ten cents an hour! I saw his starved wife and children. Slow starvation gives children starry eyes and delicate faces. I saw five men who were a few weeks ago sentenced to jail for their activity in the Vermont Marble Strike. I saw a voucher for two cents one worker got for a week's wages, all that was left after the company deducted for rent and light. I saw a pile of such vouchers. When they eat, the quarry workers eat potatoes and turnips.... In Rutland County the Overseer of the Poor is a Marble Company official.

And so I say I was wrong about Vermont. The poems in this book were written after I began to see why.

Calling Western Union, pp.xi-xxxii

Songs for the People

In the winter of 1929, at the start of Taggard's first full-time teaching appointment at Mt. Holyoke College, Wolf suffered a mental breakdown. After a number of crises and threats to the lives of his family members, he was by the end of the year admitted to Matteawan State Hospital for the Criminally Insane in New York, where he was diagnosed with paranoid schizophrenia.[1] Taggard's response to her own emotional trauma was to throw herself into her teaching and her writing, producing both her Dickinson biography and the anthology *Circumference* the following year. She applied for a Guggenheim Fellowship to give herself space and time to concentrate on her own poetry. The fellowship was awarded, and she and daughter Marcia spent 1931-32 in Mallorca, where the great socialist hope of the Second Republic had just been declared, and where she wrote many of the poems finally included in *Not Mine to Finish* (1934).

---

1   He was formally committed in 1931.

Her poem "Lark" (p.179) was written sometime in 1932, during her Mallorcan year abroad. Taggard would have been aware of the political unrest in mainland Spain, and of the growing threat of fascism in Europe through her contact with liberal and leftist Europeans like Dora Russell, who visited Mallorca in January 1932 and became a close friend. A sense of social and political apprehension colours many of the poems she created there. By the time Taggard returned to the United States, in August 1932, Philip Rahv's strident call for a new revolutionary literature, "The Literary Class War," had appeared in *New Masses*. Upon her return to the US, shortly after settling into a new job at Bennington College, Taggard wrote to Dora, "I feel that I want to do something in the radical movement but cannot quite see how it is to be done."[2] Taggard's response to that challenge was to bring an apparently lyric poem, "Lark," to the service of antifascism. First published in 1933 in the *Saturday Review of Literature*, it then appeared with some of her first radical poems of the 'thirties in *Not Mine to Finish*, and when she began a few years later to assemble her most concentrated group of politically committed poems in *Calling Western Union* (1936) she chose "Lark" to end the book, immediately after a poem titled "Revolution."

Two years before "Lark" was composed, William Empson's ground breaking book of literary criticism, *Seven Types of Ambiguity* (1930), was published. Taggard was in her first real teaching job at Mount Holyoke College in Massachusetts, and had just reviewed *A Survey of Modernist Poetry* (1928) by Laura Riding and Robert Graves for the *New York Herald Tribune* in 1929. Riding and Graves's attention to the line-by-line analysis of poetry anticipates Empson and Richards's Practical Criticism. These works, along with the essays of R.P. Blackmur, were at the foundation

---

2   Taggard to Dora Russell, [Autumn 1932], Dora Russell Papers, International Institute of Social History [online resource], item number 973-81.

of Taggard's maturing sense of critical literary judgment in this period. One of Empson's most detailed analyses in his study of the uses of various kinds of poetic allusion and inference addresses Percy Bysshe Shelley's poem, "To a Skylark." Shortly after her arrival in Mallorca, Taggard wrote asking her friend Sara Bard Field to send her books of poetry by Browning and Shelley. She will have known Shelley's poem well enough not to have to rely on Empson for it, as she had recently taught it in her classes at Mt. Holyoke,[3] but elements of his interpretation were still fresh in her mind, especially with the poem itself close at hand during her composition of "Lark."

Empson attributes to Shelley's poem a higher calling; the lark is here "outside human limitations... immortal." Flying straight up towards heaven and singing its joyful song the lark becomes for Empson a clear metaphor for the aspiration of the poet. It is this sense of expanding awareness of the mind through the senses, a revelation both sensory and spiritual, and reassurance, that Taggard plays upon in her own poem to the lark, though in her poem it is transposed to a more human register. Although she leans heavily on Christian echoes ("O Believer" and the resurrectional "The Sun is Risen"), her inferences of redemption from despair are delivered by the "spark," "shock," and power to "stun" of an overwhelming recognition of hope, a sudden religious conversion expressed with the electrical immediacy of "O lightness like a spark," an unexpected personal awakening. But that awakening, for Taggard, now needed to come by human will and effort rather than divine agency.

Taggard's poem calls upon the lark as ancient Greek poets would supplicate the gods, to wake us up, to bring us completely

---

3   Genevieve Taggard Papers, New York Public Library, Box 33, Folder 15, "Teaching Materials." Also in folder 15, Taggard's extensive notes from I.A. Richards' *Practical Criticism*.

to life; the invocation "O Lark" occurs four times. It glorifies the bird (the poetic impulse), even as it petitions the higher conscience of the reader. It is for all persons, but impersonal. It is vatic and prophetic. This is an archaic lyric in the original Greek sense, a paean to the god or gods of praise and supplication, employing "oracular speech that produces truth."[4] Taggard has gone back to the very origins of the lyric, to the beginning of western poetry, for the sacred enactment of the poem as an experience of the lyric present, employing the original hymn-like and declarative form of poetry for her modern revolutionary expression. In her poem, the invocation of the lark serves to articulate shared social values and a celebration of optimism and hope for a country in despair in the early 1930s, facing catastrophic economic depression and massive unemployment.

In the depth of the Depression, the movement towards social reform and support for the working class gained pace. The initial impetus for writers to create "proletarian art," written from the point of view of the exploited manual labourer, soon gave way to a realization that most intellectuals and artists were working from quite a different cultural base. Liberal middle-class writers recognized that they could hardly speak with any authenticity for the working class; their role surely must be to encourage and expand the ranks of bourgeois writers like themselves in order to support the social movement of and for the workers.[5] This gave rise to the Popular Front (1935-1939), which was the Communist party's political and cultural strategy to build support for New Deal legislation and to increase public awareness of the dangers of fascism. As part of this campaign, they supported leftist

---

4   Jonathan Culler, *Theory of the Lyric*, Cambridge, MA: Harvard University Press, 2015, p.49.

5   Michael Denning, *Cultural Front: The Laboring of American Culture in the Twentieth Century,* London and New York: Verso, 2010, pp.53-64.

organizations in the arts, including *New Masses* and The League of American Writers. The Popular Front was a special aspect of American culture in the 1930s, and although as an official program of the Communist Party in the U.S. it was abandoned by 1939, the sensibility it engendered persisted well into the 1940s.

Taggard engaged enthusiastically with the Popular Front through her organizational roles in the League of American Writers, her teaching in its affiliated workers' writing classes, her work with the musicians of the Composers Collective, and her collaborations with the radio writer Norman Corwin on his nationally broadcast poetry programs. Taggard was a founding member of the League, in 1935, holding a central organizing role on its Executive Committee. Her friend Waldo Frank was in no doubt as to the League's crucial mission: he told the participants at the first American Writers' Congress in 1935 that "We must have poets to sing the image of the new and truer person: the person who knows his integration with group and cosmos; the person through whom the whole speaks – the conscious cell of the conscious Communist order."[6] Taggard's desire was to be just such a person, creating poems of optimism and reassurance that would also awaken the minds of people to the need for social change.

By the late nineteen-thirties she considered "Lark" to be one of the handful of poems – songs for the people — that expressed the necessity of faith in the future, of faith in a social revolution, and it became her personal anthem of hope for a new day, culturally, economically and politically.[7] Attending the first American Writers' Congress in 1935, Taggard heard a rousing talk on

6   Waldo Frank, "Values of the Revolutionary Writer," *American Writers' Congress*, London: Martin Lawrence, c.1935, pp.71-77.

7   Taggard to Granville Hicks, n.d. Granville Hicks Papers, Special Collections Research Center, Syracuse University Libraries.

"revolutionary symbolism" by Kenneth Burke, who would also write that "the future is really disclosed by finding out what people can sing about,"[8] and she pursued this future in her poetry. She let it be broadcast over the radio in public readings, set to music in concert halls, sung in the voices of ordinary people, and read in the books she published. As with Lucinda Matlock, the character from Edgar Lee Master's *Spoon River Anthology* she performed on the radio, who "rambled over the fields where sang the larks," Genevieve would herself have asked:

> What is this I hear of sorrow and weariness,
> Anger, discontent and drooping hopes?
> Degenerate sons and daughters,
> Life is too strong for you –
> It takes life to love Life.[9]

At the end of her Guggenheim Fellowship in Mallorca, Taggard accepted a teaching job at the newly opened liberal Bennington College in Vermont. It was then that she purchased Gilfeather Farm in the small town of East Jamaica, Vermont, at the edge of the Green Mountain National Forest about forty miles from Bennington, which would become by the 1940s her permanent home.[10] The farmhouse took years to make fully habitable and initially was only used as a summer retreat, but Gilfeather provided a refuge and a return to an ancestral landscape of the sort she had perhaps glimpsed in the relationship the Mallorcans had with their own environment. As she tells us in "Hawaii, Washington, Vermont" (p.245), her forebears had lived and

---

8   Kenneth Burke, *Attitudes Toward History*, New York: The New Republic, 1937, p.335.

9   Edgar Lee Masters, *Spoon River Anthology,* New York and London: Collier Books; Collier-Macmillan, 1962 (1914), p.239.

10   Taggard to Dora Russell, November 26, 1933, Dora Russell Papers, International Institute of Social History [online resource], item number 1246-53.

died in the region a century before, and here she began to find a sense of belonging.

In its Appalachian mountain setting, Gilfeather Farm was also a place where Taggard's second husband, Kenneth Durant, felt at home, reminiscent as it was of his youth in the Adirondacks. With Robert Wolf now permanently committed to an asylum, Taggard obtained a divorce and in 1935 married Durant whom she'd known for over ten years. After graduating from Harvard in 1910, Durant had worked briefly in journalism, then on the Creel Committee, producing propaganda to build support for World War I in 1917-19, and then under Colonel House at the Paris Peace Conference in 1919. A friend of William Bullitt, who had attempted in 1919 to negotiate diplomatic terms between the US and the Bolsheviks, Durant was a committed supporter of the cause of Communism from its inception. After the war, he became the director of the Russian news agency in New York (beginning as ROSTA in 1923 and changing its name to TASS in 1925), a position he held until his retirement in 1944. The British sculptress Clare Sheridan, visiting New York in 1921, described him as "an ascetic Bolshevik" with a "face that belongs to the woods, and a soul that belongs to the world's workers. It is not always working people and workers' conditions that produce revolutionaries and world reformers."[11]

Although Durant was, by the time Taggard married him, an undeviating Stalinist with an authoritarian personality, he was also a cultured and highly educated man who could share Taggard's poetic life. It was Durant who began the work of establishing her archives with Dartmouth and the New York Public Library, and he was an intelligent reader of her poems. In 1937, when Charles Abbott, the librarian of the University of Buffalo, initiated the Poetry Collection at the Lockwood Library and

11　Clare Sheridan, *My American Diary*, New York: Boni & Liveright, 1922, p.47.

invited Taggard to be one of the first poets to be represented with a selection of manuscripts and drafts of poems, Durant took an active interest in the project, and it is notable that at the moment when Taggard's work was becoming most intensely radical (her *Calling Western Union* had been published the year before) only two of the 113 poems she sent to Abbott for his Poetry Collection, "Fantasy Before Fact" (1933) and "The Discipline" (1941), clearly reflect her politicised voice of the 1930s. At Thanksgiving in 1941, Taggard returned to Buffalo to give a lecture on "the process of writing a lyric" with examples from her work to show "stages of revision, from rough notes to finished form."[12] However firmly affiliated she was by now with Communist ideology (Durant's influence having been strongly felt after their marriage), Taggard held fast to her identity as a lyric poet, a modernist artist, and a teacher.

Taggard's marriage to Durant coincided with a new sense of political urgency in radical literary circles. She now reassessed her own political commitment and her ambitions for a poetic contribution to the revolutionary movement, declaring her belief that poetry could act as a positive force for change. In her essay "Not Mine to Finish" (p.211), she strongly admonished teachers of English to encourage young writers to live fully in the real world, rather than to take refuge in the escapist Romanticism of the past – "writing properly understood," she insisted, was "*a kind of action.*" She quoted Robert Frost's definition, "Poetry is words that have become deeds."

A few months before, in September 1934, with the *New Masses* having changed to a straightforward political weekly from the art and literature monthly it had been since 1926, Taggard's long article "Romanticism and Communism" (p.223) was published. It was

---

12   Taggard to Charles Abbott, 21 October, 1941, Poetry Collection, University Libraries, University of Buffalo, SUNY.

a response to Edwin Berry Burgum's "Three English Radical Poets" (Auden, Spender and C. Day Lewis), which assessed their relative revolutionary merits. The editors of *New Masses* found Taggard's stern denunciation of the new proletarians' apparent acceptance of their place in a history of romanticism so "provocative" that they were moved to append a three paragraph editorial afterword, calling for a more nuanced "revolutionary romanticism" by which writers could offer a vision of a socialist society. By the end of the decade, this idea seems to have taken root in Taggard's poetry, because that is what her readers would find in many of her later poems, like "Long View."

In the fall of 1939, Taggard sent the young radio editor Norman Corwin a new poem inspired by his talk to the Poetry Craft Session on new media at the recent American Writers' Congress, written, she told him, "with Radio in mind."[13] The provisional title was "Overheard and Reported" – words immediately recognizable as two aspects of the radio experience: reception and broadcast. The final title of the poem, as published in the *New Republic* (11 October 1939) was "Long View" (p.205). A prophetic poem, "Long View" offers an imagined "memory" by future pioneers of the struggles and trials of those before them who strove for the ideal state. In "The trees and rivers are on the map, but the time/Is not yet," the map proposes an ultimate goal yet to be reached, a journey not yet completed. When the poet writes "I heard us all speaking," she projects herself into this future, assimilating her own poetry with this new world, creating a sense of cultural continuity and identity. "Our own story retold" reinforces this connection and sense of historical determinism. The gift of the poet is to have this power of vision, not to dream but to prophesy: to "talk of the future" and to

---

13   Taggard to Norman Corwin, n.d. [Fall 1939], Norman Corwin Papers, Syracuse University Libraries.

convey a story of hope to the listener. It is a utopian vision in an hour of crisis. This poem, written at the end of the 'thirties, shows Taggard reaching toward a new form, something related to both song and to vernacular speech, in a concerted effort to restore faith and strengthen resolve during a terrible European (soon to be world) war.

Hope, at this moment, was in short supply for those on the left. Shortly before this poem was published, the dreams of many American Communists for the realization of economic equality and social justice had been dashed by the signing of the German-Soviet Non-aggression Pact in August 1939. The week before the *New Republic* published "Long View," it printed an article by Taggard's close friend Granville Hicks, "On Leaving the Communist Party," a traumatic but decisive break for him, as it was for so many who felt betrayed by Stalin opportunistically allying the Soviet Union to the forces of German fascism.

When "Long View" was published, Taggard received a letter from a teacher at San Francisco State College, Caroline Shrodes: "A few students," she told her, "remembered Vincent Sheean's thesis, in *Personal History*, and related his concept of the long view to your poem." Taggard's friend Vincent Sheean, at the end of his book of 1935, had described his epiphany, viewing an ancient and modern panorama from the Acropolis in Athens:

> Here you had to take 'the long view'; no other view would do, no other view was possible. ... I had known only one long view in my life. Once, for a time, I had perceived human existence to be a coherent struggle towards the reasoned control of its materials and had thought I might have a place, small but exact, in that struggle.[14]

---

14 Vincent Sheean, *Personal History*, London: Hamish Hamilton, 1969 (1935), p.436.

Taggard wrote "Long View" as an act of reassurance to the many deeply shaken believers in that struggle toward a future where hope was on the horizon, an urgent entreaty not to despair, but to trust to the idealistic, pioneer spirit she believed to be so quintessentially American and fundamentally socialist.

IV
A Nothing Vast

On Planting a Small Lilac in Vermont

Yes, this lilac I am planting signifies
The old New England rural and decayed,
Flower and leaf Frost loves, the lavender,
False-blue that Amy Lowell made
Out of mere statement purple into spray.

It's a young lilac tagged from Bloomingdale's.
The doorstep that it's by is farmer style.
I like to plant, to see the twig-roots bed.
Lilac and I will have to wait a while
Before the purpose of this planting's clear.

Planting for future people with sure hands
Is pleasure of the purest. Live and unfold!
You only seem to be compact New England —
(Her virtues stale and her intelligence cold).
I plant you for another country sure of flowers.

How well you nestled into Persian ways!
Your heart-shaped leaf ran on the border cloth.
And in this place of sunken cellar doors,
In deep grass, by deserted barns, you are both
Voluptuous and frugal like the folks.

You'll see another change. Doorstep will change.
The tight sad house will change. And in its place
I can't see much, only the doorstep edge,

Hear children talking, see a happier face
Than you can find in the working class today.

Grow for those people, lilac. Be no family shrub.

A Part of Vermont, p.16

Range, Range the Words Around

Nature is full of rhymes.
So is man's head.
In these, the evil times
The silly, the half-dead
Hum while committing crimes, —
And so to bed.

Bloody old couch. I'll write
No rhymes to pleasure such, —
Odd phrases for the night.
Wash hands to quit their touch,
Fix eyes to out-stare sight
And not say much.

Or say their guilt is mine.
The bloody couch mine too.
And have her in to dine, —
The colossal strumpet who
Spills guilt with the old wine
And the idiot new.

Range, range the words around.
How shall we fix the scale?
Long silence and no sound,
And all the risk to fail.
Then on new ground
Begin the tale.

Long View, p.5

Ode in a Time of Crisis

Now in the fright of change when bombed towns vanish
In fountains of debris
We say to the stranger coming across the sea
Not here, not here, go elsewhere!
Here we keep
Bars up. Wall out the danger, tightly seal
The ports, the intake from the alien world we fear.

It is a time of many errors now.
And this the error of children when they feel
But cannot say their terror. To shut off the stream
In which we moved and still move, if we move.
The alien is the nation, nothing more or less.
How set ourselves at variance to prove
The alien is not the nation. And so end the dream.
Forbid our deep resource from when we came,
And the very seed of greatness.

This is to do
Something like suicide; to choose
Sterility – forget the secret of our past
Which like a magnet drew
A wealth of men and women hopeward. And now to lose
In ignorant blindness what we might hold fast.

The fright of change, not readiness. Instead
Inside our wall we will today pursue
The man we call the alien, take his print,
Give him a taste of the thing from which he fled,
Suspicion him. And again we fail.
How shall we release his virtue, his good-will
If by such pressure we hold his life in jail?

The alien is the nation. Nothing else.
And so we fail and so we jail ourselves.
Landlocked, the stagnant stream.
So ends the dream.

O country-men, are we working to undo
Our lusty strength, our once proud victory?
Yes, if by this fright we break our strength in two.
If we make of every man we jail the enemy.
If we make ourselves the jailer locked in jail.
Our laboring wills, our brave, too brave to fail
Remember this nation by millions believed to be
Great and of might forces born; and resolve to be free,
To continue and renew.

Long View, p.41
First published *New Masses* (29 October 1940)

On Darkness, On Evil, on Night, etc.

Let those of poor energy
Fear night. Not I.
Night does so unmake me
Into purity of disparate parts, where I lie
Sleeping my wrong dreams my
Bad fears that they may never be.

And out of self so ill
Begin again
With the unbroken will,
The unspoiled energy of the lion's den.
Night's the recess under the hill
Where serpents uncharm men.

Long View, p.17

To an Unfoiled American Revolutionaire

*Poems should never be explained, but I will explain this
one a little, and request the reader to create in his own
mind and with these words a context in which it may
stand. Our time knows a new kind of heroism. We are
reluctant to use the word hero for the good reason that we
dislike the connotations of hero worship, the sick idea of
a God-sent savior. For this reason, we are a little slow to
see a new kind of person who now emerges as a very significant human being. The prototype is at large in humanity.
We will see him more clearly in the next few years. We are
helped by contemplating this unfoiled person; he is a part
of us, we are a part of him. And when the definition
is clear, we will not hesitate to use the word hero; it will
be a good proper word again.*

(not forgetting Whitman's Foil'd European
Revolutionaire)

Member of the people's army — a unified man.
Unlike the hollow children just his age.
Held an important outpost. At first, alone.
Alone, but not alone, with invisible help.
Knowing why he worked of what he was a part
Not alone. At times pressed hard.
Sternly and then not even sternly refused
To feel distance. Fought a long battle.
Some of it simple patience, judgment, risk.
Battle longer then lifetime; often obscured,
Perhaps at times forgotten, so hot the war.
Dwelt on none of this, never told his own story
To himself. Others, less complete, talkative persons
So placed, retreated, found some way back

And applause for the quick excuse.
Too busy to be relieved and too tireless
To risk rest. Servant with skill to devote
All, seeing a world striving to be born.
Used his head in need, made decisions like light
Having theory at heart like a passion.

Was this man real? Are we myth making?
Does one eat with a myth, walk streets with a myth, consult
A myth? Share day and danger? Sleep and wake
In resolute company because of a myth? I ask you.
History mildews in the newspaper. The radio howls.
But bad habits we had drop like ice in the sun.
Here are the new forces.... His tensile strength
Explicit love, his sanity tell us true.
Tested; we know; our young ones bring new wills.
Nothing shakes this — the world that makes this man
While he with many makes the world. Believe.

New Masses (February 18, 1941), p.28

Poet

Tragic meaning was my altitude.
Took it for mine, felt it lift
Very high, learned to live holding it behind diamond eyes,
In brain, in balance, let it eat at the vitals,
Seeing and willing events in crystal focus:
Large stars convening for nativity-eve.

Then saw the magnetic hope, and saw
Rays of power. From the saffron corpse of the tragic
Saw the new babe born, lusty, contorted.
Saw cohorts of cloud circling, dispersing,
Again circling; and space circling the perilous birth,
Until peril deepened, stained hope's country scarlet.

So refused the usual small role, knowing the nature,
The large terrain of the time. Since it is vision, since it is
Mine to say what it is, how quiet the eyes
Seeing, and the mouth open and saying:
This time, these people, the crisis hurrying
Near the defile of the evil story, this, soon and new.

Then dare to descend as by parachute, sheer
Drop down to place assigned, sheer down to fact.
Completely to relinquish vision and its piercing virtue.
Fall to the weight of one day with one life for gift.
Drawing the line from zenith to earth's tiny inches.
Suffer the limitation of beginning action. So on

Linked in unit of slow going; in the line as it stops;
With stop after step, the signal awaited. One

In the lock with all, chained but never slave.
Here sweat out struggle nothing-sweeter than history.
Web of feet working over dark bloody ground.
Heart plunging neatly, spasm on spasm.

Slow Music, p.15

Delight

In the secret place of the heart
What is it my heart most cherishes?
What image, what toto in dream, what token
     held in tight fingers?
O, one from sweet everyday, whereon I dart
Like a child, whereon no joy perishes,
Wherein no fatal bitterness lingers:

My tall man walking the meadow at night, with
     the lantern,
A solemn sleepy procession, he and I to the cabin,
Both silent, I at his heels, to return
In morning dew, in first sunrays, with the dark lantern.

And if I were Ariel come home from toils and
     circling errands,
I could laugh no more sweetly than when I inwardly see it,
My delight a trembling frame to this Attic picture.

Stern world, one rollicking image, for around this
     happy thing
Forever I turn in light handsprings of the spirit.

A Part of Vermont, p.23

This Poem

This poem, — (which contains
A world which contains a poem,
This poem which contains a poem and a versal world,
Bubble in bubble) — this poem
Must be read in a moment and
Felt in less than a moment for
Its self is evanescent. Not so, the earth.
How solid it is. And see
Issuing from the atomy globe
A phantom, kneeling and rising, forever enchanting.
It is the crisis-cross fume of our notion of her.
Who knows: is she an immortal bomb burning its
        fuse-instant?
Never to burst? Who knows? She burns at the touch of
        our minds.
We, the art of her jargon, her marvel of marvels,
Her mastering zeal, aspire... In this we suffer much
And live only when we are one, "unfolded out of the folds."
Hail, hail, unholy mother; and hail, our glory.
This is Tuesday morning; and we, the multitude
Fresco the wall of the sky into which we fade.

Slow Music, p.9

True Fable

Now make one fable of the source of love:
What finger of fire, they ask, what idiot luck,
In a waste of cults and bones and empty men....
It was poetry, poetry and the human heart.

And when a child, what filled you most with awe?
Found you a magnet-center, a golden test?
The burning bush, and the pathos of a voice:
It was poetry, poetry and the human heart.

Child loves the dazzle-frond, jumps up and down,
Not knowing flame, certain of its want,
Quick in the person of the syllables:
Poetry, poetry and the human heart.

O, long ago the keen delighting lit
An answering fire, the only deathless love,
Breathing and quiet — an inward delicate sense:
Poetry, poetry and the human heart.

Slow Music, p.27

To Ethan Allen

Sleep, Ethan, where you belong,
Allen of the little clan,
Clan of large men on lavish continent,
In the place of uncut trees and the trackless green.
Sleep to the thrush's tranquil, seasonal song.
Vermont itself is your big monument;
And also those who sing of wilderness and man;
Of intelligence and hardihood and the keen
Struggle. Song is for heroes in their time of rest.
Sleep in your granite bed under the mountain tent,
Beside your lakes and rivers; near falls that splash and flare.
Vermont was wild frontier and still contains the West.
Daily your turbulent spirit delights this air.
Sleep well in your wedge-shaped bed,
Under the slanted snow, or in spring's frequent
Vehement thunder. Sleep. A poet said,
Nature is never spent.
Neither are we, nor were you, Old Heart of Oak.
I heard your tone when first the thunder spoke.
The toil of men and women, the excited feet
Stamping at country dances, and Town Meeting Day
Chiming their biblical notes of *yea* and *nay*,
And many customs sweet
Prolong an enduring impulse this citizen took
To be his passion: to be Freedom's servant rude.
A man no Tory conclave could undo,
Founding a state and writing a troubled book.
Prisoner, freeman, leader and strategist,
Sagacious creature with uplifted fist
Against all tyrants... Those who remember you
Wish never to outgrow such servitude.
Sleep, Ethan Allen of the little clan.
Vermont in its quiet way recalls this man.

Sleep, Ethan, in the mountains where you belong.
Sleep to the thrush's tranquil, seasonal song.

A Part of Vermont, p.3

The Nursery Rhyme and the Summer Visitor

Green Mountain Mary, Green Mountain Mary
What does your garden grow?

Violets, moss, ground pine, goldenrod, briars,
Strawberries, spirea, wintergreen, ferns,
And a little bit of grass, alas.

Will you sell me your meadow?
                              Oh, no.

Who crops it?
            Deer.

See, here, Green Mountain Mary, you people are very, —
Excuse me —
Queer.

A Part of Vermont, p.5

Gilfeather Again

In Gilfeather pasture, trim with moss,
Near leafy mingle, in cove of air,
Space by our moving, flows across
Meadow to shadow; and softly there
Evening birds exchange by rote
Perfected oddments, echo pure.
I hear them open on one note,
Serene, secure.

No hurt retreats us from this calm,
Now fragile and so seasonal.
Here, healing as the scriptural balm
In Gilead, affirms the small
Invisible thrush with delicate throat —
Where we delay or return to hear it —
Of which the importunate psalmist wrote
For the broken spirit.

A Part of Vermont, p.8

Bounding Line

Silver rubs rocks and furs the twig.
All that was little is still and big.
Attention folds and stoops
To the snail, to slants and loops —
Thread of spider arrayed on the fern.

I am frost's fleck, the grain,
The fissure, the dented vein.
Here looks the insect's eye
Against lens to magnify
The stuff of frost and chill-burn.

Large swells the hoist of shade;
Infinity far overhead.
I am frost, the rim made of shine
On the twig, mercurial line
To cut the small from the big.

Small is good, rests on the ground
Small's to be seen, small has bound
In shape like crystal cut.
Crystal-frost lies white in the rut.
Crystal-frost rubs gaudy the twig.

A Part of Vermont, p.17

292

Demeter

In your dream you met Demeter
Splendid and severe, who said: Endure.
Study the art of seeds,
The nativity of caves.
Dance your gay body to the poise of waves;
Die out of the world to bring forth the obscure
Into blisses, into needs.
In all resources
Belong to love. Bless,
Join, fashion the deep forces,
Asserting your nature, priceless and feminine.
Peace, daughter. Find your true kin.
     — then you felt her kiss.

Slow Music, p.5

Aleatory Wind

Much offends,
Especially the new beauty;
The honest eye that shine and pierces
Even while it pours its honest love like a vapor of
     healing.
The bare ritual offends;
And the ritual of brotherhood
Which is the basalt sense of the world
Offends, is made to seem contrary and ugly
By means of another ritual with a flimsy deity
And a fantastic logic.
                   Where the hands have no liking
For stones and where minds are blind
To structure. Wherever the hands cease to take hold,
Where the mind backs away from the plain and the related.
This ritual will hurt
The hands of those
Who have left the wilderness of necessity,
Deep mutuality, the sense of distance,
The sense of depth.

Of the fertility of stones, their tears.
Of the electrical star, its tears.
Of the hilarity of the stone brotherhood, the activity
     of jasper,
Of the inertia of stones, the fixity of basalt,
Of the vigor of stones in their power to draw,
To test metals, to build shapes, to be in space,
To become fluid in the blood of volcanoes,
Of these I made claim...

"No art," said the European, sidestepping the
      rattlesnakes,
With ballet steps. "Unreal," said the European, "No ghosts.
No culture."

I took a stone of weeping in my right hand.
And a stone of laughter in my left.
So the ritual always began, testing the power to hold.
Holding them behind me I juggled them evenly and said
      "Choose.
Lodestones and touchstones. Magnets subtle, complex.
The greathearted jewels of the obsidian world."

And looking downward I saw a finger of wind in the dust,
Spinning the dust in a wheel, erratic,
In a funnel, a nothing of wind.

New-world dust sang a sulky little song,
But the tourist heard no song
And saw only liver-colored dust
About a foot high, suspended, in which to wade.

This stone is the electrical star,
The cleaver of space; can you, will you
Bowl it in nine-pins?
Curve it, will it to glide
In dream repetition?

We learn slowly the ritual of stones
And the tactile sense. The snap of action.
The excellent flash of the body
When it kneels and swings.

In this ritual we dance.
For we clasp our ghost, we whirl with a new music.
He is the man we murdered,
The red man. He goes. He is here.
Our ghost is our culture. And we embrace another.
He is the man we murder.
The black man. He returns and returns,
Teaching ritual. And every kind of man
Draws into this whirl. The wind veers
As if to nullify all.
The center of the earth is basalt.

Here we gaze to commune
On action's articulate bones,
Observing our guilt; the rituals of food and power
All wrongly played. Of this we know much.
Sharing aleatory wind
A thin ether,
Playing with skulls, color, gadgets
Inventions and dice.

A dangerous country. With a culture like whisky.

The European wore gloves,
And under the gloves, thimbles
On each finger — clumsy.
He turned the pages of old situations
And muttered his pity in the stony places.

Slow Music, p.54

Pacific

This child went forth to the grace-abounding sea.
I was that child, that child, in memory, me.
The sea was always dancing, never dull.
And every day the blue sea, tangible,
Swept and sustained and rinsed, with the taste of salt
Its children without hurt, in deep cobalt.

To swim was to sink and be captured taken
Through solid depths and surface dimple-shine
To the leaping edge where the instant's foam was seething.
Except near reefs where we were knocked and shaken
Until our chests were taut with inheld breathing
Fear rarely tainted that water, vast and benign.

Armed forces suffer there today — they hate
Its vasts, its depth, its sharks, its color even.
It and the enemy are both cruel and great.
Innocence is lost that called it heaven.
Their curses, their stoic quiet, taint its sweep,
And history will surely call it deep.

May the brown nations of its islands have
The joy we captured from its colored wave.
And confidence return, and children swim.
May the lore of the sea enchant again, the rim
Still be the edge of the primitive element we
Rose from, returned to and lived by: the sea.

Origin: Hawaii, p.27

Exchange of Awe

Deep cup of this cave
Heeds the moon,
Heeds the sun, tips down and up
With the tides. (So the cave rides,
The world, all gilded, glides.)
With sun, tide, moon,
With orb, quarter, crescent and the crescent wave,
Asleep, inert, a-tune.

Sunrise, the babe leaps forth,
Moonrise, he meets the maiden,
Tides, he suffers and riots,
Darkness, he recoils and dreams,
Recoils, descends
Toward the image within the image,
To devour the flower of rage,
To eat dust and taste blood,
Tight in the brackish fluid,
Brute, blind, in broken story a slave,
In the cave, the tight cave.

At noon his shadow merges with his fellows,
At noon, he toils and is heavy,
At noon he is slain and made many,
He is dismembered, he is eaten
And of others, he eats.

So he is born of man
In the realm and meaning
Of myriad man. Forgets
Oblivion, the cave,
Its residue, its after-birth; forgives

The tides their prod, accepts
Penetration of the sane sun; loves
Authority of the task,
Its antagonist fiber; dreams
His deep acquaintance with the stuff of things; adores
The burnished withering moon.

Marvelous now is man.
Wrinkles next his eyes,
Stubs of his ten fingers
Grow the exquisite skin of self.
Odors of love and sweat,
Voices of youthful creatures
Fill cups with winey light
Sweet to the lips; he drinks,
Groans in his excess
Lies prone to procreate.
Within is a great wave cresting,
The glee of the master.
He strides, an exuberant creature,
Happy at pitch, the crescent of his spanning,
Sober, with labor; defeat his skidding shadow.

Adjusted by the moon to wane,
A-down, a-dark,
Rejoicing and desponding,
Elate, afraid, shod with electric spurs,
Petitions not to die.
(For after he is slain his feeling is immortal.)
Mortal, lofty, in him, the human spirit
Repeats, repeats, petitions not to die.

Hark, and afar he feels return
The tug of tide and sun
The shock of setting moon
In solemn orb and wave, and these reply:
Lie down in nothing's cave,
Obey the grave. Undo thy self. Obey.
Now he is closing,
In mystery withers away.
Half-harking he shrivels, shrinks,
He is cradled, laved.
He is near nothing,
A nothing vast.
Now he is near pure nothing,
He is that nothing he knows never, never,
That nothing that is,
Bliss within bliss
He is no one
He is unspun.
Asleep, inert, a-tune,
A-down, a-dark,
Where pull and fuse
Forces of the tide, moon, sun.
(A gliding tide,
A moon
A swooning sun.)

Slow Music, p.59

Children of the
Hollow Men

> We are the hollow men
> We are the stuffed men
> Leaning together
> Headpiece filled with straw. Alas!
>
> T.S. Eliot, "The Hollow Men"

Christopher Caudwell, who wrote *Illusion and Reality, A Study of the Source of Poetry*, and who died in Spain, fighting with the Loyalists, understood the present stage of the culture of the world. How shall we begin to speak of these matters in the United States? He wrote:

> All art is conditioned by the conception of freedom which rules in the society that produces it; art is the mode of freedom that class has attained to.

In the closing of this book Caudwell, ten years ago, examined the deepening reactionary trend. But Caudwell, who died for freedom, says on the last pages of his book (which he left in proof sheets when he turned soldier):

Therefore the stuff of art endures as long as man. The fountain dwindles away only when men are rent and wasted by a sterile conflict, and the pulsing movement of society is halted.... The eternal simplicities generate the enrichment of art from their own bosoms not only because they are eternal but also because change is the condition of their existence. Thus art is one of the conditions of Man's realization of himself, and in its turn is one of the realities of man.

Those are the last words he wrote.

But he died – as we put it – happy, meaning that he saw beyond the blind moment and so was of good cheer, having faith in men; whereas many poets living today have not faith in freedom, nor are they in any way happy, although most certainly both they and their poetry will die. They have never become part of the world. Their writing is an impotent attempt to receive and to give, but an attempt of limited appeal. They write to display their condition, and to attack believers.

It does come back to a faith in freedom, and the particular conception of it – this large vague word is poorly defined by many who think they know its meaning.

Certain of these poets come out for a "return to the past", and they show a need in man for a static society; they want science scrapped or perhaps controlled. Most of all they skip faith in man and demand a return to some form of established religion. And they insist, of course, that without God to uphold the scale of hierarchies man collapses like a flattened blimp. One of the most important items on the agenda of this group is the destruction of democracy and the building of a rigid class society, bringing in consequence the ancient odor of poverty, obscurantism, oligarchy, or some device for rule under kings and bishops. It all stems from a hope that the movement of the world toward socialism can be destroyed.

Mr. Karl Shapiro in his *Essay on Rime*, published a year ago, touched the edges of this problem; but so far as I can understand his lines, forbade himself to think about the facts. He makes much of the confusion of belief, but fails to see the why of it, and seems content to join the fashionable intellectuals. The next step is usually a fake or real conversion, sometimes explained for the sake of "psychic security." This often amounts to a profession without a faith; and only those who practice with themselves an habitual duplicity seem to attain what we recognize as spiritual health! The sterility remains:

Finally under confusion in Belief
These headings...
...and fifth and last
The dead hand and exhaustion of our rime.

Juxtapose a book of 1840 with one of 1939. William Ellery Channing in *On the Elevation of the Laboring Classes* spoke the attitude of his friends, the poets, when he said:

A very common prejudice is that the many are not to be called to think, study, improve their minds, because a privileged few are intended by God to do their thinking for them. I deny to any individual or class this monopoly of thought.... Were the masses of men made to be monsters?

On the contrary a book published in 1939 by our leading poet would repeat in a modern tongue the same argument that Channing scotched. T.S. Eliot in setting down comments on his idea of a Christian society, sketches a picture of King and Church at the top of the pyramid, surrounded by the elite and the arts of the elite; and so on down, in the name of order, to the happy obedient peasants on the bottom of the pile, whose toil in the earth and on the sea makes education for them inadvisable. They are better off, mind you, ignorant and serene under the fatherly authority that all men desire above all, with no troublesome choices and no excruciating intellectual problems. This is Mr. Eliot's idea of freedom. The peasant's idyllic eighteen-hour day and the bliss of ignorance result automatically in obedience and adoration. What a solution for the perplexities of the ruler!

> My freedom is thy unfreedom.
> Genevieve Taggard, *unpublished poem*

Mr. Eliot desires this society in order to end our world sickness, our secular blight. He is by far the most memorable writer of our day and the sharpest critic in poetry of our capitalist democracy. If we knew it in no other way, we could clearly see by putting this book beside Channing's or any other writer of his time that something very strange has happened to the great tradition of American letters.

Consider how well set we were a hundred years ago to gather the varied and abundant harvest of experience in our Republic — how Emerson, Thoreau, Poe, Melville, Dickinson and Whitman all shone and sang like the morning stars together at the creation of a new concept of humanity. This came of a vitality released after ingestion of events and conditions peculiar to this land, and was intensified by the imbalance that resulted when these rapt and exuberant dreamers searched among the conflicts and imperfections of that stage in our society.

We see that in our time there will probably be no true continuation of this beginning. We have with us still the "Good Old Cause," but another crisis is upon us and at this moment most of our poetry abets the contrary opinion. The educated class is nearly all on the other side. And the infection has even reached some of the older poets who are still alive; those who once stood up for human beings, who saw virtue and dignity in farmers, hired men and lovers of the out-of-doors.

Mighty forces in our country will decide the issue in the battle. The labor movement and innumerable men and women who refuse to be identified with reaction push themselves into the breach. These forces do not use poetry in their meetings, their camps and schools. The lively arts are better adapted to the mass education of the trade unions. Poetry will in time reflect the rising power of this humanity; but it is now allied with the large income, and the son and daughter of the got-rich-quick-man-of-distinction. It is identified with those circles who are doing their best to bring us inflation, who use the atom bomb as a diplomatic threat, who think imperialism and talk war.

What would our kin Melville, Thoreau, Whitman, Emerson and Dickinson say about a literary world of quaint taboos and stern rituals where not to believe in Original Sin is to be considered naïve, provincial and nonliterary? And behold, to accept and preach the same is to be a star-treader, one of the elect! But more important, one of the elite!

The upside-downness of it — to enact the poor worm charade in order to achieve superiority! The tide is running against the democratic, the human power of our early literature.

Mr. Robinson Jeffers put some of this attitude in *Shine, Perishing Republic*, which opens with a picture of America settling "in the mould of its vulgarity." The poem ends

> And boys, be in nothing so moderate as in love of man, a clever servant,
> an insufferable master,
>
> There is the trap that caught noblest spirits, that caught –
> they say — God
> when he walked on earth.

Mr. Jeffers is convinced of what he says; he has neither faith in man nor in the necessity for man's increasing freedom. The pit he falls into is perfectly logical considering his premises; and the verses are extremely effective. We have not had recently anything so good from the "noblest spirits."

The demi-giants of 1912, Frost, Masters, Lindsay, Robinson and Sandburg — middle-class poets who wrote for a middle-class audience — are not as exciting as their forebears, but there is much that is good and even wonderful in their writing. They fulfilled soberly some of the task that Whitman laid upon them in "Democratic Vistas." The sadness of Robinson and the bitterness of Masters is a good herb of the wormwood variety. They offer a foretaste of the pessimism that was to come, and is now here; but their bitterness is still tonic.

Frost and Lindsay and Sandburg had affirmative things to say; two of these desired change and did not fear it, except in images of extremity. When the great gaps began to show in the world structure they were all affected. Hart Crane was a believer in a great vision of his time and culture until he was broken by the forces in that culture. The suicides of Lindsay and Crane have much to tell us. All these writers brought poetry into the company of flesh and blood, accomplishing what Wordsworth had intended, after great alterations in the structure of the English speaking world. World War I came two years after our renaissance of poetry which, being itself a reactionary war, terminated with a dangerous gas, leaking from the body politic. The Soviet Union which came into existence during that war added to the terror of the ruling powers; and the descent into black reaction was rapid. The poets led.

One member of the 1912 group was Ezra Pound. I have not the room to include what I have elsewhere written about Pound. Suffice to say that he had a vivifying influence on many disciples and that the chief of these was T.S. Eliot. The rest is history.

We should read T. S. Eliot today just as our fathers read Kipling. In Kipling they found the cluster of ideas and feelings that engendered the fantasies of empire; in Eliot we will find another cluster. The world that ends not with a bang but a whimper is already a part of the American editorial page. The sterility that grips Mr. Eliot does not prevent him from writing lines that strike the minds of men. Mr. Eliot is not the cause of the strong tide that flows in the world today, except as he shares and augments that tide. This son of a distinguished Unitarian family contradicts all the battles won by the great men of concord and Boston. He describes himself as a monarchist in politics, a classicist in literature, and a Catholic (Anglo-Catholic) in religion.

Although he has been writing for twenty years since his best expression of the crisis in belief, we miss in his writing the tone of joy and fulfilment found in Herbert, Donne, Dickinson and Hopkins. Humility is one of the Christian virtues and this virtue Mr. Eliot covets. But one is struck by the fact that Mr. Eliot has no feeling of humility or reverence for humanity as a whole; but rather just a spark of fellow feeling for the English aristocrat. And on this bad eminence the vast seas of humanity wash continually. Mr. Eliot is oblivious.

Why do I speak at such length of Mr. Eliot? Are there not many others writing today? Yes, there are; but they are still in process — we cannot yet see them plain. It is possible to speak without injustice of that brilliant sensation, Mr. W.H. Auden, who came down like a wet sky-rocket in his last book with such statements as these:

> In every act we do
> Evil as each creature does
> In every definite decision
> to improve; for even in
> The germ-cell's primary division
> Innocence is lost and Sin
> Already given as a fact,
> Once more issues as an act.

> *The Collected Poetry of W.H. Auden*

One more point. There is a great deal of slapdash inferior writing currently hailed as the poetry of democracy. It is written by those who are comfortable in the moderateness of their opinions, and they often have commercial or fame motivation. This does not sustain real people who suffer real woes, death, temptation, perplexities and toils. The writers of the anarchist, nihilist or near-Fascist schools bring the message that we are in a bad fix. We are in a bad fix. The emotional tone of their work is defeatist. In spite of the bad fix we are in, our work cannot be hymns to defeat; but people will respond to even the darkest view if it is powerfully expressed, in preference to pseudodemocratic mishmash insipid and false. We need such poets as are suggested to us by the past reality of Blake and Burns, who wrote at a time of great burgeoning and trouble and who rose from the lower classes understanding the plight of the world. Their work is full of music, naturalness, indignation and love.

The Christian Register/Unitarian 125:11 (November 1946), pp.441-442

Notes on Emily Dickinson and Emerson

She was always aware of him; he was never aware of her. He visited Amherst and even came to dinner across the hedge, but we have no record of a meeting. We do know that she read his poems when she was young and thirsty. Undoubtedly she "knew his mind" by the super-insight she cultivated. Ministers and teachers were very important to her thinking and feeling life; she says so in her Letters. Emerson was a minister of the left, of the enlightenment, and we know that she harkened unto such voices very diligently, much as we would listen to communiques today on the radio. Bulletins from the front. If there had been no enlightenment her mind might have slumbered through the years on the precepts of the local pulpit. Battle was a word she used and knew; Emerson was one of the leaders.

It is a mistake to forget all the others who filled up the landscape because they were also a part of her fare. But many of the others were stirred by this man in Concord, this not yet established but very well read master of the new schoolroom. He was able to speak to an audience formed by the same religious doctrines, faced by the same dilemmas, shaped by the same history, local and national. Emerson was hopeful and cheerful and American. He had something to say about Evil no pulpit could endorse. But he came from a soil where men had disputed doctrine since the beginning. The sunlight he let into religious feeling was in itself an event. He was a direct and also an indirect influence on the girl in Amherst.

In these notes I should like to suggest relationships and to say a little about the deep reasons for the difference in their verse and their attitudes.

We have not looked very closely to the simple matter of favorite words, symbols, habits of expression. They prove little in an absolute sense; but they hint at moments of perception, at moments of close influence. I choose two words well known to the students of Emily Dickinson's poetry: *ample*, and *punctual*.

> Ample make this bed
> Make this bed with awe;

shows her enjoyment of its largeness, its power to echo with other *a* sounds, as here with *awe*; and her valuation of *m*, *p*, *l*, so useful for building with other consonants.

> I've known her from an ample nation
> Choose one;

So, it comes out again in one of her unforgettable poems where she uses the long light ripple of the word to enhance a line which must do the same and contrast sharply with the spondaic *Choose one*, and other lines, even more marked, to follow.

The word is in the dictionary and she read the dictionary. The word is in Emerson's poems and she read the poems. His "Three Dimensions" was published in the *Dial* in 1843. There the word is a mere adjective, used clearly for meaning, not hinged upon for sound. I think few poets in 1843 were using the word. It is not the style of the day. Emerson uses it elsewhere, vaguely tending toward the taste she displayed in its use.

> Space is ample, east and west
> But two cannot go abreast.

What about that great favorite, *punctual*?

> Then punctual as a star
> Stop, docile and omnipotent ...

In Dickinson's train poem it does the work of many words. Emerson's use of it in one of those couplet lines that fail to climb to finality,

> The punctual stars will vigil keep

is characteristic.

This word matching (for instance "Wood Notes" against "Nature") yields other lesser choices; with Emerson, obscured and groping, with Dickinson used boldly, nakedly, one word pressed to its fullest possibility, uncluttered by others.

All the Emerson's Quatrains will bear re-reading for a general likeness to Dickinson's fragments. But I will not quote them here, choosing rather lines from the poems entire:

From the "Song of Nature"

> I weary of my robe of snow ...

and

> I travail in pain for him,
> My creatures travail and wait;
> His couriers come by squadrons,
> He comes not to the gate.

From "Manners"

> Too weak to win, too fond to shun
> The tyrants of his doom

311

> The much deceived Endymion
> Slips behind a tomb.

From "Beauty"

> But hovered gleaming and was gone

This is a rare instance of an echo of the rhythm of a line. Emerson's rhythm rarely interested her.

From "Waldeinsamkeit"

> And merry is only a mask of sad.

From "Monadnoc"

> The wide thaw and ooze of wrong

From "The Problem"

> And Nature gladly gave them place
> Adopted them into her race
> And granted them an equal date
> With Andes and with Ararat.

The dark grim sound of those *a*'s and the use of place names is very like Dickinson. To repeat the haunting pleasure she felt in reading such lines might well have been one of the beginning impulses to write her own. To see content of a more extended sort compare Emily Dickinson's Bee poem: "Like trains of cars on tracks of plush," with the Humble Bee; and "I taste a liquor never brewed," with Bacchus.

Such small points are of no importance if we find no larger likeness. But in deep and general ways they are very much alike. They are both rhapsodists. Ecstacy is what they are after. Emerson's plodding lines, his faintly 18th century workmanship is a horrid bar to such an end. Only when he breaks that old mould does he come nearer what he desires. Hunger and thirst, shaking, fevers, release, bliss, drunkenness — these are the states around which they both play. The idea of wine then becomes a way of materializing the need. Inaction and hope and the passive will was Emerson's solution. He was a frail man. Emily Dickinson finds conflict the condition out of which ecstacy sometimes results. She was both delicate and tough.

Ecstacy does not permit of extended passages. Both poets deal in fragments. Although Emerson tried for form it is a convention, weak, crude, bad, dead. He knew it. The "divine light" comes and goes over his verse, as is natural with one who cultivates the passive will. Only when Emerson breaks his forms does he make a channel of it. Emily Dickinson mastered form; but always in short duration; it is mastery, but often in fragments; re-asserted in life, not sustained into poems of length. Her work shows many failures to one success.

But certainly Emerson knew better than he could do. In Merlin he foretells Emily Dickinson's art, perfected by her, into points of wonderful complexity. Later in this essay I will suggest why I think it came about that he saw the problem but could not solve it, while she, lacking so many of Emerson's great virtues and right proclivities, accomplished his purpose:

> Great is the art,
> Great be the manners of the bard.
> He shall not his brain encumber
> With the coil of rhythm and number;
> But leaving rule and pale forethought
> He shall aye climb
> For his rhyme.
> "Pass in, pass in," the angels say,
> Into the upper doors,
> Into the upper doors,
> Nor count compartments of the floors,
> But mount to Paradise
> By stairways of surprise."

"Stairways of surprise" is certainly the Dickinson technique; stairways of shock. She admired the preacher who "scalped the naked soul" with his sermon masterpieces. But how well prepared the surprise in her art. When she succeeds we perceive an infinitely delicate power at work to seduce the reader to a point when the surprise will knock him off his pins. And so she does not quit "pale forethought"; in fact she does little else all her life long but plot and plan. It is a life activity; not a library device. The process becomes so deep that it has no signs of tricky intent which Emerson in his superficiality, assumes the older art to be. Rather a deep search for a way, through the material means of words, to bring about this total and devastating result.

They were rhapsodists, they aimed at ecstacy, they knew the chief art of their world, *oratory*, because it was always there in the pulpit every Sunday. Besides all those who spoke on secular matters from the chatter in the living room up to Daniel Webster himself, used the arts of rhetoric, and wit, and balance and the final word after which nothing will do but silence.

Emerson's great gift is never revealed in this form. I agree with Dr. Matthieson who writes the most penetrating analysis of Emerson that his great gift in essay as well as in verse comes in the single phrase, word or sentence. The exhilaration one gets from Emerson inheres in these stabs, these charges of superb language. The greatest passages come in the prose; still they suggest the signature of a man who should have been a poet. This Emerson knew. "I am a bard least of bards. I cannot like them make lofty arguments in stately, continuous verse, constraining the rocks, trees, animals, and the periodic stars to say my thoughts, — for that is the gift of the great poets; I am a bard because I stand near them and apprehend all they utter, and with pure joy hear that which I would also say, and moreover, I speak interruptedly words and half stanzas which have the like scope and aim: — what I cannot declare, yet cannot all withhold."

A lack of "potent concentration". Too much super-voluntary will. Too much passivity. Certainly many of Emerson's best poems evade this charge. He is often tremendously significant. Poems such as, "Terminus"; "Politics"; "Ode to Channing" bring us into the large room of Emerson's mind.

Emily Dickinson's greatest handicap resolved finally into the secret of her power. Her handicap was her extreme isolation from the world of people, from common living, from solidarity with the world, its feeling and thinking. Emerson, a very wise and great man, was a part of the world. He was protected too, and I venture that his powers could have been stirred only by a deeper participation in the active life of his time. There is too much sitting down in Emerson for the first-rank American poet. Too much thinking in the study. Too much brooding and journal writing and waiting for something to happen which never happened. No life of the body, for all the talk about it; no straining with the muscles of the back, no plunging in rivers, or lying out in thickets. Thoreau was wiser than his friend. Still the gentle sage, the dreamer, the desirer, the brooder, was nearer the real heavy handed actual world of events and clashes than was Emily Dickinson. Her life is shockingly isolated. But going to the other extreme and crying out against isolation in great anguish, and trying to adapt to it or to extract heat from cold, using its actuality as a sword against annihilation, she knows cold realities where Emerson knows only chill. This extreme makes her speak with a passion he never achieves. What is all the long work of her life, her seventeen hundred poems, but her reply to isolation? Wearisomely the poems pile up on the theme of the greatness of the self and the soul and the majesty of polar privacy, the soul admitted to itself, the infinity of consciousness. But the significant thing is that she took the pains to be an artist, which means that she at that point re-joined the human throng.

Evidently two great conflicts repeated themselves in her life without end, day after day. The first was this conflict about isolation. Until that is understood the intensity of her love for a single man cannot be evaluated. In such a light it is the truest kind of love story, in any other it is extraneous. The other conflict is most clear if we put Emerson's temperament beside her own. Guilt overwhelmed her. Enumerate the poems that identify her with wrong persons, rebels, criminals, outcasts; and then set in the other scale the reconciliation with God. This is such a complicated matter that I can only sketch at this point; and hope that others will trace the full pattern. What complicates the picture is another curious factor — a sort of hilarious innocence. Beside this range Emerson seems tepid.

Ralph Fox writing of Emily Bronte in replying to some who have placed her, as Dickinson is often placed, out of space and time says in part:

> *Wuthering Heights* is certainly the novel become poetry, it is beyond all doubt one of the most extraordinary books which human genius has ever produced, yet it is these things only because it is a cry of despairing agony wrung from Emily by life itself. The life of mid-Victorian England, experienced by a girl of passion and imagination imprisoned in the windswept parsonage on the moors of the West Riding, produced this book.

... And, commenting on the return of Catherine Linton to the Heights,

> It is the most terrible passage in English literature in the nineteenth century, but it is not, even in the intensity which gives it such life, outside of space and time. For the words of agony are wrung from Emily by her own time and no other age could have tortured her so sharply, twisted the words of aching, awful suffering out of her in accents of such terrifying force. Through the book, with the grotesque and horrid echo of a chorus, runs the complaint of the farm-hand Joseph, the canting, joyless, hating and hateful symbol of the obscene morality of his age, as though the prison walls themselves are endowed with voice to mock and spurn the prisoner.

This is near the meaning of Dickinson. Emerson saw the new forces in the real world better than Dickinson. Hers is a pretty static universe; his is somewhat tuned to the principle of change. He saw what in her language was called Evil; and his picture of its cause, source, nature, activity, is in the line of progressive thought; hers is not. But behold the complexity of literary evaluations: her poetry is more true in the feeling and the human sense, because the Evil happens to her; it did not happen to Emerson. By that difference she emerges with a power he wanted. She represents the crystallization of centuries of old doctrine, stirred with the imperatives of pain. Victory is her aim. He is the man of the new way of thinking. But to be of the new without vitality it generates in its own sons, is to be in Emerson's position.

They tell a fine story of Thoreau that when he lay dying people came to enquire if he had made peace with God. "We never quarreled," was Emerson's friend's reply. Emerson said it less sharply, fully expressing, however, his inability to quarrel with God as Emily Dickinson had, or to quarrel with any forces, of the devil, or of principalities or powers; — fundamentally reluctant to sharpen any part of himself by complete and total participation. Emerson's words run thus: "It was rumored abroad that I was penitent: but what have I to do with repentance?"

Smith College Monthly (November 1941), pp.3-6

Notes on Writing
Words for Music

I don't know how to write words for music.

I like spondees. I used them when I adapted a few lines from the poem *Long View* for the fourth movement of the secular cantata number I, *This Is Our Time*, music by William Schuman.

> We will make our peace (true peace)
> Our wealth (true wealth)
> And our justice (true justice)

It was very nice to hear these rhythms sung.

A poem called *Lark* (Collected Poems, 1918-1938), was composed on the spondee plan, but I did not write it with the idea that it would be set to music or sung. There was a primitive music in my own head when I wrote it, but when I finished the poem I closed that off as if to cut connections with chaos. This poem has been set three times, each time differently; but in each case

Excerpt from 'Lark', musical score by Henry Leland Clarke, from the frontispiece to Genevieve Taggard, *Collected Poems 1918-1938*.

the double stress makes itself felt.[1]

I have discovered that relative to other beats, spondees remain spondees when you carry them from poetry to music; I have also discovered that they are really not the same thing in both places. That I guess is the difference between music and poetry. The result is that now if I write a spondee for singing, I must foresee how it may sound musically, not poetically.

Most of the time poets do not even imagine their words spoken by a decent human unaffected voice.

Forcing us to think of our words when spoken or sung makes us better artists.

And so, you see I could learn how to write words for music, if I could keep on working with these remarkable composers, these new music people. Picking their brains, hanging on their conversation, hearing words sung in rehearsal.

---

1 By Henry Leland Clark for voice without accompaniment. By Aaron Copland, four-part chorus for mixed voices with baritone solo. By Ruth Cuthbertson, solo voice with piano.

It might be a good idea to say here which writers seem to me to know about this subject. My own experience, my learning process acknowledges Robert Burns and the Negroes, who have made up words for Spirituals and Blues, many of them nameless people. Leadbelly is a clear case of a person who knows and does. Blitzstein. Gershwin. Shakespeare. Woodie Guthrie. Earl Robinson. Cole Porter. Certain hymn writers. The writers of songs you hear in the middle of the night on the air. This is my song book. You see, I cannot learn from the "good poets" of the 19th century or of the 20th. The only exception is James Joyce with his tenor voice and his *Chamber Music*.

One should not pay much attention to the cultural fancies of semi-educated people. Among such people the sound of the long *ā* as pronounced in these United States, is supposed to be unpleasant. Watch your *a*'s they say; watch your *s*'s. Well I don't agree, and I think I could show that Milton, Shelley, Keats and many others didn't either. Ā in itself of course cannot be predicted, since meaning changes the effect of passages having identical sound. But use *a* properly and you get magnificence of tone, or so I believe. Mr. Schuman went so far as to take the sound of *a* in section III of *This Is Our Time* and build a fugue around it. The word *foundations* contained the quality, and when he set the word it sounded something like this:

Founda-a-a-a-tions

And as the fugue grew, a further extension of the *ā* resulted. Various musical and literary people predicted that this would fail. I have heard the third part sung many times, and each time it sounds better to me.

I have some general, some rather obvious ideas that I use for a guide. But a better poet can always turn them up-side down easily. All but the first idea which is:

1. Song is collective. (Poetry should be.)

2. In writing words for music, it is forbidden to try too hard. For instance, Irony and Song do not readily mix. Only special cases permit relaxing this rule.

3. There must always be some moving space around a poem-written-for-music.

4. Emphatic and impassioned speech is better than limpid, ideal and lovely language. See Poe in the "Philosophy of Composition," "Truth in fact, demands a precision, and Passion a homeliness (the truly passionate will comprehend me), which are absolutely antagonistic to that Beauty which, I maintain, is the excitement, or pleasurable elevation, of the soul." In writing words for music, one should read Poe backward.

5. There must either be a pattern organic with the thought; or there must be enough space in the structure for the composer to impose or to carve out such a pattern.

6. The writer must destroy his vanity about his literary prowess. He must admit that staleness can overtake even a perfect technician. It has overtaken most of the "names" in modern poetry; only the very miserable and passionate ones escape this. Their disquietude forces them to write badly at times, and that in turn opens their eyes to the arbitrary nature of the taste of our time. If a poet can care about the unity of poetry and music and can throw away dogmas and habits and vanities, he will be in the state to begin. He will learn the lesson of brevity, and the lesson of simplicity, and even that highest lesson of silence, its necessity and power. (All these should have been his before, part of his practice.) He will begin to

learn control of that field of emotion which can never be put into words, but nevertheless can be brought near. This is partly learned by cultivating the "grace to terminate." It is quite different from just stopping the poem.

7.   There seem to be few un-singable words. The books say avoid long e on high notes, etc., etc. I would say avoid long e in any key position, always. Whether to be sung or not.

(The only modern poet to use this sound well, so far as I know, is W. B. Yeats. Whereas all rhymesters and beginners want to use it all the time, since there are so many soft-stressed *ity*-ending words in the language. Unfortunate that our most common rhyme-sound should also be rather unpleasant, and weak in effect.)

If the word you write seems necessary, compelling, inevitable, then some composer who comes to feel these qualities can probably find a way to set the so-called difficult word.[2] But this is a new subject for me, and I have not gone far enough to reach its jumping off place. The theory is that the word's difficulty may give the composer a musical idea. Just as your difficulty in writing the off-the-path poem often brings you to the creation of a new form.

8.   There seem to be two kinds of near-song that should not be set.

A. The too packed, too complex poem, the poem full of many small organic connections, relationships. cf. Irony, number 2.

B. The complete poem perfectly realized in its own music.

(I remember hearing settings for G. M. Hopkins' *Pied Beauty* and *God's Grandeur*. Both were terrible. Perhaps the music of itself was good, I do not know. I have never heard a good

---

2   For instance *heft* in *This Is Our Time.*

setting for a Dickinson poem. Composers, feeling this matter of number 2 perhaps, choose her weak things, – another embarrassment, things like, "If I can stop one heart from breaking." I think the answer is that she shouldn't be set, doesn't need it.)

9.   There is a good little book called *Words for Music* by V. C. Clinton-Baddeley. I found it a few months ago with a review by Virgil Thompson. It's not a profound book. Just pleasantly dogmatic and sensible. I quote three passages:

> But what the poets have failed generally to recognize is that 'words for music' is a department of their art quite separate from 'poetry', and that it consists precisely in the creation of an incomplete work, in the creation of words deliberately framed for the addition of music.

and again,

> This art demands of the musician that he shall devote his music to the interpretation of the words, and not merely to the decoration of a theme suggested to him by the words. Of the poet it demands that he learn to write his words in a shape suitable for music. The incompleteness of his words must be designed to fit a similar incompleteness in music.

and again:

> If song is to be rescued from the inane indignities of the concert platform, it is an absolute necessity that the poet shall speak again with a public voice. Now it is a significant fact that the birth of a new conscience in musicians and the discovery of a new lyric voice among the poets has in fact coincided with a return of the poets to the theatre.

10. All this is fine and needs to be looked into. But Mr. Baddeley is not able to help us about the best problem of all, and the brightest possibility: our American speech, its music, its ring. Our free verse poems[3] contain a new quality and it is musical. Mr. Baddeley's advice would teach us to write nice rhymed stanzas, neat enough, regular enough for a static setting. And we certainly want to keep the knack: most popular music will have this conservative trait. But (for about thirty years) American poetry has been unable to quit a haunting and particular cadence – its own. The real triumphs may very well come in the setting of such beautiful speech rhythms as:

from E. E. Cummings' *Buffalo Bill*

and what i want to know is

how do you like your blueeyed boy

Mister Death

From Sandburg's *Cool Tombs*

Pocahontas' body, lovely as a poplar, sweet as a red haw

in November or a pawpaw in May, did she wonder? does

she remember? . . . in the dust, in the cool tombs?

and from Fearing's *Lullaby*:

Wide as this night, old as this night is old and young as it

is young, still as this, strange as this,

filled as this night is filled with the light of a moon as grey:

---

3   Mozart, that melody maker, was against rhyme words for music.

Woody Guthrie's "Talking Dust Bowl Blues": (recorded) brings up another point. Here the speech has been combined with music. Guitar and voice-chant; the rhythm is strict and the words, tied tight to the musical requirement, snap and syncopate in the most revealing fashion. If I copied them out for you, you would not be much impressed. They do not have the wonderful life of speech until the music tenses them. I wonder why poets and composers cannot study such effects.

I think I would not want to see the three poems by Cummings, Sandburg, and Fearing mentioned above set to music. For me they are right as they are and I want them left alone. But the cadences they contain are the new music of our poetry. I say study the rise and fall, the sweet intricacy of this speech and never assume that to write for music you must write copies of English Madrigals.

P.S. Perhaps the composers have not solved the problems of setting such lines.

I append a note about myself, for no reason, except that I like such notes when other people write about themselves.

I have always considered myself primarily a lyric poet. I have never been willing to stop experimenting with lyric effects.

The first song I remember is "Darling Nellie Gray." I remember because I cried when we got to "my banjo is unstrung." It was sung by my mother in 1898, the year of the Spanish American War. The time was about seven in the evening, looking at the stars from our side verandah of the house in Kalihi, Hawaii.

My people were Scotch Irish with many nonsense songs and plain and fancy ballads within easy reach. They were not self-conscious about the "value" of these songs. They just sang them now and then. I was a lazy piano pupil. But there was a lot of singing in the Hawaiian Islands and I lived there for eighteen years. At public school it was tonic *sol fa*. We sang four parts. The children gave it everything they had.[4]

I played the organ often for church and Sunday School, not hitting all the notes, but useful in a pinch. I got pretty interested in the relative merits of hymns, and their words. Luther's hymn was for many years a song I used in difficult and also happy moments of my private life.

I did not know it was written by Bach, or who Bach was, or any of the Bach music. Just this one song completely took me. We were a religious family, all kinds and conditions of hymns filled our lives. When I went to a Congregational school I found a new kind of hymn. There I picked up new tastes. "The Crusader's Hymn" became a great favorite. But we sang until I knew every property of many religious songs by Handel and Haydn and others. Our family belonged to an evangelical sect and so we sang some very jazzy hymns, too. "The Little Brown Church in the Vale," and "There Is a Fountain Filled with Blood" and "Jesus Wants Me for a Sunbeam."

Close proximity to both bad and good is the pre-requisite of growing judgment.

When I write a lyric poem, I am often conscious of the fact that I have made up a musical background. (I wrote some music down on paper when I was sixteen, but never since.) I believe in melody as well as rhythm. I would rather sing (in good company) than eat. Poetry is more important for me than words-for-music, but the two have underground connections. The same waters of life brighten them.

"Thus the developing complex of society, in its struggle with the environment, secretes poetry as it secretes the technique of harvest, as part of its non-biological and specifically human adaptation to

---

4   Will the reader stop thinking about steel guitars and ukuleles.

existence. The tool adapts the hand to a new function, without changing the inherited shape of the hands of humanity. The poem adapts the heart to a new purpose, without changing the eternal desires of men's hearts. It does so by projecting man into a world of phantasy which is superior to his present reality precisely because is it a world of superior reality – a world of more important reality not yet realized, whose realization demands the very poetry which fantastically anticipates it. Here is room for every error, for the poem proposes something whose very reason for poetical treatment, is that we cannot touch, smell or taste it yet. But only by means of this illusion can be brought into being a reality which would not otherwise exist. Without the ceremony fantastically portraying the granaries bursting with grain, the pleasures and delights of harvest, men would not face the hard labor necessary to bring it into being. Sweetened with a harvest song, the work goes well. Just because poetry is what it is, it exhibits a reality it brings to birth and nominally portrays a reality, which though secondary, is yet higher and more complex. For poetry describes and expresses not so much the grain in its concreteness, the harvest in its factual essence – which it helps to realize and which are the conditions for its own existence – but the emotional, social and collective complex which is the tribe's relation to the harvest. It expresses a whole new world of truth – its emotion, its comradeship, its sweat, its long-drawn-out wait and happy consummation – which has been brought into being by the fact that Man's relation to the harvest is not instinctive and blind, but economic and conscious. Not poetry's abstract statement – its content of facts, but its dynamic role in society – its content of collective emotion, is therefore poetry's *truth*."
— *Illusion and Reality* by Christopher Caudwell

Long View (1942), pp.102-113

Plenty Pilikia

The Hawaiian word for trouble is "pilikia." In my childhood in the Islands, if the trouble was general and of some duration we simply said, "Pilikia, plenty pilikia."

I saw pilikia turn into plenty pilikia — saw little things, trouble for our elders, turn into History. That massive word. Millions of lives go into making a gram of it, a paragraph in a book, a sentence in a communiqué. The years are so long, and the guns are so sudden.

They said, those blue-eyed statesmen of the Islands, that it was all going to be history, some day. But they were talkative old gentlemen. Our life was prodigal, sensuous, and concrete – and the straws in the wind flew by every day.

Often now in the midst of reading the Pacific news, I ask myself, "Is this the same old Pacific whose far islands lay to the west of us, in the ignorance of the great world?" A few of them were special and famous, to be sure, but most of them were mere coral atolls, heaps of guano, under swarms of yelling birds. Are these the islands Captain Schmidt told us about the day he gave us turtle eggs? The very same, name for name. And even in those days Schmidt was having clashes with the Japanese. And who, I say to myself, sitting up, transfixed by a new idea, was Schmidt anyway? Just what was he doing on those long trips? The uneasy story about Germans in Samoa joins the new idea. Is it possible? It was not for guano, we may be sure.

And so the image of islands we talked about now and then forty years ago quivers again on the mind's horizon. Is it the same Pacific? And what is history?

In this manner, with a drop of fluid personal memory, the place names of today's troubles dissolve back into reality. Into something like a water-color, as unconcentrated as any Tuesday afternoon, with time droning along towards sunset and supper.

And so one illusion laps over another. The illusion of nothing much happening — but with a feeling of suspense. The illusion of being every morning on the verge of a blow-up — always one instant delayed. And the deepest illusion of all: that we have no contact with the past, small or great.

Proust ate a cookie that sent him off on a long voyage of memory. Mangoes, purchased in the basement of Penn Station, often set me remembering in the southwesterly direction. But my decisive swing came by means of a book.

I go, in my own person, back to a time when everyone in Hawaii was speculating about the coming Pacific war, when every citizen was a statesman and a puzzler; and all were resolving to do right and behave like men and patriots.

As for remembering what others remembered, that seems too bland and gossipy for attention. Stories about the Queen and the early missionaries were almost as common as hibiscus; I forget them now. There was an old sea captain who said he pulled King Kalakaua's boots off and got him to bed many a tipsy midnight — "I said, 'Sure, King. You bet your life, King.'" Stories like that were plentiful.

My own eye-sight and ear-sound put me before the Palace steps on an August morning. I see a tableau.

I got the precise date from a shabby little book in my mother's bookcase a few weeks ago. The book was made up of a series of pamphlets entitled "Hawaii's Young People." This magazine was a fixture with us in the early days, arriving in bundles of fifty once a month during the school year, stapled within flimsy pink and green covers. It was a reading aid for the classroom, it was *Time*, *St. Nicholas*, and *Guffey's* all in a sheaf, delivered to the isolated teacher who was poor in books. In these numbers we read about the hero Maui and the goddess Pele before we heard of Demeter and Prometheus. They came from a print shop in a school on the Island of Maui. The print was cramped — the type had been set by school children — but we liked the text. If there was better reading matter we had not heard of it. The reprints were culled and the legends set down by missionaries and teachers; Osmer Abbott, Ph.D., was its editor. I paid small attention to the news items Mr. Abbott wrote up for the dark-skinned children of the grade schools. What child concerns himself with history in the making? Today the literary stuff that seemed so good tastes like over-brewed tea, whereas Mr. Abbott's notes on world events make neat reading.

On pages 117 and 145 he speaks of Aguinaldo, native rebel leader of the Philippines (who made an appeal by radio for the Japanese after Pearl Harbor in 1941); Princess Kaiulani's death is recorded; fighting in Samoa over Chief Mataafa gets a squib; so do extra sessions of Congress and a new peace plan. And then:

"China. China has been the scene of some strange stories lately. It is reported that the Emperor has been dethroned because he cut off his cue and wore European clothes. The Dowager Empress aided by Li Hung Chang did the dethroning."

At the Lahainaluna School in 1898 Mr. Abbott wrote an intelligent man's guide to the brewing history of the future, taking a world position, but emphasizing the events that might pertain to Hawaii.

"France. The Dreyfus affair is still the chief subject of talk. Some people think the army officers intend to seize the government. Colonel Henry confessed that he forged one of the papers against Dreyfus, and then killed himself."

"Washington, November 18. President McKinley has sent a long dispatch to the U.S. Peace Commissioner at Paris. It is believed he told them if the Spanish did not agree soon he would begin war again."

That, on page 29, sent me turning leaves backward, and I read at random:

"Honolulu, November 28th. The Hawaiian Sugar Planters Association met in annual session today. The sugar crop of 1897-98 was reported as 229,414 tons, — 21,702 tons less than the previous year. The labor report said that 25,000 men are employed in the plantations. More Japanese are employed than of any other nationality. There is talk of trying to get more Portuguese from Madeira and the Azores."

On the same page, opposite a moralistic little poem entitled "What I Live For" (*Require pupils to memorize this poem for recitation*), history dropped another little hint *via* Mr. Abbott: "President McKinley has issued a proclamation reserving a considerable portion of water-front in Honolulu for government use."

And so I paged backward and found myself in front of the Palace steps on the morning of August twelfth, as follows:

"Flag Raising. The flag of the United States, the Star Spangled Banner, is now floating over the Hawaiian Islands. It was raised on the 12th of August at noon, in all principal places of the Islands."

So it unblurs into focus, on sensation-waves of light, noise, curiosity, and mass emotion.

I had on a white dress. I stood to the left of the Palace stairs. I was nearly four years old; but I did not feel little. I sensed the air I was breathing — bright, translucent, warm, and cool. The Palace was a beige-white building, made of coral. In a gazebo-like bandstand stood Berger, the old pudgy German, with his Hawaiian boys in uniform, their brass instruments blazing in the sun now and then as they shuffled around for position. Palms, water sprays, and splotches of red and purple trees are at the edge of my recollection. I came because of Berger, of course; he was my Sousa: he played good and loud. The band started, and in the midst of its pleasure, I heard crying, more or less in between beats. A group of Hawaiians were standing there crying in public and on purpose. They stood some distance away from the Palace but directly opposite the stairs, almost as if arranged in rows. I took it all in. Tall men and women, clad in white with large straw hats on their heads, wept and were still dignified. I had never seen big people cry. It was shocking. Berger finished the music of Hawaii Po Nui, their song, and they fell silent.[1]

I can see quite clearly the well-swept sandy coral ground in the open space, and a few people of the sort we used to call by-standers, clustering, loafing, refusing to demonstrate. There were white men, too, in alpaca coasts and some native officials.

The behavior of those watching implied that we were seeing something of some importance; but still it seemed to be an occasion that was not very well attended. In the silence we looked up at the descending Hawaiian flag on the crest of the Palace, directly above the stairs. It came down the pole all adroop. There was another wait.

As I remember the wait now it was like this: one recording was being taken off the turn-table and another was being put into place, with a pause for technical adjustment. Then the needle of history was set into the groove of the new disc, and the Stars and Stripes went jerking up the pole. Much rustling, exclaiming, closing in, and then weeping and cheering. We all cheered, and Berger's band burst out as loud as he could play, full brasses to

---

1   This was *Hawai'i Pono'ī*, the national anthem of the Kingdom of Hawai'i before annexation, with words written in 1874 by King David Kalākaua.

match the very hottest sun, and my father said, trembling with excitement, "Come out here and salute the flag of your country."

We were living in those first days on a sugar plantation. Memory omits a good deal — it was a lonely place, and childhood had too many taboos at that time — too much was as yet untried for real freedom. The name of that place brings back a tumultuous sea-scape. Walls of white surf died down at sunset and turned level and swishing, to show cobalt open sea. When we explored in the other direction with our eyes — for we never walked far in the other direction — we saw the tall chimneys of the sugar-mill, the gigantic height of the coco palms near-by, and sheer, opal-colored mountains. The ground was like brick; I remember it best under a banyan tree.

I like-a you,
And you like-a me —

This ditty ended with a reference to a banyan tree. We hummed it, or chanted it, as we swung on its roots. But who we were I cannot remember.

There in a little house on stilts, set high off the ground, floored with clean matting, roofed with corrugated iron, and hug with mosquito netting, the two newly arrived tenderfoot teachers — my mother and father — set about adjusting and understanding their world.

Being the children of three generations of pioneers, they were prepared to be receptive. Nevertheless, they were forced to learn by a series of jolts. Here they were face to face with the much-talked-of heathen.

The big heathen worked in the sugar-cane fields and in the mill. The little heathen came to school.

At the mill the white men who worked the heathen wore boots and carried whips and clubs in their belts. The Japanese and Chinese coolies were docile; they worked long hours, sent their children to learn English, put our kind of clothing on them, encouraged them to mind their teachers. The races of children did not fight among themselves; they were affectionate and pliable. Silence and timidity were the only obstacles the teachers ever encountered. Now and then, a mother or a father said, "Sayo Nara," or "Hello," to the teachers. Who could complain of the heathen?

The overseer — called a "luna" — never seemed a pleasant man. He swore, which was evil in the opinion of Mama and Papa; he spit tobacco juice. He never went to church. Because he resembled persons in *Uncle Tom's Cabin* and smelled of liquor they classed him with the devil and sympathized with the heathen. All the heathen needed was Christianity.

And so the race problem was broken up by other attitudes from the first. One of our grandpas had had his heel shot off at Shiloh; and the other had hidden in wells and sniped at Confederate guerrillas. The temperance agitation was part of a school teacher's morality; and every missionary preached brotherhood. Mama and Papa could not join forces with the white man at the mill. "Go ye into all the world and preach the gospel to every creature," was their mandate.

Lessons in the schoolroom crawled slowly towards the far-off dream; the little foreign voices chanted the pages from New England primers, the songs and dates of American history. The multiplication tables were recited like a drone and a prayer.

1898 was dominated by the Pacific War. All Americans, Democrats or Republicans, talked politics whenever they met. Only sea captains and lunas who had married Hawaiian women were supposed to represent a purely local point of view. All the others conferred spontaneously, forgetting their deep, timidly hidden reservations, concerning religious affiliation. Catholics, Congregationalists, Mormons, Episcopalians, Carmelites, even scalawags, if they were sober and clean, drew close together for long, long dissertation. The Islands were dots in a very big ocean; and the ocean washed the shores of Asia.

When a steamer came in, the news of the world was dumped ashore, and all set to work, shredding it, ruminating.

Being an eaves-dropper, an intruder into Papa's lap when after-dinner conversations were begun, I tested the smoothness of the shave on Papa's chin against my ear and heard Papa's acquaintance utter the phrase "color line", and again "color line".

"Draw the color lone in politics," he said. "Mark my words, Taggard, mark my words. God's raised up the Anglo-Saxon race to spread civilization and Christian liberty. That's a fact. Look at the war, now. Mark my words." But Germans, Canadians, Dutch, and English persons were a trifle suspect, too. Who had not coveted the Islands before they were made secure by the revolution of 1893? Honolulu was full of men of these nations, who had once planned a career of their own under a flag of their own — not the one then flying over the Palace.

Out of that world, and for that world, Mr. Abbott wrote:

"Egypt. The utter defeat of the Khalifa near Omdurman by the English Egyptian army under General Kitchener, places the whole Nile region in the hands of the English. The French are going to leave the valley of the Nile entirely in the hands of the English. The danger, if there was danger, of war between France and England has passed away."

"Germany. Prince Bismarck died at his castle on Saturday the 30th of July."

Asia was the brooding presence — who indeed knew Asia? The Chinese (not *our* Chinese, but the Chinese Chinese) were opium fiends and murderers of missionaries. The Japanese were — perhaps worse, perhaps better. It was debated. Our Chinese man, woman, and child were visible enough but need not be closely examined, for they seemed to blend into the landscape. It was the Japanese man, woman, and child who set the problem. The other races were to be seen too, walking around here and there, doing this and that; they were not central to the problem either.

Once in seven days the face of our city changed. It became an Occidental world, a white world. Where did they all hide away on that day? Only if you went through Palama did you see kimonos and obis and sandals and clogs; cues, parasols, and oiled pompadours. Sunday school and church created its one day in seven with the ancestral image, non-tropical, on the dark-brown side, genteel. The old hymns told us we were Protestant and American; broadcloth was a uniform of the man of God; one contemplated the ladies' hats, the home-made dresses, the faintly small-town rig of the whole congregation. Diction blended to fit the flavor of the King James translation of the Bible; pidgin English was walled away as if it were never spoken. Until sometimes in the midst of doctrine, the un-English quality of the Old Testament, or the picture of an Apostle in flowing robes, emerged with the startling suggestion of something alien — and behold, the Bible itself was an Oriental story book, fabulous and full of color. How puzzling it all was, if you ever stopped to think of it.

In 1898 we were fleet-minded. Two uncles passed through Honolulu on their way to the Philippines; their stop-over was a time of jollification; of special cooking; jaunts, service stories, and tension. How handsome they were in their campaign hats, bent at the brim, their cotton gaiters, their insignia! Soldiers were in style. They flooded the palm-shaded streets, wore hibiscus behind their ears, and "took-up" with Hawaiian girls. "The boys" brought some ribald songs to hymn-singing Hawaii:

> My Mama told me
> That she would buy me
> A rubber dollie,
> A rubber dollie.
> I dare not tell her,
> I got a feller,
> Or she won't buy me
> That rubber dollie.

The boys were tough, the songs were tough — it was a new, tough era.

The khaki uncles were Army. Fine as that was, patriotic frenzy and all, fireworks and all, nothing done for them could excel the mute adoration of the battleship *Oregon* when she finally docked. The battleship was an emblem of power and intention larger than the flag.

On the *Oregon*, in 1898, we children were introduced to guns. It was a reverent display. The gun was inspected, the gunner opened the breech, reciting his lecture meanwhile, waiting patiently as all peered into the greased interior. The gun was patted, and kodak pictures were taken, over and over and over; little girl with gun, citizen with gun, little girl with sailor; citizen, sailor, little girl with gun.

The battleship had a certain smell, the sailors had a certain look. It was so unlike the tropics. We came to feel a little simple-minded in this awe of the ship. Everybody went to look — even those in bare feet. If a Chinese or a Japanese owned a panama hat and a white suit he went, too. Otherwise not. Spain was the enemy; old feudal undemocratic Spain. So we went down to see what it was that could triumph over Spain. We experienced together a vast mechanized, scrubbed, and painted object. This was the signpost to the Twentieth Century. This was the super U.S.A. come out across many Pacific waves to give us better dreams.

Mr. Abbott was very keen about this battleship. He told the school children of the Islands about a long debate that had been going on in Congress for years. Were the Sandwich Islands important? Congress asked first. Will the Islands be American or Asiatic? Congress couldn't make up its mind. Before Annexation, there were phrases as worn smooth as thin dimes: *coolie labor, contract labor, sugar tariff, Manifest Destiny, color line, yellow peril, heathen Chinee, little Jap*. The battleship was supposed to be an answer to all the queries that lay behind those phrases.

I walked the holystoned decks and consented to be lifted up repeatedly by the sailor boys to look through the narrowing barrel of the big guns. My father and I went everywhere they would let us go. What made us do all that? My father's kind of man loves a ship — any ship. Still that was not the nub of the matter. The *Oregon* was for my father a fascinating thing because it was a paradox. My father hated war.

Mr. Abbott reprinted a paragraph from the *New York Herald* giving the area and population of "Our Coming Empire," including eight Pacific islands or archipelagos besides Alaska, Porto Rico, and Cuba. And to link up with the dates in the history lesson, he added: "The coffin of Christopher Columbus with its remains has been taken from the Cathedral in Havana to be sent to Spain. They were brought to Havana when Spain lost Santo Domingo."

No matter how many items of interest the great wide wonderful world contained, the unsolved problems of the Pacific and Asia were clearly the dominant ones. They were worries that began like distant twisters at sea – water-spouts, typhoons, running at you suddenly, or perchance gliding off who knows where.

"Honolulu, May 9th. After the 1st of October the government will not allow the Japs to be more than one half the workers on a plantation. The rest must be of different nationality. It is proposed to pay American $18 and board to work as plantation laborers."

"Washington, January 2nd. Naval men plan to make San Diego, Honolulu, Pago Pago, Guam and Cavite bases of supply for coal, etc."

"Honolulu, February 6th. Lord Charles Beresford is in town. His plan of an 'open door' in China is being talked about all over the world. He means by this that the tariff duties shall be the same for every nation sending goods to China, so that a German will not have to pay less than an Englishman, nor a Russian more than an American. He wants England, United States, Germany and Japan to agree to compel the 'open door,' and to organize the Chinese Army so that it will keep peace in China and protect missionaries and other people who live there."

"Brazil. *The Oregon* and the *Iowa* have started southward from Rio Janeiro on their journey to Honolulu."

"Manila. February 23, 1899. Aguinaldo has issued orders to his men to kill all American prisoners. This shows that he is really a savage.

"Dewey has asked the *Oregon* to hurry to Manila. He seems to fear the German fleet."

"Honolulu. In the last few weeks almost every piece of land that had any water has been made a plantation. Not that cane has been planted but that the owners are getting ready. There has been much buying and selling, some of it foolish and wicked.

"Italians are to be brought here to work on the plantations."

"Hilo. A chest containing 25,000 Mexican dollars has been taken from Aguinaldo. It is said that this was his money for the war...."

"Two companies of Filipinos have enlisted in the American army."

"Manila, May 10th. Aguinaldo is said to have run away."

"London, March 5th. The bubonic plague is raging in Bombay. There were nearly a thousand deaths from it last week."

My bound volume, the prop for my memory, ends with the May issue, 1899. Still without it I can remember the day we heard the news of McKinley's assassination. Our school was like a chapel; and the children put the flag at half-mast. We wound the frame of the President's chromo with black and white cheese-cloth. The cloud of chalk dust was down. We sang dirges and were unified — Japanese, Chinese, Korean, Porto Rican, Portuguese, and Hawaiian children. Those children are today the loyal citizens of Hawaii, where not one act of sabotage has been reported since 1941.

I remember the Black Plague — the news of it first in whispers like the whispers about leprosy. There were two scourges. The plague-rat with its flea companion reported by Mr. Abbott managed to crawl up a hawser in an Indian port and crawl down another hawser when the ship came to Honolulu. I remember the second time because then the plague came into our home. Haya Shida, our Japanese servant, came down with a bubo.

We saw the death wagon beyond the hibiscus hedge, then men with gloves on; and they carried him out across the lawn and shoved him in at the back door, while the horses stamped and swished. He was still alive; but he would die in a few hours. We went out then. He wife knelt beside him. He lifted his head up high enough to look at all of us. We held him there as long as we could, not moving, not crying, speaking with restraint and politeness; and he, in an old gray kimono, a thing he never wore when he worked, propped up on his elbow, thanked us, ducked his head, and was taken away. Haya Shida was no "little Jap" and no militarist. Every Island child has memories of coolie Japanese that contradict the cartoons.

We saw bits of the old order, the discards of monarchy. The de Sota family lived next door. Their house was an abode — Pacific style chateau, with stables and a general air of panoply. Papa de Sota had been in the Queen's cabinet, we surmised; he was a personal follower, at any rate. And the legend about the flag pole lit up the gloom of the old estate: he had vowed to leave it flat, in the long grass for the mongooses' habitat, until the Queen was back on the throne. The characteristic vow of the old courtier. Displeasure, withdrawal. The flag pole was never visible, only a long ridge of ragged grass, as long as a train of cars.

Papa de Sota was *passé*. He was ousted by fine old men from New England, men who remembered Emerson as a Red, although they quoted him. In their alpaca coats and their panama hats and whiskers they were to be seen on Honolulu's streets, on Bishop, Bethel, and King, Beretania and Alakea, with the morning "Advertiser" in their pockets, local affairs in their talk; public-spirited men they were, who had converted the Hawaiian heathen, written him an alphabet, and collected for him his legends. They were Americanizing the people of the Islands, they were bankers, sugar-planters, scholars, churchmen, citizens. Indeed, they were somewhat like the battleship *Oregon*. And they were doomed to pass away, gradually — outmoded by the problems they had created.

Some of them had homes at Pearl Harbor. My Pearl Harbor was a big leaf of shallow blue inlets where we sailed and fished. Beyond the reefs the Japanese brought up the pink and purple fishes that went to the market. We did not venture there. We had heard of sharks. And once, we were told how they found in a shark's belly part of a kimono and a straw slipper. So we caught crabs on twine near the piers, and sailed for sailing's sake. It was a crabs-and-coconuts-for-supper life.

I recall a sailing day when we went nearer the Harbor's mouth than was our custom. And there we puzzled about a brownish hulk, rigged with travelling buckets on a crane. "And what, what, what is that?" we inquired, butterflying near.

"A dredge," they said, "to open up the harbor, to make a place for ships."

"Ships?"

"Battleships."

"Will battleships ever, ever, ever come to Pearl Harbor?"

"Oh, yes, certainly."

"How funny!" we said. And just then we caught a good breeze that sent us rippling.

With equal astonishment to us, the young ones, came the morning in August, 1914, when Papa came down a sweetly shining pathway, transfixed by the front page of his *Advertiser*. There were headlines, and over his shoulder we saw a three-column picture of European War – billowing smoke, and a general with a sword on a white horse. "World War," said Papa. "World War."

Then he dropped into pidgin English. "Plenty pilikia," he said.

The Yale Review 35:1 (September 1945), pp.48-60

A Homecoming

In 1935, the Vermont Marble Company in Rutland County, north of the Green Mountains and Taggard's community of East Jamaica, responded to the economic pressures of the Depression by cutting the pay of its workers to less than a living wage. The workers' strike that ensued took place during the coldest winter for years. As a member of the United Committee to Aid Vermont Marble Workers, Taggard gave testimony at the public hearing at West Rutland Town Hall, on February 29, 1936. Her visits to the families of the striking workers deeply impressed upon her the terrible privations they were forced to endure. These impressions found a voice in one of her most intensely politicized poems, "A Middle-Aged, Middle-Class Woman at Midnight," published in *Calling Western Union*: "Porcupines eat salt out of wood in winter. Starve/ So our children now…. See the set faces hungrier than rodents." When she wrote in her memoir "Hawaii, Washington, Vermont" that she felt "not a true member of [her] Vermont community," she had perhaps not yet experienced the full societal trauma of the Marble

Worker's Strike that winter, but in joining the campaign to aid their cause, she certainly found a secure sense of belonging there.

When the chairman of the committee, the artist Rockwell Kent, published an article in *New Masses* in the spring of 1936 to raise support for the miners, he invoked the memory of Ethan Allen, who had "evicted the British" from Ticonderoga in 1775, and asked (in the face of pending evictions of miners' families) where this Vermont hero of the American Revolution would stand today?[1] Taggard's 1945 book, *A Part of Vermont*, begins with her poem "To Ethan Allen" (p?), celebrating him as a political leader who, with his band of local militia, the Green Mountain Boys, rebelled against wealthy New York land speculators in the 1770s, defending the rights of simple farmers (as Taggard's own ancestors had been), finally winning statehood for Vermont in 1791.

In Taggard's poem, Ethan Allen's "big monument" is "Vermont itself"; he is intimately identified with nature in a subtle reference to Coleridge's *Christabel*: "one green leaf, the last of its clan," and to the nature poets of New England, Emerson and Thoreau, in the lines "those who sing of wilderness and man." When Taggard writes "A poet said, '*Nature is never spent*,'" she quotes directly from Gerard Manley Hopkins' "God's Grandeur" (1871), which continues, "There lives the dearest freshness deep down things." This sense of hope is confirmed in the line "Vermont was wild frontier and still contains the West," evoking the spirit of a pioneer people retaining an unshakable faith in a new day dawning, a new land to be discovered.

In "To Ethan Allen," Taggard uses a heroic character out of the New England revolutionary past to represent her hopes for working class victory against forces of capitalist oppression in her own day. What looks like a conventional elegiac poem has a

---

1   Rockwell Kent, "In the Name of the Great Jehovah," *New Masses* 29:1 (31 March, 1936), pp.13-14.

social sting in the tail, as backwoods rebellion is girded with proletarian heroism. "To Ethan Allen" was therefore a perfect leading
poem for Taggard's poetry collection celebrating her home state
of Vermont as a true foundation for American democracy, but
also an important contribution to the book *Time in New England*
(1950). Taggard had supplied the title for the book, a collabora-
tion between her friend the photographer Paul Strand and the
photography critic Nancy Newhall.[2]

In his application to the Guggenheim Foundation in October
1943, Strand expressed his desire to make through photography a
"portrait of [an] American environment in terms of the character
of the land itself, the people who live on it, the things which they
have made and built."[3] Taggard was one of his referees, having
known Strand since the 1930s: she was listed on the Board of
Advisors for Strand's film company, Frontier Films, in 1936, and
an early cut of Strand's and Leo Hurwitz's film *Native Land* (with
musical score by Taggard's friend and member of the Composers
Collective Marc Blitzstein) was shown at the New School for Social
Research on the occasion of the American Writers Congress of
1939. At the Congress, Taggard organized a special session on
writing for the "new media" of radio and film. In her statement
of support to the Guggenheim, she described Strand as a great
artist with rare powers of observation, brought to the task of pre-
senting this New England cradle of democracy:

> They tell a story of him in Vermont, the farmers tell it, those
> who watched him hover over his camera for hours and hours,
> near the corner of a barn waiting for a cobweb to hang still
> enough for picturing. It puzzled them, but they respected him

---

2   Strand and Newhall also selected one other Taggard poem for the book,
"The Nursery Rhyme and the Summer Visitor."

3   Paul Strand, Application for 1944 Fellowship, October, 1943. Guggenheim
Foundation Archives.

having seen him at work.... The purity of Vermont needs only his tender lens and his austere eye.[4]

Strand, she believed, possessed a perceptiveness uniquely sensitive and uncompromising to do justice to Vermont, which was for Taggard the essence of New England, and her adopted home.

There were many happy connections between Taggard and Strand in this period: at Taggard's invitation, Strand visited Gilfeather farm and rented a room nearby for several months in 1944, very taken not only with the place but also with Taggard and Durant with whom he shared an unshakable commitment to left politics. When *A Part of Vermont* was published, Taggard sent Strand a copy. And when *Time in New England* finally appeared in 1950, it included two poems by Taggard, two photographs taken at Gilfeather Farm and a portrait of Taggard's friend and neighbour Ed Bennett. Although Taggard did not always understand Strand's subtle use of symbolic natural forms to pose a social metaphor, she was clearly struck by his intense power of attention to things before his lens and his ability to render them with clarity and intensity. In "Bounding Line" (p.292), we can see Taggard achieving in a poem what the straight objectivist photographers of the Thirties (of whom Strand was a leading light) were creating through photography.

The bounding line of the poem's title defines forms, bringing us into intimate awareness of things around us. The poem concerns itself primarily with perception, and with a quality of attention that makes "big and still" those things that were small or unnoticed, or in motion. In the first stanza, both the snail and the spider leave their characteristic lines, tiny delineators of the active principle, drawing the viewer in. Here attention slows down and magnifies experience; by bringing the visual event "against" the "lens," it makes vision a conscious act of seeing rather than

---

4   Taggard, statement of support in Strand, Application for 1944 Fellowship.

an occasion of passive looking. To "cut the small from the big" is to extract the particular from the general, and this is where photography excels, especially in the hands of an artist like Strand.

In another poem from *A Part of Vermont*, "On Planting a Small Lilac in Vermont" (p.275), Taggard takes the lilac which in T.S. Eliot's *Wasteland* is forced out of the dead land of a degraded culture, and instead makes it a messenger of life and hope. Taggard's lilac is lovingly planted for "future people with sure hands," and she enjoins both plant and people to "live and unfold!" With its implicit reference to Whitman's "When Lilacs Last in the Dooryard Bloom'd," the poem directly confronts the early modernist poets, Amy Lowell and Robert Frost, with the suggestion that neither imagism nor nature-idealising regionalism will do, when it comes to standing on the threshold of a new world. Though the lilac is tagged at Bloomingdale's (the ultimate capitalist emporium) it finds itself planted in a rural setting "farmer style" at a "doorstep edge" that signals a transition to a richer, more rewarding kind of life, where it will witness happier faces "Than you can find in the working class today." Written in 1935, this is one of the poems that herald Taggard's increasing determination to "do something for the radical effort" in literature (as she wrote to her friend Dora Russell in 1932), while reminding us of her firm sense of her own place in the history of American poetry.

A major creative influence on Taggard's in the 1940s was the posthumous book by the Marxist critic Christopher Caudwell, *Illusion and Reality* (1937), which traced the roots of Western poetry in the forms of society, finding them shackled to the structures of capitalism. She finished her essay "Notes on Writing Words for Music" (at the end of her book *Long View*) (p.319) with a long quotation from this Marxist study, which testifies to Taggard's sincere belief in the social value of poetry. For Caudwell, as she quoted him, the peasant workers' "harvest song" created through the celebration of labour an example of a higher and more complex reality to which working men may aspire:

Poetry describes and expresses... the emotional, social and collective complex which is the tribe's relation to the harvest. It expresses a whole new world of truth, which has been brought into being by the fact that Man's relation to the harvest is not instinctive and blind, but economic and conscious. Not poetry's abstract statement — its content of facts, but its dynamic role in society — its content of collective emotion, is therefore poetry's truth.[5]

Caudwell's idea was that in tribal, pre-capitalist societies, poetry and production existed as one whole, split in two through the centuries, each aspect lost without the other and yearning to be reunited. He believed that only socialism would accomplish that reunion, in a society where every individual was both worker and poet.

When Taggard included the poem, "Image" (p.202) in her *Collected Poems* (1938), she dedicated it to Caudwell. Like so many of what she considered her best poems written in the 1930s, "Image" gives the marching labourer a heroic, poetic voice, in "glorious oracle!," "Joy just-spoken," "Clarion throat eloquent," and "soul of Hallelujah" with its sense of religious and emotional release. The "image" of the poem's title is the face of the marching, jubilant revolutionary worker, but by the end of the poem it has been transformed into the star (symbol since 1917 of Communism) on flags, and all aspects of culture including technology, currency, and extending to the natural world itself: "Let it shake large and quiet in star-water." (Keats's epitaph in Rome reads: "Here lies one whose name was writ on water.") The "star-water" in Taggard's poem is both the reflection of the flag, and the reflection of the sky, the heavens — making it both particular and universal, political and lyrical.

During the spring of 1945, the Museum of Modern Art in New York held a retrospective exhibition of the photographs of Paul Strand. The show concluded with a group of twenty photographs

---

5   Christopher Caudwell, *Illusion and Reality*, London: Lawrence & Wishart, 1973 (1937), p.38.

Paul Strand, "Mr. Bennett, East Jamaica, Vermont", 1943.

titled "Vermont 1944," including Strand's portrait of Taggard's neighbour, Mr. Ed Bennett, one of the images he made for *Time in New England*. Although Strand was probably not aware of it when he photographed him, Ed Bennett had recently been diagnosed with terminal cancer, and Strand's portrait therefore took on an added tragic quality when he died the following year. When Taggard died herself soon after, the magazine *Masses & Mainstream* (the Marxist monthly replacing the recently ceased *New Masses*) printed Strand's photograph of Mr. Bennett on the cover and in its pages featured the poem, "Exchange of Awe" (p.298), which Taggard had written as a response to Strand's photo – the photograph and poem forming one elegy, now publicly dedicated to Taggard.

Taggard took the title "Exchange of Awe" from a letter written by Emily Dickinson to Frances Norcross in 1873, an expression of sublime wonder at the polar explorer Captain Charles F. Hall who had died in Greenland two years before. Taggard's poem takes the life trajectory of one man as a microcosm of the slow progress of human society, "the realm and meaning of myriad man," from barbarism and slavery, through war and strife, to finally accepting "the sane sun" (emblem of the intellect) and glorying in the "authority of the task," an authentic individual completely integrated, in harmony with the rhythms of nature.

In the second stanza, the "image within the image" is the symbol or the type, in the imagination or dream of the subject, in his state of darkness, and a reference to the shadows in Plato's cave – those fragments of reality human beings can only perceive through mere sensory perception. Only through release from enslavement by the unconscious forces of nature (and history), the poem suggests, can the individual and the society develop spiritually and intellectually.

"Marvelous now is man," with its seventeenth-century tone, proclaims the ideal perfection of the human creation, thrown into the focus of a sharper reality with the subsequent line: "Wrinkles next his eyes." The subject of the poem, Blake's "Everyman," stands as a clear-seeing witness to human experience, but Strand's photograph of Mr. Bennett enlarges him in the poem to an individual, with all his literal humanity and unique characteristics: slightly unshaven, with a piece of string in his buttonhole. And in Strand's image Taggard finds the perfect type of the common man, the worker, the laborer in the fields. This was, after all, the aim of the popular front: to express the hope of a new world in communism for, and through, the ordinary citizen. In the sixth stanza, opposing adjectives are deployed for maximum contrast: "elate, afraid," "rejoicing and desponding," "immortal, mortal," to supply the whole range of human feeling, and to lift one man's life to the scope of mankind's story. Perhaps the metaphysical basis of the poem is that the "awe" which is exchanged is not the Shakespearean condition of unconsciousness in death, life being "rounded by a little sleep," but the "bliss within bliss" at both ends of life, encompassing and embracing him. When "He is unspun," he is unwound, unravelled, his story goes back to the beginning. And in that place, he now finds himself at the end, where "Forces of the tide, moon, sun" (the instinct, the unconscious mind, the intellect) fuse and become one powerful continuum through life and death.

The critic Samuel Putnam, in his review of Taggard's 1942 book *Long View*, saw her poetry bridging the metaphysical precision of *Circumference* (which he associated with Emily Dickinson) and the broad range and expansive voice of *Long View* (where he recognized the sound of Walt Whitman).[6] In *Slow Music* (1945) this is further demonstrated by poems of a similar scope: from the specificity of nature in "Gilfeather Again" to vast, declarative poems like "Aleatory Wind" and "Exchange of Awe." In so many of her later poems, the poet leads the reader confidently onto that bridge, within easy access of both modes of her work. In the fall of 1946, Taggard, who had been struggling with hypertension, went on leave from her teaching job at Sarah Lawrence College, and in January the following year she resigned. In November of 1948, after months of illness and hospitalisation, she died. Her memorial brochure was printed with a copy of "Exchange of Awe," accompanied by a poem by Emily Dickinson and one by Walt Whitman.

Gladys LaFlamme Colburn, a poet and a friend, wrote after Taggard's death that the current of truth running through her work was her deep and unshakable belief that there would eventually come a time when "man might realize the heroic impulses of his being," and that she had worked tirelessly to transform her vision of this new world into "an authentic poetry."[7] That authenticity would naturally reflect her commitment to both the ethical and

---

6 Samuel Putnam, "Poet's Vision," *New Masses* 43:10 (9 June, 1942), pp.23-24.

7 Gladys LaFlamme Colburn, "Introductory Notes to Reading Genevieve Taggard Poems," 19 March, 1951, Genevieve Taggard Papers, New York Public Library, Box 42, Folder 8.

metaphysical aspects of her nature. Taggard at various points regarded herself as a revolutionary — first, of bohemian free love and reformist socialism, then of the new world offered by Communism. But she was, even in her most radical moments, first and foremost a poet, and for her the main focus of the revolution was going to be not so much upon social levelling as on the liberation of human creativity. In a statement of 1940, Taggard referred to herself straightforwardly as a "radical" whose fondest hope was to live to see America "achieve economic democracy" and "lay a foundation for a great culture."[8] By achievement of "economic democracy" she meant, of course, the exchange of the existing capitalist system for a new socio-economic order (Communism), but in order to ensure a fair and equal society in which that great culture could flourish free of market constraints, something for which she never gave up hoping.

In 1938, Ernest Hemingway had written to Taggard, "You are a good poet, Jed, but you also have a very good heart. It's pretty fine there is somebody with a good heart that knows their Marx and can write poetry."[9] Taggard always considered herself "primarily a lyric poet,"[10] but also knew that a change was needed in a failing social and economic system and worked hard to express that need through her poems. Her good heart will be for her readers to discover.

---

8   Fred B. Millett, ed. *Contemporary American Authors*, London: George G. Harrap, 1940, p.603.

9   Hemingway to Taggard, 28 October, 1938, Genevieve Taggard Papers, New York Public Library, Box 7, Folder 6.

10   Taggard, "Notes on Writing Words for Music," *Long View*, New York and London: Harper and Brothers, 1942, p.110.

Bibliography

Books by Genevieve Taggard

For Eager Lovers, New York: Thomas Seltzer, 1922.

Hawaiian Hilltop, San Francisco: Wickoff and Gelber, 1923.

Words for the Chisel, New York: Alfred A. Knopf, 1926.

Travelling Standing Still: Poems, New York: Alfred A. Knopf, 1928.

Not Mine to Finish: Poems, 1928-1934, New York: Harper & Brothers, 1934.

Calling Western Union, New York: Harper & Brothers, 1936.

Collected Poems, 1918-1938, New York: Harper & Brothers, 1938.

Long View, New York: Harper & Brothers, 1942.

Falcon: Poems on Soviet Themes, [excerpted from *Collected Poems, 1918-1838* and *Long View*], New York: Harper & Brothers, 1942.

Slow Music, New York: Harper & Brothers, 1946.

Origin: Hawaii, Poems, Honolulu: Donald Angus, 1947.

355

To the Natural World, by Genevieve Taggard (Introduction by Marcia Liles, Note by Josephine Miles), Boise, Idaho: Ahsahta Press, Boise State University, 1980. Available online at https://scholarworks.boisestate.edu/cgi/viewcontent.cgi?article=1046&context=ahsahta (accessed 6 November 2022).

Biography
The Life and Mind of Emily Dickinson, New York: Alfred A. Knopf, 1930.

Anthologies
Continent's End: An Anthology of Contemporary California Poets (with James Rory and George Sterling), San Francisco: Book Club of California, 1925.

May Days: An Anthology of Masses-Liberator Verse, 1912-1925, New York: Boni & Liveright, 1925.

Circumference: Varieties of Metaphysical Verse, 1456-1928, New York: Covici Fried Publishers, 1929.

Ten Introductions: A Collection of Modern Verse (with Dudley Fitts), New York: Arrow Editions, 1934.

Acknowledgements

The Taggard, Durant, Liles, and Benét families were associated for many years through work and marriage. I am deeply grateful particularly to Judith Benét Richardson for her encouragement, and for allowing the publication of copyrighted materials owned by the estate of Genevieve Taggard.

For their unfailing assistance in archival research, I am most thankful to Tal Nadan of the Manuscripts and Archives Division, New York Public Library, and to Eric Esau, former reference librarian at Rauner Special Collections Library, Dartmouth College. And sincere thanks, too, to Professor Susan Fiske of Princeton University for information about Taggard's first husband Robert Wolfe.

I am also very grateful for the advice and guidance of Dr. Craig Howes of the Center for Biographical Research, University of Hawai'i. Special thanks are due also to Dr. Christopher Kelsey and Dr. Michele M. Penhall for their unstinting long-distance research assistance, and to Mike, who was always there for a seminar.

Genevieve Taggard (1894-1948) was an American lyric poet, critic and short story writer who went on to become one of the most active and committed of radical poets of her generation.

Terese Svoboda is the author of 20 books and has numerous prizes, including the Bobst Prize in fiction, the Iowa Prize for poetry, an NEH grant for translation, the Graywolf Nonfiction Prize, a Jerome Foundation prize for video, the O. Henry award for the short story, and a Pushcart Prize for the essay.

Dr. Anne Hammond is an independent writer and Visiting Research Fellow at the Centre for Fine Print Research, University of the West of England, UK. She is the author of *Ansel Adams: Divine Performance* (Yale University Press, 2002).

GREETINGS FROM JAMAICA, VERMONT

To Test the Joy: Selected Poetry and Prose
By Genevieve Taggard

First published in this edition by Boiler House Press, 2023

Part of UEA Publishing Project
Poems and prose copyright © Genevieve Taggard, 1919-1948
Introduction copyright © Terese Svoboda, 2023
Editing and critical essays copyright © Anne Hammond, 2023

Portrait photographs of Genevieve Taggard: Studio of Arthur
Muray, New York, c.1928. From Genevieve Taggard Papers, Man-
uscripts and Archives Division, New York Public Library. Repro-
duced with permission of the New York Public Library.
Paul Strand photograph, "Mr. Bennett, East Jamaica, Vermont.":
From the Paul Strand Collection, Philadelphia Museum of Art.
Copyright © Aperture Foundation, Inc., Paul Strand Archive.

Cover Design and Typesetting by Louise Aspinall
Cover image by David Clode via Unsplash
Typeset in Arnhem Pro

ISBN: 978-1-915812-02-5

Milton Keynes UK
Ingram Content Group UK Ltd.
UKHW022240130923
428613UK00012B/141

9 781915 812025